PRAISE FOR THE FIRST EDITION OF U&ME

John Stewart has done it again with *U&ME: Communicating in Moments that Matter.* He has written another book about communication that is at once highly readable, grounded in the latest research and thinking, original, and deeply practical. With the focus on people meeting in moments of communication, he has reached a new high in relating the best of theory to the everyday lives of real people, like you and me.

> ~ Gerry Philipsen, Ph.D.
> Professor Emeritus of Communication, University of Washington

There is genuine interpersonal communication and what passes for communication in everyday life. Throughout his distinguished career, Dr. Stewart has drawn our attention to the difference. In *U&ME*, he discuses the benefits of not settling and how we can achieve genuine contact.

> ~ Paul R. Falzer, Ph.D.
> Clinical Epidemiology Research Center, V.A Connecticut Healthcare System

In *U&ME: Communicating in Moments that Matter*, Dr. Stewart has distilled a career of teaching, research, and practice in interpersonal communication into a highly readable discussion of the problems and opportunities of relationships in families, at work, and other settings. The book contains clearly worded principles and engaging vignettes, both of which are invaluable in helping readers apply the concepts.

> ~ Kenneth N. Cissna, Ph.D.
> Professor Emeritus, Department of Communication, University of South Florida

In *U&ME: Communicating in Moments that Matter*, Stewart extends the reach of his earlier work to include the everyday of our on-line lives, courtship and dating, family and friends, leadership, spirituality, and politics. Written in an accessible style with useful personal examples, stories, and exercises, *U&ME* is a must read for those committed to improving the quality of their relating, their relationships, and, consequently, their lives.

> ~ Kimberly Pearce
> Co-Founder and President, CMM Institute for Personal & Social Evolution, Author of *Compassionate Communicating: Poetry, Prose & Practices*

New & Revised!

U&ME

Communicating in Moments that Matter

John Stewart, Ph.D.

Taos Institute Publications
Chagrin Falls, Ohio

U&ME: Communicating in Moments that Matter
New & Revised!

Cover and Design Layout: Debbi Stocco

Library of Congress Catalog Card Number: 2014941973

Taos Institute Publications
A Division of the Taos Institute
Chagrin Falls, Ohio
USA

ISBN-10: 1-938552-26-1
ISBN-13: 978-1-938552-26-7   Printed in the USA and in the UK

Taos Institute Publications

The Taos Institute is a nonprofit organization dedicated to the development of social constructionist theory and practice for purposes of world benefit. Constructionist theory and practice locate the source of meaning, value, and action in communicative relations among people. Our major investment is in fostering relational processes that can enhance the welfare of people and the world in which they live. Taos Institute Publications offers contributions to cutting-edge theory and practice in social construction. Our books are designed for scholars, practitioners, students, and the openly curious public. The **Focus Book Series** provides brief introductions and overviews that illuminate theories, concepts, and useful practices. The **Tempo Book Series** is especially dedicated to the general public and to practitioners. The **Books for Professionals Series** provides in-depth works that focus on recent developments in theory and practice. **WorldShare Books** is an online offering of books in PDF format for free download from our website. Our books are particularly relevant to social scientists and to practitioners concerned with individual, family, organizational, community, and societal change.

— Kenneth J. Gergen
President, Board of Directors
The Taos Institute

Taos Institute Board of Directors

For information about the Taos Institute and social constructionism visit:
www.taosinstitute.net

Taos Institute Publications

Taos Tempo Series:
Collaborative Practices for Changing Times

U&ME: Communicating in Moments that Matter, New & Revised! (2014)
by John Stewart

Relational Leading: Practices for Dialogically Based Collaboration, (2013)
by Lone Hersted and Kenneth J. Gergen

Retiring But Not Shy: Feminist Psychologists Create their Post-Careers,
(2012) edited by Ellen Cole and Mary Gergen

*Developing Relational Leadership: Resources for Developing Reflexive
Organizational Practices*, (2012) by Carsten Hornstrup, Jesper Loehr-
Petersen, Joergen Gjengedal Madsen, Thomas Johansen, Allan Vinther
Jensen

Practicing Relational Ethics in Organizations, (2012) by Gitte Haslebo and
Maja Loua Haslebo

*Healing Conversations Now: Enhance Relationships with Elders and Dying
Loved Ones*, (2011) by Joan Chadbourne and Tony Silbert

Riding the Current: How to Deal with the Daily Deluge of Data, (2010) by
Madelyn Blair

*Ordinary Life Therapy: Experiences from a Collaborative Systemic
Practice*, (2009) by Carina Håkansson

Mapping Dialogue: Essential Tools for Social Change, (2008) by Marianne
"Mille" Bojer, Heiko Roehl, Mariane Knuth-Hollesen, and Colleen
Magner

*Positive Family Dynamics: Appreciative Inquiry Questions to Bring Out the
Best in Families*, (2008) by Dawn Cooperrider Dole, Jen Hetzel Silbert,
Ada Jo Mann, and Diana Whitney

Focus Book Series

When Stories Clash: Addressing Conflict with Narrative Mediation, (2012)
by Gerald Monk and John Winslade

Bereavement Support Groups: Breathing Life into Stories of the Dead,
(2012) by Lorraine Hedtke

The Appreciative Organization, Revised Edition (2008) by Harlene
Anderson, David Cooperrider, Ken Gergen, Mary Gergen, Sheila
McNamee, Jane Watkins, and Diana Whitney

*Appreciative Inquiry: A Positive Approach to Building Cooperative
Capacity*, (2005) by Frank Barrett and Ronald Fry

*Dynamic Relationships: Unleashing the Power of Appreciative Inquiry in
Daily Living*, (2005) by Jacqueline Stavros and Cheri B. Torres

*Appreciative Sharing of Knowledge: Leveraging Knowledge Management
for Strategic Change*, (2004) by Tojo Thatchenkery

Social Construction: Entering the Dialogue, (2004) by Kenneth J. Gergen, and Mary Gergen

Appreciative Leaders: In the Eye of the Beholder, (2001) edited by Marge Schiller, Bea Mah Holland, and Deanna Riley

Experience AI: A Practitioner's Guide to Integrating Appreciative Inquiry and Experiential Learning, (2001) by Miriam Ricketts and Jim Willis

Books for Professionals Series

New Horizons in Buddhist Psychology: Relational Buddhism for Collaborative Practitioners, (2010) edited by Maurits G.T. Kwee

Positive Approaches to Peacebuilding: A Resource for Innovators, (2010) edited by Cynthia Sampson, Mohammed Abu-Nimer, Claudia Liebler, and Diana Whitney

Social Construction on the Edge: 'Withness'-Thinking & Embodiment, (2010) by John Shotter

Joined Imagination: Writing and Language in Therapy, (2009) by Peggy Penn

Celebrating the Other: A Dialogic Account of Human Nature, (reprint 2008) by Edward Sampson

Conversational Realities Revisited: Life, Language, Body and World, (2008) by John Shotter

Horizons in Buddhist Psychology: Practice, Research and Theory, (2006) edited by Maurits Kwee, Kenneth J. Gergen, and Fusako Koshikawa

Therapeutic Realities: Collaboration, Oppression and Relational Flow, (2005) by Kenneth J. Gergen

SocioDynamic Counselling: A Practical Guide to Meaning Making, (2004) by R. Vance Peavy

Experiential Exercises in Social Construction—A Fieldbook for Creating Change, (2004) by Robert Cottor, Alan Asher, Judith Levin, and Cindy Weiser

Dialogues About a New Psychology, (2004) by Jan Smedslund

For book information and ordering,
visit Taos Institute Publications at:
www.taosinstitutepublications.net

For further information, call:
1-888-999-TAOS, 1-440-338-6733
Email: info@taosinstitute.net

Table of Contents

PREFACE

EVERYBODY KNOWS THAT COMMUNICATION is important. Some of our best memories are of a heart-to-heart talk with a good friend, the first time we heard "I love you" from someone outside our family, and sincere public praise from a boss.

We also know that communication can be frustrating and painful from disagreements with a dating partner and shouting matches with a son or daughter.

Unfortunately, our communication can feel so habitual and second-nature that we sometimes believe problems like these are inevitable, or are the other person's fault, and that there's nothing we can learn that will really help improve things. So a manager who has problems keeping employees can attend a helpful seminar about listening and come away saying, "That was all just common sense, and most of the time I already do what they said anyway," while morale in his unit continues to decay.

Like good parenting and good managing, good communication *does* involve a lot of common sense. Yet, if you look around you,

you'll see enough bad managing and dysfunctional families to demonstrate that communication skills might be simple to understand but they're sure not easy to do well. Most of us do have something to learn about the everyday, commonsensical topics of listening and speaking.

One fact it helps to learn is that communication problems get worse when we try to improve them by focusing on what we think is "behind" how we listen and speak. Many mistakenly believe that the key is to start with the right *ideas* and then to figure out a good way to communicate them. Or, we believe, if the *feelings* of love are there, a couple's problems will eventually get better. A work-life version of this same mistake is the conviction that, if a manager *intends* to do the right thing, her communication will show it. In all these situations, the mistake is believing that what's most important are the thoughts, feelings, ideas, commitments, and intentions "behind" what's said, texted, Skyped, or written.

The truth is, the family, friend, and work relationships that are so important to us are built and destroyed, wounded and healed in the specific ways we listen, speak, read, and write. Even when your spouse wants the two of you to have equal power, if he habitually interrupts, your relationship will be hurtfully unequal. If a well-meaning manager almost never rewards or encourages people, workplace relationships deteriorate, despite her best intentions. In every part of our lives, relationships are created and crippled in the actual listening and speaking between friend and friend, wife and husband, manager and subordinate, student and teacher, accountant and client, parent and child. Nothing is more critical to the quality of our lives than our relationships, and nothing is more critical to our relationships than how we communicate.

Impersonal and Personal Communicating

This book helps you improve the quality of your life by showing you how to manage the quality of your communicating. It won't necessarily help make your communication more speedy or eloquent, although these qualities might improve. But *U&ME* will show you how to make your communication more *personal* and less *impersonal*, which is the key to quality communication and a quality life.

Impersonal communicating happens when people only fulfill their roles—server and diner, teller and bank customer, usher and concert-goer, teacher and student, manager and worker. While this kind of communication is vital for getting many things done, it doesn't connect people *personally.*

Personal communicating connects people as unique individuals who are making choices, experiencing feelings, and being reflective and mindful about what's happening. This kind of communication is vital between spouses, among business partners, in families, among friends and work team members, in learning situations, in spiritual and religious gatherings, and in many important political and multi-cultural settings. Why? Because personal communication can enhance the satisfaction, productivity, understandability, and contact-quality of every human meeting. This book's overall goal is to encourage and empower you to make your communication as personal as possible in each of the life arenas it discusses.

This doesn't mean that you have to wear your heart on your sleeve or pry into the other person's private life. As the following pages show, it just means that you encourage more direct contact with many of the people you meet.

Chapter 1 explains what Moments that Matter are, and why they're important. Then Chapter 2 shows how the quality of each person's communication is directly linked to the quality of their lives and to the Big Question: *What does it mean to be a human being?*

Today's brain scientists agree that humans are the only beings we know of who can connect with everything around us in two powerful and different ways. We can relate to the world rationally, logically, analytically, and impersonally which, at its extreme, is what Spock does in the *Star Trek* series. And each human can also relate to the world directly, holistically and personally—like, at their best, a child or the Dalai Lama. Philosophers have celebrated these twin talents for centuries, and neuroscientists are now demonstrating how these two ways of relating are possible because of the structure of the human brain.

Most of the time these two capabilities are blended, but we can tell which one is mainly operating by the ways we listen and speak, read and write, smile and scowl, look directly and look away, shout and whisper, rush and pause, keep our distance and hug. Specific communication behaviors vary in important ways from culture to culture. But in much of the Western world, when we are mainly connecting with what's around us impersonally, we speak and write labels and facts, are likely to shout more than whisper, often rush more than pause, and tend to look away and to keep our distance. When people in these cultures are mainly connecting with what's around us personally, we write and speak owned opinions and choices, pause to let the other person talk, look into the other's eyes, check our understandings, and let our faces and voices show our feelings.

THE CHALLENGE

The challenge we face in the 21st century is that widespread cultural pressures are pushing us to connect impersonally most of the time. We're hard-wired for both impersonal and personal contacts, but our communication lives are out of balance.

At work, long meetings plod rigidly through boring agendas. Marketers greet clients with phony smiles and empty flattery. Teachers give dry lectures to bored students. Parents don't listen to their teen-agers. Spouses believe they "know just how she'll react" and "We can't change how we've always done it." And the internet encourages 10-second video Snaps, filtered Instagrams, hundreds of superficial "friends," non-stop connectivity, and speed, speed, speed.

This book shows you how to enhance the quality of your life by restoring some of the balance that's been undermined by widespread objectification, depersonalization, mass strategies, and the need for speed.

How to Read U&Me

After the introductory part, you may want to read only the chapters about the life arenas that are most important to you. Or you could read the first two chapters to get the overall approach, the chapter about the life arena that interests you most, and then the last chapter. But the book as a whole offers understandings and skills that you can apply throughout your life. What's here grows out of my work as a facilitator, trainer, teacher, researcher, consultant, spouse, parent, and friend. I've reported these findings in scholarly articles, chapters, and books; I've tested these understandings and skills across several decades; and I continue to revise and fine-tune them. You'll find references to my other writings, videos, contact information, and my interpersonal communication blog at http://www.johnstewart.org

ACKNOWLEDGEMENTS

All my forty years' of interpersonal communication study and practice happened with family, friends, colleagues, students, critics, and clients, and most of these people helped me learn. This means that there's half a lifetime of people to thank for what's here. It would be tedious for you if I listed them all, and I'd be sure to forget some.

So what follows hits the highlights, and I ask forgiveness from those I've omitted.

Allen Clark introduced me to Martin Buber, and Helen Felton, Barbara Keely, Tamar Katriel, Milt Thomas, Maurice Friedman, Ken Cissna, Marcelo Dascal, Karen Zediker, Ron Arnett, and dozens of students encouraged me over the years to continue studying and applying his work. Karen has been an especially helpful good friend.

Many other colleagues and friends have lived with me through moments that mattered, including George Diestel, Frank Bussone, Sam Bradley, Lyall Crawford, Paul Falzer, Gary D'Angelo, Blake Emery, Eric Oksendahl, Faith Smith, Ken White, Jeff Kerssen-Griep, Susan Dyer, Dale Reiger, Lisa Coutu, Kathy Hendrix, Dick Stuart, Amanda Graham, Laura Black, Laura Manning, Jody Nyquist, Gerry Philipsen, Donal Carbaugh, Ann Darling, Bill Wilmot, Bob Arundale, Mike Held, Karen Barnes Ellison, Judy Heinrich, Jeff St. John, Fr. Ralph Carskadden, Bill Burgua, John Paul Olafson, Todd Kelshaw, Cindy King, Joanna Brooke, Melanie DeBond, Ken White, Michael Lane Bruner, John Gastil, Theresa Castor, Barbara Warnick, Lori Joubert, Saskia Witteborn, John Shotter, Alan Scult, Chip Hughes, Jeffrey Bullock, Peter Smith, Barnett Pearce, Sallyann Roth, Tom Fisher, Dale Easley, Ferdi Businger, and Cy Yusten. Thank you for all the ways you've helped shape my life.

Special thanks to John Angus Campbell for being my colleague and brother over our 43-year friendship. Special thanks to Walt Fisher for being my teacher, mentor, and friend. Special thanks to Aimee Carillo Rowe for helping me to learn important lessons about critical race theory and white privilege.

Special thanks to Becky Sisco for encouraging me to begin this book and doing all she could to break me of my worst academic writing habits. Special thanks to Kim Pearce, whose personal presence and professional expertise continue to energize and support my thinking and writing. Special thanks to the St. John's writers' group for pushing me to keep it simple.

Special thanks to my family—especially Marcia, Lisa, Lincoln, Barbara, Brad, and Dorothy—for helping me remember that this project is worth the effort. And the most special thanks to Becky Johnson-Stewart who, seemingly without effort, lives a life of dialogue, and, to my stupendous good fortune, lives it with me.

PREFACE TO THE REVISED EDITION

U&ME was first published in September, 2013, and by early 2014 my conversations with a number of readers convinced me that it needed improvements. For one thing, the second chapter was too dense to easily understand. The original edition also had no chapter on multicultural moments that matter, and demographic changes in the U.S. and other countries are making them increasingly common and often challenging. Readers told me that the chapter about political communicating said nothing about what to do when a friend or family member starts spouting political ideas you disagree with, so I added a discussion of those experiences. Studies of the two different ways our brains interpret everything around us had progressed to the point where I wanted to add a little to what I said about that, too.

I also wanted the chance to go back through every chapter to make sure what I wrote was as clear as possible. I want *U&ME* to be easily understandable to everybody who is interested in enhancing the quality of their life by improving how they communicate. So I scoured the pages to get rid of needless jargon, repetitive explanations, and too-long sentences.

I hope that the result is a new revision that is even more helpful. See what you think!

Chapter 1

MOMENTS THAT MATTER

I WAS VISITING THE UNIVERSITY *Health Center when a student greeted me in the hall. Kent was a sophomore who had been hit by a car while biking to class. I'd heard about the hit-and-run, but it still shocked me to see the stump where his left leg had been amputated. When I expressed my concern about what happened, Kent told me his story.*

He described his bike, a classic fat tire Schwinn that he loved, and recounted how he pedaled it up to a normally-busy intersection that looked empty. A car appeared from nowhere, and he couldn't dodge it. Kent thought it was strange that he remembered his helmeted head bouncing off the blacktop as he watched the car's wheels pressing the Schwinn's crossbar through his thigh. As he finished, we both stood there in silence, me on two legs and Kent on crutches and one. "Shit" was all I could say. After a pause, he replied, "Yeah." And more silence.

Over the next month, each time I visited the Center, Kent and I would hang out for a while. In the time Kent and I spent together, I learned about how painful physical therapy can be, I shared his frustration with the slow police investigation, and I got an introduction to artificial legs. But most of the time we just talked about everyday topics. I remember that he was planning to change his major from engineering to pre-med. We talked because we cared about each other.

Kent and I have long since lost contact. But at our first meeting, we were propelled from strangers to friends by a moment that mattered. For a moment, in our talking and listening, we met, not as able-bodied and disabled, or student and teacher, but just as human beings—persons. I experienced what some writers call "the feeling of being felt,"[1] and I believe he did, too. Over the time we conversed, we created several more of these moments together.

I also biked to work every day, and I'd dodged plenty of rude drivers. Like him, I was grateful for my helmet, even though it looked silly. I shared many of Kent's feelings, including his anger at the driver, his frustration about not being able to get back his leg, and some of his fear about what was coming—the painful rehab, learning to walk again, coping with a prosthetic, being treated as handicapped. As I think back, I can only guess what our short relationship meant to Kent. But at the time, we just met, and the contact enriched both of our lives.

"Enriched both of our lives" is pretty lofty language, I admit. But that's what this book is about. Quality of life is a term for personal satisfaction, happiness, and a person's sense of being alert and energized. It's about our health, joy, self-esteem, and longevity, about love in our life, and our being at peace in the sense of *shalom*. Although money can make life easier, many wealthy people have a lousy quality of life, and many with modest incomes are healthy and happy. The difference is close relationships. As one writer puts it,

*Research. . . shows there is only one experience in life that
increases happiness over a long time. It's not money, above
a base survival amount. It's not health, nor is it marriage or
having children. The one thing that makes people happy is the
quality and quantity of their social connections.*[2]

Another research team confirms, *"people who have few close contacts with others have a lower quality of life and die sooner than people engaged in organizations and involved with family and friends.*[3]

You and I regularly make big and small decisions that affect our
quality of life—whether to join a group, change jobs, lose weight,
break up with an abusive partner, spend time with loved ones. Most
of these decisions are about our relationships. Quality of life becomes
especially important when we're facing death. The questions that will
matter most on your deathbed and mine are ones like, What kind of
wife was I? What kind of husband? What kind of parent? What kind
of friend? Whom did I love and who loved me?

*Nothing is more critical to our quality of life than our rela-
tionships, and nothing is more critical to our relationships
than how we communicate.*

Years ago, Kent's life and mine were enriched by our brief relationship. Together, we created several moments that mattered. His
struggle to recover was less lonely, and I got to enter another human's
world and to contribute another human side to his hospitalization.

I also remember an experience that taught me how moments that
matter can sometimes be painful. It happened in a session my wife
and I had with a counselor named Ellen, when we were trying to sort
out what made our marriage stressful. *Ellen asked me why I'd arrived
late for the session, and I described what had happened on the way.
I'd rushed to my car, realized I'd forgotten my keys, slid my briefcase under the locked car while I ran back to my office, returned with
the keys, and driven off. Part way there, I discovered what I'd done,*

returned to the lot, and discovered that my briefcase was gone. I was definitely frazzled when I got to the counseling session. Ellen sympathized with me some and then gently asked me how much "dignity" I thought there was in my life.

Her question struck me like a slap in the face. I was embarrassed and angry at the thought that my life might be "undignified." "What are you saying?" I snapped defensively. Ellen didn't push the idea on me; she just planted it and helped me think out loud about it.

Pretty soon, I began to see that she had really hit a nail on the head. She had listened to me deeply enough in earlier sessions that she'd come to know part of me better than I knew myself. Here again, I had the profound "feeling of being felt." Her point was not that I needed to be stuffy or snooty, but that I should respect myself enough to slow down, be more mindful, and move through life with more grace. Ellen talked about learning a similar lesson in her own life, and she shared some of the ways dignity smoothed things for her. It felt like a talk with an older sister. Although it was painful, this was another moment that mattered, another conversation that enhanced both our lives.

MOMENTS THAT MATTER

Every human being, just because we're human, is primed for moments that matter. Each human infant experiences this quality of contact with our parents and other primary caregivers. These moments are utterly normal, part of almost everyone's first sense of "the way things are." These communication events crucially shape the kind of persons we become.

Sometimes these events are so brief or deceptively simple that they can be lost in the crush of texts, emails, calls, memos, and other demands. This is why I call them *moments*.[4] They may last only a second or two. Sometimes, when this quality of contact happens several times in a longer conversation or a relationship, the people involved adopt a positive pattern. Then the communication in this relationship has this quality much or most of the time.

These moments usually happen face-to-face, but they can also occur on Skype or cellphone, on email, through Facebook, and via some other technologies. They occur most often between two people, but sometimes several members of a family, work group, athletic team, or performance ensemble connect in this way. Whenever and wherever they occur, these moments enrich the quality of our lives. That's why I call them moments that *matter.*

Moments that matter are some of the most *human* events we experience. In a moment that matters, we are confirmed as the person we are, acknowledged as unique, recognized as significant. In a positive moment, we feel supported or loved. In a negative one the pain or embarrassment we feel is accompanied by the realization that, although I don't like what's happening, it's clear that the other person "gets" me.

They Commonly Happen in Talk

Picture in your head someone you care deeply about. Your friends would say that your face lights up when you see this person. You feel a twinge of excitement when the two of you meet or talk —maybe sexual excitement. You would probably say that the two of you love each other.

You can happily tell many stories about how you met, interests you have in common, activities you like to do together. One of these stories is probably about the first time you said and heard, "I love you." This was a moment that mattered, a communication event of direct contact. The words that were spoken and heard captured and reinforced wonderful feelings, and your eyes, touch, tone of voice, and face all reinforced what the words said. The two of you really *connected.*

For a few people, the first "I love you" in a relationship just pops out or bubbles up in the middle of an otherwise normal conversation. But many people worry for days or even weeks about whether it's time to speak these words, and exactly how. Some manipulative men and women strategize the time, place, and tone of voice of their first "I love you" in order to get what they want—sex, money, drugs, or damaging personal information. But most of us don't just throw the first "I love you" into an everyday conversation, because we know that these three words embody an important commitment and invite a serious response.

The spoken words "I love you" are important enough that they've been identified by hundreds of research subjects as one of the important "turning points" in a romantic relationship.[5] Turning point research has identified several kinds of events that significantly change a relationship by marking a point at which it moves from, for example, "acquaintance" or "friend" to something more—or less. Some of the highest-impact turning points happen in *talk*, when romantic partners first say to each other, "I love you," or, on the other side, when one says, "I'm dating someone else," or "I want a divorce." These negative and positive moments are distinctly memorable. The words that were said when we were dumped can stick with us for years. And many couples celebrating 50 or 60 years together still distinctly recall their first "I love you." At the moment when these words are said and heard, we feel them in our bodies. Some people's heart races, their stomach jumps, their face feels hot. Why? Just because of the *talk*, what's being *spoken and heard*.

What's spoken and heard can have a similar impact in some very different situations. The alcoholic quickly learns in her first Alcoholics Anonymous meeting that each person who speaks during the meeting is expected to begin with, "My name is _____, and I'm an alcoholic."

At her first AA meetings, Jessica can't bring herself to utter these words, not only because of the shame she feels, but also because she doesn't want to hear the group's response. It will simply be, "Hi Jessica," but in this context, the spoken response *means*: "We accept you *as another alcoholic, just like us*." At first, this contact experience is too painful for Jessica to risk. Eventually, when Jessica feels more at home in the 12-step program, this moment becomes comforting and reassuring. Exactly what comforts and reassures her? The *talk*, the words that she speaks combined with the spoken responses she hears in this particular context. The saying and hearing create a moment that matters.

Talk Includes More than Just Words

When I say that these moments happen in talk and we feel them in our bodies, I mean to highlight more than just the words themselves. Word choice can be very important, as is shown by the big difference between "I like you" and "I love you." But "talk" means that the words are *spoken*; they happen in a certain tone of voice, at a certain volume, with certain timing, and accompanied by other markers such as facial expression eye contact, posture, distance, and sometimes touch. Take volume and vocal inflection, for example. Occasionally, "I love you!" will be shouted out in frustration when the other person doesn't seem to realize the love that's there. But usually the words are spoken softly and gently, accompanied by direct eye contact and similarly soft, gentle, and even suggestively erotic touch. All these *nonverbal* features are part of every instance of spoken words. So *talk* is verbal and nonverbal.

Another result of talk being spoken is that it's heard rather than just seen and read. This is important because we experience information from each of our five senses differently, and the differences can be important. For example, seeing gives you information about only what's in front of you, while hearing takes in what's all around you.

Seeing requires light, but we hear whether it's bright or pitch black. These features can make heard experiences more encompassing and high-impact. If you're using seeing to read, you're taking in information from left to right, right to left, or top to bottom, while sound comes at you all at once. Seeing is also easier to control. You can shut your eyes easily, while it's harder to shut out all sound. So heard experiences often happen *to* you, whether you want them to or not. Although the experience of being caught up in a group or crowd involves both seeing and hearing, the parts you experience through hearing—shouting in unison, singing in harmony, group silence—often affect you more. And while bright flashing lights are almost impossible to ignore, hearing your name called out, especially when you don't expect it, can be even more riveting. Moments that are spoken and heard often matter most.

Talk and Public Contacts — Throughout our lives, there are situations where *talk,* as I'm describing it here, can create contact experiences with high impact on our lives. For example, in weddings, spoken questions and responses can create important connections. In every tradition, in order to marry each other, the partners must show up at the right place and time in front of an official and witnesses, exchange tokens—usually rings—and most crucially and importantly, exchange vows.

"Vows" is the label for the *talk*, the public spoken promises that people being married make to each other. In some traditions, vows consist mainly of a series of questions to which each partner responds, "I do." More frequently, the two each say their vows aloud to each other. Married couples witnessing a wedding often get emotional when they hear the vows being spoken, because they are reminded of the feelings they had when they said their own vows. But the strongest impact usually happens to the couple themselves, who are sometimes overcome enough by the weight of the situation that they find it hard to speak. For many of us, this is one of the most important moments in our lives.

In court, spoken and heard words can be just as important, but in other ways. When you're worried about what you're going to be asked as a witness at a trial, it can be hard to respond out loud to the bailiff or clerk's question, "Do you promise to tell the truth, the whole truth, and nothing but the truth, so help you God?" There's something about *saying* "I do," out loud in that courtroom that can be scary. What happens if, after that public commitment, you leave something out or inadvertently lie, and you get caught? On the other hand, if you're eager to tell your side of the story, the same moment between you and the bailiff can be empowering. In this situation, the bailiff's spoken question—"Do you promise. . . ?" and your confident "I do" can give special weight and credibility to everything you say next.

Talk in Families — Outside the sacred space or courtroom, families often have spoken mini-rituals that help keep them connected to one another. Before a Thanksgiving meal, each family member may say out loud one special thing they're thankful for. At the moment that these words are being spoken and heard, the fullest meaning of "Thanksgiving" can happen, right in this talk among the people around the table. At Christmas, my family re-kindles memories of our immigrant German forebears by singing together the German words of "Silent Night." All of us have to follow the text on the well-worn pages that are handed out just before we sing, because we've lost our grandparents' native language. But the foreign sounds we sing together still bring Grandma and Grandpa Hoffman into our presence, and, most importantly, the singing and hearing of these sounds together *connect* us as family. It's a moment that matters.

Moments that Matter Online — I noted earlier that, as individuals and as a species, humans originally experience moments that matter face-to-face, in verbal and nonverbal speaking and listening. This kind of talk is obviously not possible on some online technologies. In fact, some digital options are crowding these moments out of many people's lives. But in those cases where a person wants to encourage a personal connection online, for example, in an email, extended Facebook exchange, or a Skyped conversation, he or she will translate qualities of what is experienced in live talk into the digital contact.

As I'll explain in Chapter 3, some online options promote moments that matter and some don't. Because of the limitations of some social media, several groups I've talked with recently told me that they are now closing their accounts and re-committing to email, telephone contacts, and even snail mail and face-to-face meetings. Some researchers are getting increasingly worried that over-dependence on texting and short videos is crippling people's vital conversation skills.[6] Wedding guests are now being asked to turn over their cell phones before a ceremony to inhibit distractions during the event. At least one restaurant in Los Angeles is offering diners a 5 percent discount on their bill if they dump their digital devices before being seated.[7] Savvy online communicators are learning which media to use in which cases and how to balance the speed, efficiency, and effectiveness available online with the persistent and healthy human need for personal contact.

In short, moments that matter are some of the most human events we experience. They can be positive or negative. They are usually brief, but they can significantly affect our lives. Characteristically, they happen in talk, in the speaking and listening that we experience in the various arenas of our lives—families, business, religious and educational settings. Online options sometimes help these moments happen, and they often do just the opposite. For example:

MIS-MEETINGS

A man I know recently took his daughter and a group of her classmates to a concert in a nearby large city. Since they were graduating high school seniors, he treated the young women to dinner at a fancy restaurant before the concert. Right after the group was seated and before the server took their orders, each senior reached into her purse and pulled out her smart phone. Without saying anything to anyone at the table, each began texting, and two of them at the table were texting each other. Kevin was completely excluded from this part of their interaction.

From the young women's point of view, they were acting normally. It's fun to connect with your peers, and smart phone technology empowers you to enjoy almost constant contact. But it's digital rather than personal contact. Even acronym- and emoticon-laced texts, tweets, or Instagrams are pale reflections of what could have happened around the table. Neither the women nor their digital partner could see each other's face—wrinkled noses, raised eyebrows, dancing eyes, frowns and smiles. Except for the two texting each other, they couldn't hear each other's laugh or sarcastic groan; they missed the pauses in each other's talk and the wordssherantogether; they couldn't smell the fragrance each was wearing or playfully touch each other's arm.

Mis-meetings are missed opportunities for meeting, times when a moment that matters could have happened, and it didn't. Mis-meetings occur in many places. A parent has been longing for a close conversation with his son, the son says something briefly encouraging, and the dad is unable to follow through. Or, husband and wife both know that the husband's mom won't come out of the hospital this time, and yet they fall asleep without conversing about this significant event in their lives.

You may notice how often mis-meetings occur when you spend time with work colleagues or party guests who exchange superficialities rather than having genuine conversations, or you see a cafeteria full of high school or college students stooped over their smart phones and iPads. You may have heard about books like *The Shallows: What the Internet is Doing to Our Brain*[8] that document how social media and gaming have permanently altered reading, critical thinking, and communicating patterns. You may have read Sherry Turkle's book *Alone Together: Why We Expect More from Technology and Less from Each Other*[2] that reports thousands of cases of people substituting digital simulations for actual human contact. You may even find yourself texting rather than talking, using Snapchat rather than texting, or spending more time on Facebook than directly engaging with important people in your life. If so, understanding mis-meeting can help.

MARTIN BUBER'S CONTRIBUTIONS

I've taken the word, "mis-meeting" from a story told by a communication philosopher named Martin Buber. Buber was a very influential writer; for a time, his book *I and Thou* was third in world-wide sales only to *The Bible* and *The Qur'an*, even though Buber's book is not mainly religious. The "Thou" in the title is a translation of the intimate form of the German pronoun, "you," and his book is mostly about human relationships. The story Buber told is about a profound moment in which he learned what mis-meeting was.

Buber's parents divorced when he was young, and he was raised by his grandparents. When he was four years old, he was talking with his babysitter, a neighbor girl. Buber was missing his mother, and he asked his caregiver when she would return. More than 75 years later, Buber remembered word-for-word the sitter's reply, "No, she will never come back." Late in his life, Buber wrote about this moment, "I know that I remained silent, but also that I cherished no doubt of the truth of the spoken words." The four year-old Buber couldn't articulate exactly what he learned ("I remained silent"). But this painful moment of direct contact with the babysitter left him with a profound understanding ("I cherished no doubt of the truth") that lasted the rest of his life. What he learned in this moment was that he would never be able to connect with his mother in the same way he had just connected with the neighbor girl. As a child, he longed for this kind of contact with his mother, and the truth was, it would never happen.

As Buber put it, this truth "remained fixed in me; from year to year it cleaved ever more to my heart." Then "after more than ten years I had begun to understand it as something that concerned not only me, but all [people]. Later I made up the word, "Vergegnung"— "mismeeting," or "miscounter"—to designate the failure of a real meeting between [people]."[10]

The word that Buber coined combined the German word *begegn*, which means "meeting" or "encounter" with the prefix *ver*, as in the German words *verfehlen*, "misdirect," *versagen*, "misfire," *verwalten*, "mismanage," *verwenden*, "misappropriate," and *verdrucken*, "miscarriage." The concrete, human situation that birthed this spoken word and the way it was coined combine to give its meaning. Like "misfire," "mis-meeting" labels a defining event that should have happened and didn't. Like "misdirect," "mis-meeting" names a happening that went awry or astray. Like "miscarriage," "mis-meeting" is a word for an occurrence that violates legitimate expectations. Mis-meetings are missed opportunities for human contact. And they can profoundly affect the quality of our lives.

For example, a mis-meeting at work can lead us to question our competence or our importance to the organization. A mis-meeting at home can raise fears of abandonment or betrayal. A mis-meeting in the classroom can kill a student's motivation or lead a teacher to wonder if the job is worth the effort. Because we're all social animals, we know in our bones what personal contact feels like, and when we expect this kind of moment and it doesn't occur, the effect can be profound.

The Truth of the Spoken Words

Importantly, both meeting and mis-meeting can have the impact they do because of the way they're experienced. Buber highlights this point when he talks about suddenly recognizing "the truth of the spoken words." These words capture a kind of understanding that we have all experienced and that can be very powerful. It occurs when we are "struck" by something, or we have an "Aha!" experience. What we learn in these cases stands out and sticks with us. The insight is "in our face." It's impossible to ignore.

Unfortunately, we usually overlook this kind of experience when we think about why something is "true" for us. Usually, we recall how something becomes "true" because of the facts that support it and what the logical arguments are. But I'm talking about a different kind of understanding. Buber experienced "the truth of the spoken word" another way, in a moment that mattered. He learned about mis-meeting in this moment. This direct, immediate, "Aha!" way of understanding and learning becomes more important as we move through this book.

Buber knew that what the babysitter said was true, but not because she was a well-known authority or because she cited facts to back up what she said. The *truth* of what Buber learned in this meeting struck him directly and immediately; it "cleaved to his heart;" it enabled him to make sense of key parts of his life. He experienced this truth holistically and in his body. This is different from the kind of "truth" we learn from facts or logical arguments.

It is like the experience you've had when you've encountered a great piece of music or painting, an impressive building, a classic sculpture, or a moving poem. Take a beautiful temple or cathedral, for example. When you're standing in front of it taking it in, you are probably not objectively analyzing it. You're not noticing specific details like the harmonizing proportions of the roof lines or the relationships among the decorative statues. Instead, you're struck by the building in an immediate and holistic way. Your response is probably something holistic like, "Wow!" "Incredible!" or awe-struck silence. You can *feel* the meaning of the structure—that the humans who built it were truly devout and grateful to the deity it honors. You experience the truth of the building immediately, directly, and holistically.

I'll say more about this way of understanding in Chapter 2. My point here is that Buber experienced the spoken words of his baby-sitter immediately and holistically. When she said his mother was never coming back, he was left with "no doubt of the truth" of what he learned. All of us understand some truths in this same way, and I highlight it here, because this kind of understanding is what helps create moments that matter.

QUALITIES OF HUMAN CONTACT

Contact Quotient or CQ

One way to think about the differences between a moment that matters and one that doesn't is with the term Contact Quotient or CQ. CQ is the quotient that expresses the ratio between the quality of contact you experience and the quality of contact that's possible. In other words,

$$\frac{\text{Richness, intensity, or quality of contact achieved}}{\text{Richness, intensity, or quality of contact possible}}$$

For instance, a husband and wife who have been married for 40 years have a huge CQ denominator (the number below the line)—let's say 10,000. When they're angry with each other and one is giving the other the silent treatment, their numerator (the number above the line) is painfully small—maybe 15. So their CQ in this instance would be 15 / 10,000—pretty low. They are mis-meeting rather than meeting. But when they spend an afternoon and evening together in conversation, mutually enjoyed activities, and lovemaking, their numerator is very high—maybe 9,500—and their CQ approaches 10,000 / 10,000.

Moments that matter can be thought of as communication events with high CQ scores, where the people involved are taking full advantage of whatever contact-potential exists. But whether you think of the quality of your contact as a numerical ratio like CQ or as an un-quantifiable feature—awesome, rich, amazing, delightful, disappointing, thin, constrained, crappy—the point is that the quality of the contacts we experience varies widely.

Impersonal & Personal Contact

Buber's point in *I and Thou* was that humans have the capacity to connect with the world around us and with each other in two qualitatively-different ways.[11] It's easiest to understand these options with the help of a sliding scale, with the ends labeled "Impersonal" (Buber called it "I-It") relating and "Personal" (Buber called it "I-Thou") relating. At the impersonal or I-It end of the scale it's common to experience mis-meetings, while at the personal or I-Thou end of the scale you often experience a moment that matters.[12]

QUALITIES OF CONTACT

I-It or Impersonal------------------I-Thou or Personal

As I mentioned in the Preface, Impersonal communicating happens in the cafeteria line, with a ticket-taker, and usually in the bank or government office. The people involved connect with each other as role-fillers rather than as persons. By contrast, Personal communicating is connection between *persons*, unique, choice-making, reflective beings who bring to their meeting personal qualities, feelings, and second thoughts, and who notice some of the personal elements of those they're connecting with. I'll say much more about this in later chapters.

QUALITY OF COMMUNICATION AND QUALITY OF LIFE

My main point here, though, is *that there is a direct relationship between the quality of each human's relating and the quality of his or her life*. Humans become who we are in our relations with others, relations that can be placed along the Impersonal----Personal scale. Our most formative moments that matter happen in contact with others—mother and father, siblings, teachers, mentors, lovers, spouse, children, grandchildren. It's true that human life requires day-to-day, goal-directed, impersonal connections with more-or-less faceless others. It's also true that a full human life emerges most completely from direct, present, candid, personal connections—moments that matter.

For those of us who can hear and speak, most of these moments happen as spoken and heard, verbal and nonverbal contact—when he gently *says* "I love you" to her and she reciprocates, when AA sponsor and member *say* the serenity prayer together, when supervisor and subordinate profoundly connect in a performance evaluation conversation, when bride and groom share their vows with each other. Those who cannot hear or speak experience this same quality of contact nonverbally, for example in American Sign Language or with touch. These moments are not mysterious, they do not require any special knowledge, and we are all naturally capable of creating and experiencing them. They *can* happen via some digital technologies, but not all of the ones that people currently use or may use in the future.

Today, many people using social media report that they are online not to supplement their face-to-face contacts but to replace them. Given the history of technology, by the time you read these words, Snapchat, Instagram, and Facebook may be obsolete. But one thing that can be confidently said about their technological replacements is that many will facilitate more mis-meetings than moments that matter. Such is the natural tension between technology and what makes each of us human.

As I write this, I use two email accounts every day, I have two Facebook sites, a website, and a blog, Becky and I FaceTime with our family, and I Skype fairly often. So I'm definitely not an enemy of electronic communicating. And yet I know that many digital options mislead us into paying primary attention to speed and quantity over quality.

Image-management is crucial in cyberspace. For many people, two screens—or three—are better than one (tv + smart phone + tablet). Digital overload drives some of us to over-control our contact time by keeping people at a distance with the help of 10-second limits, texting shorthand, and the ready accessibility of virtual respondents—avatars, automatic status updates, and other non-human interaction options.

Off the internet in the face-to-face world, mass mailings, rigid business meeting agendas, large lecture classes, polarized political exchanges, and depersonalized religious services also distance us from the people we work with, vote for, learn from, and worship with. Mis-meetings clutter, clog, and infect our lives. They make us believe we're connecting with those we love when we're not. They frustrate our ability to reach our goals as parents, friends, managers, and spouses. Mis-meetings make work a chore. They separate us at family gatherings. They reduce our desire to worship. They make it easy for us to be absent from organizations whose goals we support. They alienate us from people we'd like to love. In all these ways, they diminish the quality of our lives.

You and I experience only a fraction of the high-quality moments that we could experience as friends, spouses, lovers, parents, neighbors, support group members, colleagues, worshippers, supervisors, managers, students, club officers, committee chairs, voters, and, representatives. To put it another way, across all the kinds of communication we experience, our CQ scores could be much higher than they are.

As a result, the quality of our lives is much lower than it could be. In the abstract, we don't fully realize our human potential as creatures who become who we are in our relationships with others, beings whose greatest potential is to love and be loved. Much more concretely, we ache from the lack of direct, personal contact with our sons, daughters, and spouses; our children, parents and grandparents are confused by some of our decisions because they don't know us as well as they could; work is a drag because we almost never have the pleasure of collaborating on a smoothly-functioning team; and we leave the annual meeting, monthly conference, or weekly prayer service with a strong sense that, although we smiled at and spoke to several people, we seldom really *connected*. We spend time with others, and we're still lonely. This book can help you reverse these trends.

PREVIEW OF WHAT'S COMING

In the next chapter, I describe how to recover some of what's been lost. Chapter 2 begins by connecting communication to the question, "What does it mean to be human?" and then details the crucial differences between every human's two ways of understanding that I've already introduced. It shows how our holistic, direct way of understanding empowers us to communicate personally. From this chapter, you'll learn generally how you can help make more of your communicating as personal as possible.

The largest part of the book is made up of eight "Applications to Life" chapters. Each provides concrete and practical suggestions for how you can encourage and experience more of these moments in eight arenas of your life: Chapter 3 explains how you can use the communication understandings and skills developed in Chapters 1 and 2 to enrich your online communicating. Chapter 4 is about dating and courtship. Chapter 5 focuses on family life. Chapter 6 addresses business life, Chapter 7 on your life as a learner and teacher, Chapter 8 on your political communicating, and Chapter 9 on multicultural situations. Chapter 10 is about spiritual and religious contexts.

Chapter 11 re-connects all the understandings and skills to who we are as humans and leaves you with three general guidelines to help make more of your communicating as personal as possible.

Two Important Reminders

Remember the point about common sense. You may already know a lot of what's here—at least in your head. But if effective communication were mainly a matter of common sense, the divorce rate would be much lower, there'd be less bullying in schools, fewer people would be taking drugs for depression and stress, and the culture would be investing much less money, time, and stress coping with painful relationships. No doubt you already do some—maybe even a lot—of what I suggest in the chapters coming up. And I'm also sure that both you and I can do a better job of communicating in just about all the situations we encounter. I invite you to join me in this project of making more of our communication as personal a possible!

Finally, although I'm sharing these ideas in the form of a book, I hope that you won't stop with just the words on these pages. What's here is meant to be discussed with family and friends, tested at home and at work, and applied, in real time, with *talk*; that is, in your listening and speaking, texting and Skyping. Hugh Prather effectively described what's involved in this application process. He wrote,

> Ideas are clean. They soar in the serene supernal. I can take
> them out and look at them, they fit into books, they lead me
> down the narrow way. And in the morning they are there.
> Ideas are straight—
> But the world is round, and a
> messy mortal is my friend.
> Come walk with me in the mud. . . .[13]

Chapter 2

MAKING YOUR COMMUNICATION AS PERSONAL AS POSSIBLE

THE BIG QUESTION: WHAT DOES IT MEAN TO BE HUMAN?

YOU PROBABLY WOULDN'T THINK that personal communication is connected with what it means to be a human being, but it turns out it is.

The connection surfaces every year in an unexpected place, the international test of the question, "Can computers think?" Artificial Intelligence researchers try to answer this question with what's called the Turing test.

In the Turing test, a panel of judges use keyboards and screens to interview a pair of unseen respondents, one a human confederate and the other a computer program designed to carry on a conversation—a chatbot. The judges try to figure out which is the human and which is the computer. The originator of the test claimed that if and when a chatbot was able to fool 30 percent of the judges after five minutes of

39

conversation, "one will be able to speak of machines thinking without expecting to be contradicted."[14] *This hasn't yet happened, but in the 2008 contest, the top program missed the mark by just one vote.*

Brian Christian was a confederate in the 2009 test, and, as he explains in his book The Most Human Human, the Turing test forces computer programmers, judges, and confederates to confront the question, "What does it mean to be human?" and to communicate in ways that reflect their responses. This is why the Turing test can help show what personal communication actually is.

In their five-minute online conversations, each Turing test participant has to plan and carry out questions and responses that, on the judges' side, test for distinctively human characteristics, and on the programmers and confederates' sides, try to demonstrate them. What best communicates humanness? Is it emotional content that the messages need to ask for and display? Uniqueness? Moral values? Self-reference? Humor? Awkwardness? Interruption?

Besides determining whether computers can think, the answer to The Big Question also affects a lot of other basic judgments. For example, if you agree with the ancient Greek philosopher Aristotle that the answer to the question is that humans are "rational animals," then logic and reason are more important to who we are than emotions, hopes, or dreams. On the other hand, if you answer to the question, "What does it mean to be human?" by saying that we were created by God, Allah, or some other higher power, then there are realities beyond what humans experience; it's possible in some ways to know your creator; and it makes sense to hope for a life after death, even though that may not be "rational."

Answers to The Big Question

So how's the Big Question been answered? Over centuries, the best thinkers have come up with responses that say humans are *two-sided.*

Analytic and Holistic Understanding — Several philosophers and political theorists have answered The Big Question by saying that humans are the beings who understand what's around us in two different ways: analytically and holistically.[15]

Analytic understanding finds order and meaning through the use of rationality, logic, and verifiable fact (e. g., using a checklist), and holistic understanding finds order and meaning through the use of analogies or stories (e.g., "This organization has tight little groups, just like my high school," or "The answer here is like Goldilocks— not too little, not to big, but just right."). Humans naturally do both. Analytic thinking works by breaking things into parts, and holistic understanding grasps things as-a-whole. Analytic thinking is distanced and objective, while holistic understanding is immediate, participatory, and is often expressed in statements that are feeling-laden and subjective in other ways. Analytic understanding emerges from purposeful studying and holistic understanding often feels like it "happened to" the understander in some kind of "Aha!" moment. Analytic understanding emphasizes similarities and generalizations, while holistic understanding emphasizes individual differences. We have no evidence that any beings other than humans can understand in both these ways.

Impersonal & Personal Understanding — Another two-sided answer to The Big Question comes from neuroscientists. These researchers focus on the human brain, because it is the part of the body that most sets us apart from all other beings.

In many ways, the scientific answer to The Big Question echoes the philosophical one. The simplest version of the neuroscientists' answer emphasizes differences between the human brain's right and left hemispheres. Electronic pictures of human brain operations demonstrate that the right hemisphere comprehends unique things-as-a-whole and in their context, where the left hemisphere understands things broken into parts. As brain scientist Jill Bolte Taylor explains,

> *Moment by moment, our right mind creates a master collage of what this moment in time looks like, sounds like, tastes like, smells like, and feels like. . . to the right mind, no time exists other than the present moment, and each moment is vibrant with sensation*"[16]

Taylor continues,

> *In contrast, our left hemisphere is completely different in the way it processes information. It takes each of those rich and complex moments created by the right hemisphere and strings them together in timely succession. It then sequentially compares the details making up this moment with the details making up the last moment. By organizing details in a linear and methodical configuration, our left brain manifests the concept of time whereby our moments are divided into the past, present and future.*"[17]

Another brain scientist adds, "And it also turns out that the capacities that help us, as humans, form bonds with others—empathy, emotional understanding, and so on. . .are largely right-hemisphere functions."[18]

A more up to date version of the neuroscientists' answer emphasizes the importance of what brain researchers call "mirror neurons." These are brain cells that fire not only when a person performs an action like drinking a glass of water but also when the same person watches someone else performing the same action. Importantly, mirror neurons are not located in just one hemisphere; they are parts of complex circuits that connect various areas of the brain. Several brain scientists believe that mirror neurons are what permit one person to understand the other person "from the inside." As one puts it, "Our brain seems to make sense of other people through shared circuits. . . . It's through this capacity that you get this intuitive understanding of other people's goals."[19]

This brain research gets tied to communication when neuroscientists label these two kinds of understanding "the personal versus the impersonal."[20] The main reason one is called *impersonal* is that it groups things and people into categories like "evergreen and deciduous," "beautiful and ugly," "big and little," or "male and female, " while the other kind of understanding recognizes uniqueness, like "the tree where the swing's always been," "uncle Al," or "mom." Another reason for the distinction is that *impersonal* understanding breaks things and people into parts, while *personal* understanding is holistic, like we recognize songs or faces. In short, decades of research and clinical experience lead these brain scientists to answer the Big Question this way: *Humans are the beings who are able to understand everything around us both personally and impersonally.*

TWO KINDS OF HUMAN UNDERSTANDING

Analytic or IMPERSONAL understanding	Holistic or PERSONAL understanding
• Comprehends using analysis, logic, & facts	• Comprehends using images & story
• Breaks things into parts	• Understands things as-a-whole
• Distanced and objective	• Immediate, participatory, and subjective
• Results from intending to "get it"	• Often happens to you as an "Aha!"
• Emphasizes similarities, groups, and generalizations	• Emphasizes one-of-a-kind features

Both kinds of understanding operate together, and yet it's easy to find examples that emphasize each. Analytic understanding is mainly operating every time you decide on a big purchase by researching different brands and models and analyzing various features, functions, and warranties. Judges instruct attorneys to present them with only "the relevant facts." And as the 2011 film "Moneyball" illustrated, many professional baseball teams now select players by using "sabermetrics" to amass statistics describing almost everything a player does. These are all examples of analytic, impersonal understanding.

But, as films like Clint Eastwood's 2012 feature, "Trouble with the Curve" shows, many good decisions about baseball players are not purely rational or analytic. Juries also base their decisions not just on individual facts but on the most believable *story* that connects the various pieces of evidence into a whole.[21] This means that judges and especially juries also understand the story of a crime holistically. Similarly, patriotic men and women regularly join the armed services even when it might not make analytic sense to do so, because of their love for their country. Some people choose a ride because of "car lust." Those who act on personal understandings often report that the key insight—the patriotic urge to serve, love for a car's styling—does not emerge from any systematic process of rational decision-making. Instead it "struck them" in an "Aha!" moment and later "felt right."

And perhaps most commonly and most importantly, people make lifetime commitments to their husbands, wives, and partners not because the facts add up, but because they've fallen in love. "Fallen," as in it happened *to* them. These are all examples of personal understanding.

Both personal and impersonal understanding are vital to effective and happy human living, and in practice, they often overlap. *And*, while impersonal understanding is unquestionably necessary, personal understanding is tied most closely to the quality of our lives.

OUR TWO WAYS OF UNDERSTANDING LEAK OUT IN OUR LISTENING & TALKING

These two ways of understanding show themselves in our verbal and nonverbal, spoken and heard communicating. Talk reveals *impersonal* understanding when it includes a lot of labeling—*"the administrative assistant," "one of the servers," "somebody in sales," "another politician"*—because labels treat people as types or categories, rather than unique individuals. Impersonal understanding also emphasizes measurable qualities of the person—how old, short, or heavy they are, or the person's ethnicity or gender. So stereotypes result from impersonal understanding. This kind of understanding also surfaces in absolute judgments about whose fault it is or why something happened—*"She's bad for you," "Don't buy anything from them." "If you can't trust them, just do it yourself."*

At other times, we understand and relate to the things and people around us *personally*, that is, holistically, with immediacy, relevant feelings, positive or negative caring, and sometimes with love. *You ask your friend how his day is going, and genuinely listen to his response, rather than immediately dumping your troubles on him. Your boss asks you for an evaluation and you care enough about her future success to tell her truthfully that she's sometimes too intense to work with comfortably. You search for ways to comprehend your teenage son's fascination with Goth dress because you want him to understand your fears about the risks of this subculture. You spend time having coffee with your sister rather than always tweeting or texting, and while you're together you both turn off your screens.*

As I've said, most of us live significantly imbalanced lives that involve much more impersonal than personal understanding, and as a result, our lives involve much more impersonal than personal communicating. This is true both globally and locally. From a global perspective, Oxford professor, physician, and neuroscientist Iain

McGilchrist offers hundreds of pages of documentation to support his claim that impersonal modes of understanding have come to dominate Western culture to the point where both art and science are dangerously out-of-balance.[22]

Locally, the imbalance is easier to see. As I've noted, it makes sense to relate *impersonally* with bank tellers, ticket-takers, bus and taxi drivers, many customer service people, retail clerks, and most of the people with whom we have purely social role-relationships. But this depersonalized quality of contact happens in too many of our tweets, texts, Facebook postings, and emails, and in too much of our other communication. The imbalance is obvious in the way mismeetings clog and infect our lives.

Since humans have the capacity to relate to what's around us both impersonally and personally, whenever we spend our lives stuck in either mode, we fail to realize our full human potential. This is what's at stake. There may be some rare persons whose relational lives are unbalanced by too much personal relating. If these people exist, they would benefit from *fewer* moments that matter. But for most of us, the opposite is true. As a result, more of these moments can profoundly enhance our lives.

So How Can We Best Encourage Moments that Matter?

In a few paragraphs, I'll provide a simple model that can guide your practical efforts to encourage moments that matter in every arena of your life. This model combines the impersonal----personal distinction I've just outlined with two additional important points.

The first is that communication is **continuous.** People have been talking and listening ever since we evolved from apes. Versions of the communicating we experience every day were going on when we were born and will continue after we die. This means that none of us completely *originates* any specific communication contribution. In fact it can often helpful to think of all our communicating as a *response* to some of what came before it. So the irate husband's, "Get the hell out of here!" isn't just an order or an attack; it's also a *response* to what preceded his outburst.

Responses have both a backward-looking and a forward-looking part. The irate husband's outburst is clearly designed to end that conversation; that's what he wants to happen *next*. If he'd added, "Plaster's falling off the ceiling!" the next thing he might have heard is "Thanks!" The important point is to realize that you're always in the middle of an ongoing flow of communicating, and if you want to understand what's being said or done, you need to think of it as part of this flow from what has happened to what might happen *next*.

"Continuous" also means that, so long as we are within the hearing, seeing, smelling, tasting, or touching distance of someone else, we cannot *not* communicate. If you and I were sitting across from each other and I asked you to stop communicating with me, you could not do what I asked. Why? Because anything you did—look down, be silent, leave the room—would mean something to me. Whenever anyone can perceive us, they can (and do) build meaning from what we do and don't do.[23] Communication is *continuous* in both these senses.

The second important point is that all communication is **collaborative.** This obviously doesn't mean that people always agree, but that communicators "co-labor" to produce meanings, even when they disagree. This happens even when one person has much more power. Regardless of how carefully the manager plans a meeting, one or more people might have agendas different from his. Regardless of how clearly I write or speak, you may still interpret what I say as confusing. Even a dictator whose orders are consistently followed can't control how people feel about his or her demands. Mixed martial arts competitors are also collaborating by showing up at the same time, agreeing to the involvement of the referee, and following the rules. Conversation partners are usually co-laboring more than this, regardless of how much they agree or disagree. So whether you're thinking about written or spoken communication, face-to-face or digital, conflict or cooperation, the process basically involves humans continuously and collaboratively **making meaning together.**

Give Up Blaming —When people forget that they're continuously collaborating on meanings, they tend to oversimplify their understanding of communication. One prominent oversimplification is the belief that a communication outcome can be accurately blamed on one person's actions—"It's her fault that we're lost," "He made me forget the meeting," or, as I heard a few days ago, "She made me have that affair." When you understand that human communication is *continuous* and *collaborative*, you cannot coherently blame just one person or one set of actions for whatever is happening.

For one thing, in order to say that someone caused an outcome, or that "It's all her fault," you need to assume that whatever happened *began with the guilty person's action.* But since communication is *continuous,* that can't be. So the person whom you say is at fault because he didn't call you back to confirm the meeting may be remembering your complaints about "getting all those annoying calls."

Fault and blame also ignore the fact that communication is *collaborative*. When directions are unclear, for example, it's due to both the direction-giver and the direction-receiver. Did the receiver ask about what confused her? Did the giver check the receiver's understanding? It may have seemed perfectly legitimate to one person to assume that the family would gather for the holiday dinner just as they had in the past. But others might have different legitimate assumptions that led to different interpretations.

Does this mean that when there are problems, nobody's responsible? No, not at all. Individual responses still make a difference, and some are more ethical, appropriate, or humane than others. But it's important to replace the oversimplified and distorted notions of fault and blame with a broader focus on both or all "sides" of the communication process. I do not mean to replace "It's her fault" with "It's his fault," "It's both of their faults," or "It's nobody's fault." Instead, I'm suggesting that you give up the notion of fault and blame altogether, at least when you're thinking or talking about human communication, because it drastically oversimplifies the process.

I hope you can get a sense of the significance of the fact that communication is continuous and collaborative. When you forget these features, problems almost inevitably arise. And if you can work to eliminate these problems, I guarantee that your CQ scores will climb. Here's a poem I wrote about this idea.

The backstory: Two lovers, forced by prior commitments to be 2000 miles apart for six weeks, talk by phone every day. Although they understand that "absence makes the heart grow fonder," they dislike the separation. Three weeks into the separation, he writes a poem for her and when he reads it to her over the phone, she cries. After their conversation about that poem, he writes this one.

BETWEEN

"You make me cry."
"You make me write."
Lovers touching over miles,
Each reports a personal truth,
And each distorts what's real.

Her tears aren't caused by him,
Like a hammer drives a nail
Or the moon moves tides.
His writing's not caused by her,
Like heat boils water,
Or a lever lifts a weight.
Neither makes the other cry or write.

Crying happens when her love meets his words.
Writing blooms from his love of words and her.
Both emerge between.

Her crying shows her love:
Others wouldn't weep,
Some wouldn't even read.
His writing shows his love:
Others might tweet or sing.
Some wouldn't even blink.

So it is between these two,
And everywhere that humans walk.
Count all that's individual,
Track each psychic piece
Trace every singularity,
And what remains counts most;
The syn- in synergy
The function in math,
The green when yellow meets blue—
The between.

Don't shape your world to fit the lie
That "person" equals "island,"
That Adam's only one,
Separate, individual,
Disconnected from partner Eve.

Asian thinkers have it right:
The smallest human unit's two.
We're products of connections.
What's real for each is co- and syn-
Jill's world is built with Jack
And his with her.

So what?
Don't shift from blame to guilt—
"It's all my fault" or "I screwed up."
That's just another lie,
Obscuring what's between.
Instead, refigure fault and blame,

Re-own your role in joys and pains,
Embrace your partnered life.

Giving Out and Taking In

This model also appropriates the simple distinction between what communicators "give out" and what we "take in." All communicating involves both these processes, whether we're face-to-face, online, on the telephone, or writing. Each person communicating in all these contexts is simultaneously "giving out" verbal and nonverbal cues, and he or she is also "taking in" cues from others.

The "giving out" part includes the amount you write or say; your word choices; your tone of voice; how loud and how fast you talk; the white space, caps, punctuation, and emoticons in your writing; and your body language when you're face-to-face or video-connected—eye behavior, facial expression, posture, gestures, etc.

The "taking in" part includes everything your senses pick up—what you hear, see, smell, and in some cases what you touch and taste. "Taking in" also includes all your listening behaviors, including how and how much you focus on the other person, whether and how you encourage her speaking, how open you are to what she says, whether and how you reflect back what you hear, the questions you ask, and how you interpret what's said. Within the constraints permitted by the medium being used, communicators are always both "giving out" and "taking in" communication cues.

MAKING YOUR COMMUNICATING AS PERSONAL AS POSSIBLE

A moment that matters happens when the people involved *collaborate to make the communication between them as personal as possible.* This is the basic understanding that the rest of this book explains how to apply. When communicators "give out" and "take in" only their *impersonal* qualities or features, then the contact between them will be *impersonal*. When the alternative happens, when the people involved engage their holistic, personal mode of understanding in order to "give out" and "take in" more of their own and the other's *personal* qualities or features, then moments of matter will happen.

Exactly what are our "impersonal" and "personal" features?

A MODEL OF QUALITIES OF COMMUNICATION Impersonal ------------------------Personal	
When self & other are treated as:	When self & other are treated as
Interchangeable	*Unique*
Measurable	*Having ESP (emotions, spirit, psyche)*
Reactive	*Responsive*
Unreflective/Mindless	*Reflective/Mindful*

You can put every instance of your communicating somewhere along the model's line between impersonal and personal. And the model shows you how to move your communicating in whichever direction you prefer. When people communicate positively or negatively with respect, caring, candor, empathy, and presentness, they "give out" and "take in" significant *personal* features—uniqueness, ESP, responsiveness, and mindful reflectiveness. The result is that the contact between them is personal and their contact quotient (CQ) is higher. And when they give out and take in only interchangeable, measurable, reactive and unreflective/mindless parts, then the contact between them is impersonal.[24] Let's look at each of these features.

FEATURES OF "THE PERSONAL"

Uniqueness

Humans can definitely be treated as if we were interchangeable parts, but each of us is unique in at least a couple of ways. One is genetically. Unless two persons are cloned or are identical twins, the probability that they would have the same genetic materials is 1 in 10 to the ten-thousandth power. That's less than one chance in a billion trillion!

But even when persons have the same biological raw material, each experiences the world differently and develops a unique identity. You verify this every time you get to know identical twins. If you've done this, you've undoubtedly found that even though their DNA may be the same, they have individual preferences, styles, patterns, weaknesses, and strengths.

When Turing Test confederate Brian Christian was challenged to convince the judges that he was a human and not a computer program, he focused centrally on "giving out" uniqueness. One day, a round of the competition was delayed by fifteen minutes, and Christian immediately mentioned the delay in his texting. He was the only one who mentioned it. None of the chatbots could be reprogrammed quickly enough to follow suit. As Christian writes,

> *"Part of what makes language such a powerful vehicle for communicating 'humanly' is that a good writer or speaker or conversationalist will tailor her words to the specifics of the situation: who the audience is, what the rhetorical situation happens to be, how much time there is, what kind of reaction she's getting as she speaks, and on and on. . . . [The opposite] is part of what makes the language of some salesmen, seducers, and politicians so half-human."*[25]

Christian extends his experience beyond the Turing Test when he concludes, *"I suppose when you get down to it, everything is always once in a lifetime. We might as well act like it."* (Christian, p. 98) This is great advice!

When people are communicating with each other *impersonally*, they are overlooking most of this uniqueness.[26] Our familiar first conversation moves—"Hey!" "Hi! How are you?" "Good, how are you?" "Good!"—

are ways to get to the point where we can experience the unexpected, the idiosyncratic turns that give life to our exchange; they enable us to move past formalities and patterned gestures into the real thing.

Our ability to understand uniqueness is one of the gifts we receive from the personal parts of our brain. As McGilchrist puts it,

> *In general. . .the left hemisphere's tendency is to classify, where the right hemisphere's is to identify individuals. . . .The right hemisphere's version [of experience] is more global and holistic. . . whereas the left hemisphere identifies single features that would place the object in a certain category in the abstract.*[27]

Each time you recognize uniqueness, each time you notice, understand, "get it" both *that* the person you're talking with is unique and something of *how* he or she is unique, your understanding becomes more holistic, immediate, and personal. It's more holistic because you don't notice uniqueness by adding up a critical mass of distinctive attributes; you grasp a whole. In addition, this kind of understanding often happens *to* you when a person's uniqueness smacks you upside your head; you're surprised and struck by it. *For example, recall the last time that you were intently listening to a friend so carefully that you were about to finish a sentence for him and he finished it in a way you could never have predicted.*

Uniqueneness is the primary "feature of the personal" that makes communication personal. Moments that matter happen most fully when the people involved notice and respond to each other as unique individuals. The personal capabilities of our brain give each of us, without any special training, the ability to understand elements of the other's uniqueness immediately, holistically, and in-the-present, and to access aspects of our own uniqueness that are relevant to the conversation. As a result, when you want to move your communicating toward the right-hand side of the sliding scale, listen and talk in ways that enable you to recognize and affirm the other's uniqueness and to make some of your uniqueness available to your conversation partner.

In future chapters, I'll suggest specific ways to attend to and demonstrate uniqueness online (Chapter 3), when dating (Chapter 4), in your family (Chapter 5), on the job (Chapter 6), in multicultural situations (Ch. 9), and so on.

Emotions-Spirit-Psyche (ESP)

Objects are measurable; they fit within boundaries. An event lasts a measurable amount of time. Although it's difficult to measure some things directly—the temperature of a kiss, the velocity of a photon, the duration of an explosion—the objective features of a phenomenon can be described in space-and-time terms. This is what blueprints and spec lists do.

It's different with persons. Even if a medical team accurately identifies Jack's height, weight, temperature, blood pressure, serum cholesterol level, hemoglobin count, and all his other data right down to the electric potential of his seventh cranial nerve, the team will not have captured the person Jack is. Many scientists, social scientists, philosophers, and theologians have made this point. Some cognitive scientists, for example, include in their model of the person components they call "schemata," or "cognitive patterns" that don't have any space-and-time (measurable) existence, but that can be inferred from observations of behavior. Others call the unmeasurable element of a person the "human spirit," "psyche," or "soul." But whatever you call it, it's there.

I call this feature ESP to help it stick in your mind. I do not mean "extra-sensory perception" as in telepathy or clairvoyance. Here, ESP labels the everyday, readily-observable qualities or features of persons that can't be directly measured but are nonetheless very real—our emotions, characteristic spirit, and individual psyche.

Emotions or feelings are the clearest observable evidence of this unmeasurable part. Instruments can measure data related to feelings-- "Pulse 110, respiration 72, Likert rating 5.39, palmar conductivity 0.036 ohms." Although these may be accurate, they don't capture what's going on in you when you encounter somebody you can't stand or say goodbye to somebody you love.

When people are connecting person-to-person, some of their feelings are in play. This does not mean that you have to pry into your conversation partner's darkest secrets or wear your heart on your sleeve to communicate personally. It just means that when people are making personal contact, some feelings and other parts of the peoples' ESP are appropriately acknowledged (taken in) and shared (given out).

Responsive

Objects can only react; they cannot respond. The difference is that reactions don't involve choice and responses do. A ball can go only where it's kicked, and if you are good enough at physics calculations, you can figure out how far and where it will go, on the basis of weight, impact, velocity, and aerodynamics. But what if you kick a person? You cannot accurately predict what will happen, because when persons are involved, the outcome depends on response, not simply reaction.

The human range of responses is limited, of course. We can't instantly change sex, become three years younger, or memorize the contents of Wikipedia. *And* we *can* decide whether to use a conventional word or an obscene one; we can choose how to prioritize our time commitments, and choice is even part of the feelings we experience.

As I mentioned earlier, responses have a forward-looking element. This means that your choices help determine what happens next. No matter what's happened before and no matter how bad things currently look and feel, you always have the option to try a *next* step that moves the conversation forward. No matter how long two people have not been speaking to each other, the next time they meet, one of them could speak.

Sometimes people make remarkable ethical choices in extreme situations. *Rais Bhuiyan, a Muslim man living in Houston, was shot in the face in a hate crime following the 9/11 terrorist attacks by Mark Stroman, an admitted white supremacist. As Bhuiyan describes the shooting, "He asked me 'Where are you from?' and I said, 'Excuse me?' As soon as I spoke, I felt the sensation of a million bees stinging my face and I heard an explosion." Bhuiyan lost the vision of his right eye in the attack, but now, as he puts it, "I forgave Mark Stroman many years ago. In fact I never hated him. I never hated America for what happened to me either. Islam calls us to forgiveness and compassion." Stroman was sentenced to death for killing two other men in similar, hate-crime incidents. Bhuiyan, along with others in the Muslim community and beyond, campaigned to have Stroman's death sentence communed to life without parole. They were unsuccessful. Just before he was executed, Stroman acknowledged the changes that Bhuiyan's campaign had made in him. "Hate is going on in this world and it has to stop," he said to prison witnesses. " Hate causes a lifetime of pain."*[28]

Bhuiyan's experience is obviously an extreme one. But small choices are also important. The more you realize your freedom and power to respond rather than simply react, the more you can make your communicating as personal as possible. Sometimes it's easy to fall out of touch with this freedom and power. You feel like saying, "I *had* to shout back; he was making me look silly!" or "I just couldn't say anything!" These statements make it sound as if you don't have any choice, but even when circumstances are exerting pressure, persons still have some freedom and power to choose how to respond. It may mean resisting a culturally-rooted preference or breaking some well-established habit pattern, and it may take courage and practice. But it's possible to become aware of your options and, when you choose, to change them. The reason this point is important is that when you're just reacting, you've lost touch with an important part of what it means to be a human being.

Reflective/Mindful

A fourth feature of humans is that we can be reflective and mindful. These two words identify different parts of this distinctive element of our humanity. The term "reflective" means that we are not only aware of what's around us but also that we are characteristically *aware of our awareness*. Wrenches, rocks, and rowboats aren't aware at all. Dogs, cats, armadillos, and giraffes are all aware of their environments, but we don't have any evidence that they are aware of their awareness. They can't make the "meta-move" that humans make whenever we are proud of our courage or ashamed of our cowardice, feel pleased by our progress or frustrated at the time we've wasted, or whenever we have "second thoughts" about a choice or decision we've made. So far as we know, only humans naturally and regularly compose and save histories of their lives, elaborately bury their dead, explore their extrasensory powers, question the meaning of life, and speculate about the past and future. All these practices grow out of human reflection, awareness of awareness.

Mindfulness is related to being reflective. Mindfulness is "the awareness that emerges through paying attention on purpose, in the present moment, and nonjudgmentally to the unfolding of experience moment by moment."[29] Mindfulness means "being here now." It's the opposite of living life on automatic pilot. It is a psychological state and a skill that has been the focus of centuries of Eastern thought, especially in Buddhist traditions, and it is now being actively researched, taught, and practiced by Westerners dedicated to personal and interpersonal well-being.

Psychiatrists, neurobiologists, educators, and communication scholars have discovered how powerfully mindfulness can affect many aspects of our lives.

Buddhist practice often begins by helping people be mindful of their breathing. Zen master Thich Nhat Hanh explains,

> *As you breathe in, you can say to yourself, "Breathing in, I know that I am breathing in." When you do this, the energy of mindfulness embraces your in-breath, just like sunlight touching the leaves and branches of a tree. The light of mindfulness is content just to be there and embrace the breath, without doing it any violence, without intervening directly. As you breathe out, you can gently say, "Breathing out, I know that I am breathing out.*[30]

This focus on breathing sounds strange to some Westerners. But mindfulness can be applied to washing the dishes, jogging, cooking, driving, and every other daily activity. When you are in a mindful state, there is a great deal of evidence that many aspects of human life improve, including your level of stress, immune functioning, ability to heal, resistance to eating disorders, and interpersonal attunement.[31] When you increase your mindfulness, you can enhance the quality of your life.

When people are ignoring the fact that humans can be reflective and mindful, their communication usually shows it. For example, a person may stick with superficial topics—the weather, recent news items, gossip—topics that don't require much reflection. Or two people might carry on a several-minute conversation that moves on automatic pilot—*"How are you?" "Fine." "What's been happening?" "Not much. How about you?" "Oh you know: Same old, same old." "Did you have a good summer?" "Great. You?"* And so on. These ways of relating keep you on the left hand side of the impersonal----personal scale.

On the other hand, when you mindfully take active account of your own and others' reflectiveness, you can significantly enrich what's going on as you communicate.

You can encourage mindfulness by slowing down, pausing to reflect, taking time to consider the complexities of both the topic and your conversation partner. You can also try focusing your own and the other person's attention on the present—*"What are you thinking?" "How are you feeling now about this plan?" "What doesn't sound quite right to you?"* Mindfulness also includes acceptance of what's happened and what's unavoidable. Even though you might have wished that she didn't say that, or that the deadline hadn't passed, when she did, and when it has, you can focus on what might happen *next.*

The point is that humans are distinctively able to be reflective and mindful, and communication that embodies this feature is more personal than communication that doesn't.

SOME EXAMPLES

It's fairly easy to locate examples of impersonal communication that would fit on the left-hand side of the sliding scale in the model. Here is a simplified text of an impersonal conversation among five high-school friends:

Nancy:	*We had like a light lunch. No, you had a steak today!*
Vicki:	*Shawn ate lobster this afternoon.*
Nina:	*Really?*
Matthew:	*He did?*
Shawn	*Yah*
Nina:	*Where at?*
Vicki:	*A half Maine lobster in the mall? They have this place. . .it was Café Mandarin?*

Matthew:	*Yeah?*
Vicki:	*So he had this special. So he thinks that the lobster's gonna be all cut up and everything, an' he'll just stick it and. . .*
Nina:	*Yeah. . . .*
Vicki:	*eat it, and here they bring this animal. . .*
Matthew:	*Was it a whole lobster?*
Vicki:	*It was a half*
Shawn:	*A half a lobster.*
Vicki:	*But it was all, you know*
Shawn:	*One claw and then: half, you know*
Matthew:	*How, how much?*
Vicki	*Nine ninety-five*
Vicki:	*It was with appetizer an' soup*
Matthew:	*Really?*
Shawn:	*I got everything*
Vicki:	*Chicken chow mein, rice, and the lobster*
Nina:	*Wow!*
Shawn:	*Ah, It was a full meal*
Matthew:	*Wow*
Shawn:	*Nine ninety-five. I can't believe it.*
Nancy:	*Such. . .a. . .deal*
Shawn:	*Yeah.*[32]

At other times, these friends' conversations may well fit on the personal side of the model. But in this exchange they give out and take in mainly impersonal stuff. The whole exchange sticks to a fairly superficial topic and doesn't reveal much about any of the people's uniqueness. The story is about Shawn's experience, but there's little here that reveals how Shawn felt about what happened (ESP), other than that he was impressed at the price. Matthew and Nina function mainly as foils for Vicki (reacting). Vicki frames the story as a joke on Shawn, but this element is left undeveloped. The conversation could have happened between just about any group of friends.

By contrast, consider this brief exchange from the stage play, *The Diary of Anne Frank*. The play is based on the true story of how Anne, her Jewish family, and some family friends hid from the Nazis in a secret apartment on the top floor of a building in Amsterdam during much of World War II. The diary ends when the family is discovered by the Gestapo and sent to the camps to die. This conversation occurs between Anne and her sister Margot, after it has become obvious that Anne and Peter Van Daan, who is also hiding there, are developing a relationship.

Anne:	*I'm sorry, Mother. I'm going to Peter's room. I'm not going to let Petronella Van Daan spoil our friendship.*
Margot:	*Why don't you two talk in the main room? It'd save a lot of trouble. It's hard on Mother, having to listen to those remarks from Mrs. Van Daan and not say a word.*
Anne:	*Why doesn't she say a word? I think it's ridiculous to take it and take it.*
Margot:	*You don't understand Mother at all, do you? She can't talk back. She's not like you. It's just not in her nature to fight back.*
Anne:	*Anyway. . .the only one I worry about is you. I feel awfully guilty about you.*
Margot:	*What about?*
Anne:	*I mean, every time I go into Peter's room, I have a feeling I may be hurting you. I know if it were*

> *me, I'd be wild. I'd be desperately jealous, if it*
> *were me.*

Margot: *Well, I'm not.*

Anne: *You don't feel badly? Really? Truly? You're not*
jealous?

Margot: *Of course I'm jealous. . . jealous that you've got*
something to get up in the morning for. . . . But
jealous of you and Peter? No.

Anne: *Maybe there's nothing to be jealous of. Maybe he*
doesn't really like me. Maybe I'm just taking the place
of his cat! Wouldn't you like to come in with us?[33]

Anne is uniquely present to Margot here in the way she "gives out"
her feelings about her mother—"I think it's ridiculous to take it and
take it"—and about Margo—"I have a feeling I may be hurting you."
Ann shows some elements of reflection when she says, "I mean, every
time I go into Peter's room, I have a feeling I may be hurting you."
Anne also invests energy" taking in" Margot's feelings—"You don't
feel badly? Really? Truly? You're not jealous?"(ESP) Anne reveals
her questioning (reflectiveness) when she wonders, "Maybe there's
nothing to be jealous of. . . ." Margot shares some of her uniqueness,
too, in her feelings—"Of course I'm jealous. . . ." One of Anne's
choices is evident when she says, "I'm not going to let Petronella Van
Daan spoil our friendship." Margo inserts their mother's feelings into
the conversation when she says, "It's hard on Mother. . . ." Margo
shares some of her understanding of Anne's uniqueness when she
says, "She's not like you."

This conversation is not particularly warm and fuzzy, but it does
capture a moment that matters between Anne and Margot. To the degree
that Anne and Margo "give out" and "take in" each other's uniqueness, ESP (feelings, etc.), responsiveness (choices), and reflective-
ness/mindfulness (questions), the contact between them is personal.

CONCLUSION

This chapter provides the basic, general answer to the question, "How can I help create moments that matter?" The rest of this book offers more specific and concrete ways to understand and promote these moments in many life arenas.

I've shown how the quality of our communication is directly linked to the quality of our lives, and translated this link into a model you can use to evaluate and improve your communicating. To summarize:

- The answer to the Big Question, "What does it mean to be a human?" is that humans are the beings who can relate to what's around us both impersonally and personally.

  ◆ These ways of relating surface every day in how we talk and listen.

  ◆ Twenty-first century communicating is much more impersonal than personal. This imbalance diminishes us as humans. Moments that matter can help restore the balance we've lost and significantly enhance the quality of our lives.

- When you want to move the quality of the communication between you and somebody else toward the Impersonal end of the sliding scale, engage your rational and impersonal understanding by

  ◆ "Giving out" *impersonal* cues, which are those that show how you are interchangeable with others, measurable, unreflective, and reactive. And, at the same time,

  ◆ "Taking in," listening for, and noticing only *impersonal* aspects of the other person, including ways he or she is interchangeable, measurable, unreflective, and reactive.

- When you want to move the quality of the communication between you and somebody else toward the Personal end of the sliding scale (that is, when you want to encourage a moment that matters), engage your holistic, and personal understanding by

- ♦ "Giving out" *personal* cues, which are those that show your uniqueness, your ESP aspects, your responsiveness and your reflective/mindfulness. And, at the same time,

- ♦ "Taking in," noticing, and listening for the *personal* aspects of the other, including ways he or she is unique, has ESP, is responsive, and is reflective/mindful.

This, in a nutshell, is how you help manage the quality of the communication you experience, and thus, the quality of your life. It's an outline for how you can promote moments that matter.

Chapter 3

MEETING AND MIS-MEETING ONLINE

In EARLY SEPTEMBER, 2011, NEWS SOURCES *around the world carried the shocking story of an air crash in Russia that killed 43 people, including 27 well-known hockey players, 2 coaches, and 7 hockey club officials. It was one of history's worst plane crashes ever involving a sports team. The dead included players and coaches from the St. Louis Blues, the Vancouver Canucks, and Czech, Swedish, and Latvian team members well-known to hockey players and fans. NHL Commissioner Gary Bettman issued a statement saying, "Though it occurred thousands of miles away from our home arenas, this tragedy represents a catastrophic loss to the hockey world—including the NHL family, which lost so many fathers, sons, teammates and friends." Russian NHL star Alex Ovenchkin tweeted: "I'm in shock!!!!!! R.I.P."*

Notice the unintentionally hollow quality of this tweet. The crash seriously affected at least hundreds of thousands of hockey players, coaches, and fans, and the deaths were personal, family tragedies for many in the relatively small international hockey community. The Commissioner's statement captures some of the anguish people felt. Alex Ovenchkin undoubtedly lost some close friends in the crash, but when he chose to *tweet* about it, the result was such a trivial, superficial comment that it almost dishonored the memory of the people who died. Twitter can do great things, but this event was totally not what Twitter's made for.

Many of the heaviest users of social media recognize these limitations. In a 2012 letter to the editor of an Oregon newspaper, Tuyen Bolton wrote:

> *I'm a high school senior who enjoys the current technology but I've found that people—particularly teenagers—have lost their sense of connection with those they see regularly. . . .*
> *As you sit down at the table together, you discover what was supposedly a 'dinner and discussion' becomes a conversation between a Blackberry and an iPhone. Before phones became so futuristic, talking face to face with someone wasn't unusual, and answering the phone during a conversation was considered rude. Technology is killing the art of communication. Nothing beats seeing the twinkle in someone's eye. So the next time you're about to answer that text, think about communicating with the person you're with and not with your phone.*[34]

BENEFITS OF ONLINE OPTIONS

The technology that Tuyen's complaining about has major benefits. One of them is that the 21st century gives most of us more of many things. Few people get more time, of course, and many don't get more money, or more of the things money buys. But the Internet and increasingly-affordable digital technologies have provided even low-income U.S. citizens, Afghan tribespeople, and sub-Saharan Africans access to more information, more connectivity, and more global engagement.

For example, in 2013, 1.2 billion people world-wide were using Facebook, and over 70% of those connected to the internet in the U.S. had Facebook accounts. Almost a quarter of Facebook users check their account more than 5 times a day, which is partly why American spend an average of 37 minutes daily on social media, more than on any other internet activity. Over 40% of online adults use multiple social networks, and the 2013-14 favorites were Snapchat, Twitter, Pinterest, Tumblr, and LinkedIn.[35] Skype reported 133 million users making almost 40 billion minutes of calls per month.[36] Mobile Internet use via smartphones was projected to increase 50-fold between 2010 and 2015.[37] An estimated 70% to 85% of viewers were using mobile devices—"second screens"—while watching TV,[38] a trend that tightly connected television viewing with social media.

This communication revolution is helpful in many ways. Cell technology enables parents to stay safely connected to their school-age children. E-mail, texting, and Skype help aging relatives stay involved in family conversations, reducing their loneliness, increasing their safety, and helping keep the family connected. Skype also empowers millions to reduce the distance between military families, far-flung colleagues, and collaborators on other continents. Social media sites enable millions of people to broaden their personal and professional networks. Families find each other via Facebook and establish or re-establish important connections. On-line simulations like *Second Life* not only gave people opportunities to explore alternate identities and exercise their imaginations, but also provide companies like IBM with a platform to hold productive, problem-focused meetings with gen-x and gen-y employees.[39]

ONLINE THREATS

And there are widespread abuses, including superficial tweets about genuine tragedies, people in the same room keyboarding each other, traffic deaths due to texting, and adolescents and adults consumed by Facebook, IM, and online gaming. In 2011, almost 60% of Facebook users under 20 reported that they communicate more online than face-to-face, and this pattern was spreading to those over 35, who made up more than 30% of Facebook users.[40] This means that a majority of this group is voting with their bodies not just for speed, control, and convenience, but for indirect rather than direct contact, for brief and often superficial messages rather than conversational exchanges, for print connections rather than *talk*.

These threats have helped create a backlash. In late 2011, increasing numbers of young people and adults were identifying themselves as "non-Facebook people," and "face-to-facers."[41] In 2012, Clay Johnson's book, *The Information Diet* advised heavy media users how selective media detachment can help prevent digital versions of obesity. Thousands of people made New Year's resolutions to go on an information diet, which emphasizes that the threats of media multitasking continue to be real.

Many people now recognize that 21st century communicating is much more impersonal than personal and online communication options are one of the primary forces pushing us in this direction. This imbalance matters, because it can diminish us as humans. Moments that matter can help restore some of the balance we've lost and significantly enhance the quality of our lives.

Preferring the Virtual Over the Real

For many, the most attractive feature of online options is control. You can manipulate who you appear to be on Facebook, show just a snippet of your life on Snapchat, choose how to respond to texts and tweets, and connect without letting others see your dress, facial expression, eye contact, or gestures, or smell your breath. It's undeniably empowering to have this kind of control. Unfortunately, when such control comes because the contacts are online rather than face-to-face, many people expand their specific inclination toward texting or messaging to a general preference for the virtual over the real. A 2011 study of 2300 British young people revealed that almost half prefer their online lives to reality. As one British teenager put it, *"if you don't like the [online] situation, you can just exit and it is over."*[42] *"That's why so many people hate the telephone,"* a U.S. seventeen year old adds. Shelly Turkle clarifies why: "The best communication programs shield the writer from the view of the reader. . . .It's a place to hide."*[43]

Hiding has consequences. As Chapter 2 underscores, humans become who we are in our contacts with others, and connections based on hiding and control can diminish the quality of our lives. Interestingly, two German words offer insight into why this preference for the virtual over the real is ultimately dangerous. In the German language, both *Erlebnis* and *Erfahrung* mean "experience." But *Erlebnis* is generally used to talk about the kind of experience a person *has* and *Erfahrung* labels experiences that *happen to you.*[44] All human life includes both. We choose whether to have the experience of an IMAX movie or to sample sushi *(Erlebnis)* and many people first experience grief as it overcomes them when a pet or relative dies *(Erfahrung).* Tweeting, Instagrams, and texting are primarily *Erlebnis* experiences. You do them when and how you want to. Both an "Aha!" moment and a violent thunderstorm are *Erfahrung* experiences; they happen *to* you.

People who consistently choose the control that the virtual world gives them can mistakenly be thinking that most or all their experience can be *Erlebnis;* that is, that they can control not only what they do but also what happens *to* them. This is a dangerous mistake for two reasons. The first is that this level of control can't exist in the human world. Not only can earthquakes, tornadoes, and floods occur almost anywhere, but human life is also routinely punctuated by mechanical breakdowns, cancelled flights, traffic tie-ups, rising gas prices, and important people who surprise us with their complaints, disagreements, support, and love. Shit happens. So does joy. The second reason it's bad to consistently escape online is that you miss many of the richest, most gratifying experiences humans can have: Moments that matter.

Depleted Brain Functioning

There's also another set of threats generated by extensive online communicating. Nicholas Carr's *The Shallows: What the Internet is Doing to Our Brains* is just one of several similar post-2008 books that describe them. It is now clear that heavy digital media use diminishes critical thinking capabilities, cripples problem-solving, and reduces the richness of imagination, all skills that employers value highly.[45]

Extensive engagement with hypertext also permanently alters reading patterns. As Carr puts it,

> *"I used to find it easy to immerse myself in a book or a lengthy article. My mind would get caught up in the twists of the narrative or the turns of the argument, and I'd spend hours strolling through long stretches of prose. That's rarely the case anymore. Now my concentration starts to drift after a page or two. I get fidgety, lose the thread, begin looking for something else to do. . . . The deep reading that used to come naturally has become a struggle" (pp. 5-6).*

Without some patience, willingness to engage, and ability to focus, personal contact-in-talk is as impossible as extended reading. Carr concludes, *"As we come to rely on computers to mediate our understanding of the world, it is our own intelligence that flattens into artificial intelligence" (p. 224).*

Objectifying People

The combination of a dramatically increased number of communication options, plus the combined technologies of hypertext and multimedia deliver "hypermedia," a term for words plus images, sounds, and moving pictures that demand a kind of divided attention that strains human brains. Early on, theorists believed that these "rich media" experiences would deepen comprehension and strengthen learning. The more inputs the better. But research has demonstrated just the opposite. Learning is diminished, understanding is weakened, and those engaged in these media environments feel overwhelmed, bombarded, and afraid for their productivity, effectiveness, resilience, and in some cases, their sanity. As one neuroscientist puts it, ". . . *when people do two cognitive tasks at once, their cognitive capacity can drop from that of a Harvard MBA to that of an eight-year-old.*"[46]

This pressure forces us to invent ways to manage the bombardment, and the default choice is often to distance and objectify other people. In this way, we fail to take in or give out uniqueness, which makes our communication impersonal. As Sherry Turkle puts it,

> *the connected life encourages us to treat those we meet online in something of the same way we treat objects—with dispatch. . . .when we Tweet or write to hundreds or thousands of Facebook friends as a group, we treat individuals as a unit. Friends become fans. A college junior. . .says, "I feel that I am part of a larger thing, the Net, the Web. The world. It becomes a thing to me. . . . And the people, too, I stop seeing them as individuals, really"*(p. 168).

Some evidence indicates that this objectification is symptomatic of increasing general detachment. A 2010 analysis of data from over 14,000 college students over the past thirty years shows that since 2000, young people have reported a dramatic decline in interest in other people. Today's college students are far less likely to say that it is valuable to try to empathize, to put themselves in the place of others or to try to understand their feelings.[47] Since empathy is obviously a key element of personal communication, these data are evidence that, at least among college-age people, more and more communication is moving in the direction of increasingly *im*personal contact.

BALANCED MEETING ONLINE

Despite these threats, I am definitely not saying that people should stop communicating online. As I said in Chapter 1, I'm online every day, on one of my computers or my smartphone. But I try to use digital options in ways that are appropriate, e.g., for scheduling a meeting, and in ways that enhance my face-to-face relationships.

Chapter 2 emphasizes that we have the ability to relate with everything around us in both impersonal and personal ways, and this means that *both* qualities of contact are necessary for optimal human health and growth. How can we promote both personal and impersonal contact online? How can we achieve the balance here that is our birthright as humans and one key to the quality of our lives?

Coping With the Fear of Bombardment

A first step is to figure out how to cope with the dozens or even hundreds of digital messages we get every day. Often, media multi-taskers and other well-wired individuals are seriously stressed by the amount that's coming in. Some react in a knee-jerk way by objectifying people, closing off, and shutting down, and in the process, they significantly impoverish themselves and the people in their lives.

If media bombardment is an issue in your life, it helps to respond from your personal rather than your impersonal side. Rather than throwing out the baby with the bathwater, manage your digital media life by adopting what psychologists call an *internal* rather than an *external* "locus of control." "Locus of control" is about where you think the power in your life is located. People with an external locus of control are convinced that their destiny is determined by outside forces such as fate, powerful other people, or the vibration of their smart phone. People with an internal locus of control feel empowered to shape their own life, to make positive decisions in the face of, or even despite challenging circumstances.

An 18-year old named Samantha and her fiancé, Ryan, were originally attracted to each other by their shared belief that their generation spends way too much time online. *In her 8th grade year, Samantha and her girlfriend discovered how easy it is to lie online when a "17 year old boy" they exchanged online information with—likes and dislikes, hometown, family secrets—turned out to be a 50-year old stalker. That scary reality stuck with Samantha, and when she saw how online over-use was socially crippling her younger brother, she began a mini-campaign against it. You won't find Samantha and Ryan on Facebook or Twitter, because they are convinced that these and other online seductions keep most young people from learning, as they put it, "basic social skills like interviewing for a job and carrying on a meaningful conversation." Several of Samantha's friends now agree with her that "Angry Birds is the dumbest thing!" and they have learned that if they let a ring-tone interrupt a conversation with her, they'll at least get a "Come on, girl!" and probably also, "Do you realize what you're doing to yourself?" Samantha and Ryan prefer face-to-face exchanges, and do most of their online communicating via email.*[48] This couple demonstrates that, even though media bombardment is real, you can use an internal locus of control to minimize its impact and use the resulting relief to enrich your most important contacts.

Media use patterns will continue to change. Some ways of connecting online will fade away, as did Myspace. But the growth curves of other digital technologies will continue to be steep, at least for the foreseeable future. As Turkle puts it, "We have to find a way to live with seductive technology and make it work to our purposes" (p. 294).

IT MATTERS

As we work to "find new paths toward each other," we need to jerk ourselves out of the naïve conviction that it doesn't matter, that "It's only Facebook," "The telephone demands more than I can deliver," or "I've got to control how much other people can get close to me." Each time we choose one medium over another—Instagram rather than email, tweeting rather than texting, texting rather than calling, exchanging messages over a contrived and beautified Facebook site rather than using something more direct—our choice affects the quality of our lives, who we are as persons. It's good for our health, our sanity, and our time management to be able to manage the crush of information that bombards us daily. *And* it's good to experience moments that matter, to be vulnerable enough to be touched authentically, to experience "the truth of the spoken word," to *feel* some of what another is feeling, to viscerally sense our commonality, to experience the security of partnership and the intense sense of connection that can be part of a disagreement, even if its just about weekend plans or a money decision, to touch. It *matters*.

VERTICAL AND HORIZONTAL MEDIA

One concrete way to manage your online life effectively is to know how to choose the right medium, and to exercise reflective choices. Remember that communication becomes more personal as it moves from talking and listening about general ideas, stereotyped understandings, mechanical and objective facts, mindless reactions, and unreflective comments toward listening and talking about *unique* perceptions, *emotions-spirit-psyche (ESP)*, *responsive* choices, and thoughtful *reflections*. Some media help you make your communication as personal as possible, and some don't.

Horizontal media like Facebook, Snapchat, and Twitter are cross-sectional and facilitate status updates, quick connections, commercials for products and services ("like us on Facebook"), political recruiting, short text messaging, and entertainment-based content, including soft news. These can be functional and useful, *and* their basic form does not usually promote personal contact.

Vertical media are those that allow participants to deeply engage in the subject matter and the relationship, such as blogs, dedicated websites, and subject-specific social networks like user groups and professional and specialized discussion forums.[42] Video conferencing, Skype, and cellphone conversations can all facilitate contact in *talk,* as that term was described in Chapter 1. Email can also be a vertical medium that can support in-depth connections.

Both can be useful. Horizontal media can continue to offer some relief from the demands that come from functioning in a variety of social system roles. You can use these kinds of media when you are distinguishing between casual and serious topics and between an acquaintance and a friend (family member, sibling), for example, by using tweets or texts for more superficial contacts.

Over extended time periods, regular Facebook postings can sometimes provide part of the depth that's common on vertical media like email. *Each day last November, as a lead-up to Thanksgiving, many Facebookers posted a reason they were thankful. By mid-month, friends were responding, and ESP was moving in both directions. I'm one family member who treasured some of these messages, and they prompted several instances of personal contact.* Facebook messaging or chat functions can also serve as real time email.

This kind of contact is even easier on vertical media. When you want to connect more closely, your general approach should be to focus on listening for and talking about uniqueness, ESP, responses rather than reactions, and mindful reflectiveness.

All four require at least a minimal amount of fullness, and this is a main reason why it can be difficult to engage personally on horizontal media. *Brian Christian won the "most human human" award partly because he worked hard, within the five-minute limit of the Turing test, "to make as much engagement happen in those minutes as I physically and mentally could. . . . In other words, I talked a lot. I only stopped typing when to keep going would have seemed blatantly impolite or blatantly suspicious"* (p. 191). This commitment can obviously be carried to an extreme, which is why it is not a compliment to hear that someone thinks you "talk [type, text] too much." But, persons are complicated; we are at least unique, have ESP, are responsive, and can be mindful and reflective, all at once. Text-based media also eliminate most nonverbal cues. It stands to reason that, when you want to connect person-to-person, you'll need to engage over time with more than one-sentence, 10-second, or 140-character questions and responses.

ENCOURAGING PERSONAL CONTACT ONLINE

Uniqueness

Uniqueness is the key element to personal contact online. On your side of the communication transaction, you can choose the specific medium, not just because it's handy or everybody is doing it, but because it works best for your needs and the people with whom you're connecting. You can bring individual insights and experiences into the content you share, rather than parroting what others have said, only repeating widely-shared stories, gossiping, passing along stereotypes, or mouthing platitudes. When you limit yourself in these ways, you get something like this exchange from Facebook, which includes almost no uniqueness and is pretty impersonal, even though it happens between friends:

> Jenny: *I understand that the drug companies wanna make money. But I don't wanna hear about old*

> *people having problems with SEX! I know I will*
> *be there some day but come on. Those ads can*
> *come on after midnight. Not all day long. I can*
> *hear my nieces saying "Mommy what's erectile*
> *difficulties" GROSS*

Ann: *Lmfao. I know right... Who wants to hear about*
        erectile disfunctions [sic]. Surely not I. Lol

Both these Facebookers seem to be just repeating what everybody says about ED and advertising. When you're thinking about taking in and giving out uniqueness, though, you can bring your own distinctive life-events into what you communicate. What's your individual take on Duck Dynasty? Or the death of 3-D TV?

You can also invite others to bring their uniqueness into the communication. Focus consciously on what's distinctive about their talk—not only about the opinions they express but also about how what they say emerges out of their unique experiences. Although millions may be "Totally tired of hearing about Lindsay Lohan," for example, each person who holds this opinion brings to it a unique set of contextualizing experiences. Listen and watch for them, and where it's relevant, probe for them. Remember that, if you really want to understand someone in depth, you need to get them speaking in sentences that you can't finish.

Taking In the Personal

When you want to promote a moment that matters online, work to take in personal aspects of the other(s) (uniqueness, ESP, responsiveness, reflectiveness). This is much more difficult on horizontal media than on vertical ones. But in both cases, you can focus on, read, and/ or observe what you receive to identify possible layers or elements of meaning behind or beneath what's immediately apparent. Even the tweet, "Still at Six Flags with all the kids," might indicate that the writer is weary ("still") and a bit overwhelmed by the number of people to deal with ("all" the kids). Every part of a text or e-mail that does more than just inform may give you some insight into how the writer *feels* about what's being discussed, which of his or her *choices* are relevant, and what *questions* about the topic remain for him or her. When you're communicating with someone you know pretty well, try "reading with your ears," which means sensing what's written as you would hear it if it were *said* by your communication partner. Vocal intonation, even if it's projected by you, can provide important clues to what your conversation partner might mean.

Also pay attention to the nonverbal elements of the other person's posting, text, e-mail, or talk. When Skyping, watch and listen between the lines for tone of voice, pauses, volume, and other cues to how they feel about what they're saying. Pay attention to these and to all the other nonverbal parts of their communicating, including facial expression, gestures, posture, and eye behavior. In Skype sessions, most people understand that direct eye contact means looking into the camera while you're talking and listening. Even texting and email provide some nonverbal cues. How long does it take for them to reply to you, and what does their timing say? Which acronyms and emoticons are authentic and which seem forced?

As you interpret a written message, also work as holistically as you can. Interpret what's said in its context, where the context can include time and timing, previous comments about this topic, and relationships between this comment and larger values and opinions held by your conversation partner. Avoid reacting to a single inflammatory, or otherwise striking message. If the context isn't obvious, ask the person to "say more." Holism is part of personal thinking, and it's important and useful when you want to understand a person as more than just a combination of objective features and social roles.

As you're taking in cues, remember that good listening is about

30% talk. For instance, effective face-to-face listeners provide sounds ("Mmhmm," "Ahhh"), encouragers ("Good point" "For example?"), and nonverbal cues (direct eye contact, forward lean, appropriate touch) to indicate *that* they are engaged and *what* they're perceiving. They also use clarifying questions, probes, and other encouraging responses to "pull" more talk from their conversation partner. These guidelines can be adapted to online contacts.

One book usefully summarizes four "power listening tools:" Ask, Mirror, Paraphrase, and Prime (AMPP).[50] The Ask step means that good listening starts when you make room for the other person to express themselves, and encourage them. You pause, avoid interrupting, ask open-ended questions, and appropriately probe their responses.

Mirroring can take two forms. The simplest is to mirror an important word or phrase in what the other person just said. This happens when she says, "I've always been confused by that requirement," and you respond, "Confused?" This kind of question will almost always encourage elaboration and detail and is easy online.

Another kind of mirroring happens when what the other person's saying seems inconsistent with what he's said before or what he seems to be feeling. *"You seem angry to me,"* can be helpful if it's said in a genuinely supportive way, like holding up a mirror so they can hear how they sound. Or, you might suggest, *"It sounds like you're nervous about confronting her. Are you sure you're willing to do it?"* The goal is not to "nail the person in a contradiction" but to encourage him or her to say more about something that seems conflicting.

Step #3, Paraphrasing is one of the most powerful listening tools, whether you're online or face-to-face. A complete paraphrase has four parts: (a) A restatement of the other person's idea or content, (b) that includes some of what he feels about the content, (c) expressed in your own words, (d) followed by a verification check. *"So you're upset because I've said I'm concerned about some of the clothes you wear, and this seems out of date and controlling to you. Right?"* On-line or face-to-face, asking, mirroring, and paraphrasing can all encourage the other person to respond interpersonally by increasing his or her feelings of safety.

When the other person is still not saying much, you can try the fourth tool, Priming the pump. Just as you used to have to pour some water down an old-fashioned water pump to get it working, you can make a contribution to the conversation that encourages the other person to respond honestly. Priming means taking your best guess at what the other person might be thinking and feeling, saying it in a way that shows it's okay to talk about it, and then going on from there. *"Are you thinking that the only reason I'm saying this is that I want to blame you for what happened?"* As the AMPP authors conclude, "Priming is an act of good faith, taking risks, becoming vulnerable, and building safety in hopes that others will share their meaning" (p. 169).

Asking questions —As you consider what questions to ask online, remember to avoid the ones that do more to squelch personal contact than to promote it. The first is a "Why?" question. Some research indicates that a question that begins with "Why" tends to promote defensiveness.[51] Of course, there are exceptions, but listen for yourself to the difference between "Why did you decide to do that?" and "How did you decide to do that?" The former seems to be asking for a moral justification, while the "How" question focuses more on the less threatening mechanics of your choice. You can make the same inquiries and diminish defensiveness by using "How did you decide to. . . ?" or "What's your rationale for. . . ? instead of "Why?"

The second kind of question to avoid takes the form, "Aren't you glad you didn't do that?" or "Isn't that what you mean?" I call these "pseudoquestions," because they are statements masquerading as questions. What looks like a question is really a statement, something like "I believe that was a dumb move; don't you agree?" Or "I understand what you said better than you do." Express your opinions or concerns as statements, and ask genuine rather than pseudoquestions when you want the other person to elaborate, be more specific, provide an example, clarify, or otherwise enhance what he or she's saying.

Dialogic Listening —You can also apply an online version of what I've called dialogic listening.[52] When you're listening *empathically*, you're focusing on the *other* person's thoughts and feelings. *Dialogic* listening goes beyond this to an attempt to "sculpt mutual meanings," which means actively collaborating on the pool of meaning that's created in the conversation. So when listening dialogically, you don't focus mainly on where the other person's coming from but what the two of you are constructing together. The basic stance that promotes dialogue is *letting the other person happen to you while holding your own ground.*

This metaphor can be useful. "Letting someone happen to you" requires you to be vulnerable, at least at this time and on this topic. You give up some of your control over the communication situation. You experience the communication as *Erfahrung,* not just *Erlebnis.* When you let someone happen to you, it shows that you trust the other person enough to listen with care and thoroughness. You can listen patiently and fully to opinions and ideas that are far from what you believe—even ones that disgust you—without agreeing with them, because understanding is very different from agreement. The risk that it takes to do this is relatively minor. And doing so can be a real learning experience. Plus, this is only the first part of dialogue; *while* you're letting the other person happen to you, you also "hold your own ground." I'll talk about this in just a minute.

When you want to practice dialogic listening online, start by letting the other person happen to you. What specifically does it mean to "let another person happen to you?" Well, as the previous paragraph indicates, I mean this suggestion to appeal to your personal mode of understanding. Ease whatever white-knuckle grip you have on your own convictions, and postpone building a case against your conversation partner until you've heard her out completely. It's important to be confident enough—living enough out of an internal locus of control—to allow yourself to be subject-to her communicative influence. As I mentioned, it takes a little bit of courage. The potential payoff, though, is that, when you let the other person happen to you and also hold your own ground, the two of you may possibly meet profoundly, even intimately.

Giving Out the Personal

"Holding your own ground" means expressing yourself assertively. Assertiveness is a communicative stance that's in the middle between aggressiveness and non-assertiveness. You're neither a dictator nor a doormat. In your verbal/nonverbal talk you are present, authentic, and as candid as the situation permits.

Being assertive means saying what matters most to you in this situation, and why. You don't beat around the bush, and you present ideas in ways that make them clear, not ways that promote victory over your conversation partner. This kind of writing or speaking includes the complexity of your motives, preferences, and ideas, which means that assertiveness is difficult to do on horizontal media. Assertiveness presents conclusions provisionally rather than with certainty, which means, in part, that you avoid "always" and "never" language.

Assertive speaking and writing also includes concrete examples of the points you're making, not just generalizations, vague labels, or exaggerations. This kind of communication is liberally sprinkled with I-statements that own opinions, take responsibility for choices, and in other ways demonstrate a healthy internal locus of control. Often assertive communication begins with a paraphrase of what the other person's said, to demonstrate the assertive person's understanding of the other person's perspective, and it ends by asking for a paraphrase, so your conversation partner is encouraged to say back to you what she's just heard you say.

Relevant feelings are also part of assertive communicating. You can include excitement, concern, commitment, hesitation, eagerness, affection, support, and caution in your online postings. The point is not to "bleed all over the screen" but to make the feeling sides of yourself at least partly available to the people you're communicating with, and to respond to feelings they express. An authentic, "I'm totally psyched!" or "Sounds like you're really worried about that" can help move a conversation toward personal contact.

Another reason to exploit opportunities to share thoughtful reflections on vertical media is that this practice speaks to some of what's most human about us—our abilities to have perceptions about our perceptions (reflectiveness). As I said in chapter 2, we can engage "second thoughts" to decide not to say something because it might be hurtful, to feel gratified because we said exactly what we meant, and to wonder if we should take-back or explain more fully something we just said. Each of these—the decision, the feeling of pleasure, and the questioning—reflects a perception about other perceptions. This is what it means to be *mindful* and *reflective,* and this kind of content can help make communication more personal.

All these specific suggestions about what you "take in" and "give out" are ways that you can do your part to *make your communication as personal as possible* online. Each of the specific suggestions I've made can be adapted to, and applied with the full range of online communication options.

EMAILING WITH AUNT DOROTHY

Email is one vertical digital medium where personal contact can happen. I'm lucky enough to live out this possibility, week-to-week, in my exchanges with family members two thousand miles away. I especially enjoy connecting with my ninety-five year old Aunt Dorothy. Despite the fact that it's increasingly difficult for her to live independently, she continues to enjoy the small house on the lake that has given her so much pleasure since she and Uncle Julius built it in 1940. Especially because she's the only remaining member of my mom's generation, I treasure our regular contact.

See if you can identify in the following exchange examples of Dorothy and I "taking in" and "giving out" elements of who we are as persons: uniqueness, ESP, responses, and reflections. I think there are several. As prompts, I've identified a few in brackets.

To help you follow the thread of the conversation, Lynn is a cousin of mine; Debbie is Lynn's daughter; and Lincoln is my son.

Hi John and Becky

"Tis really time to hit the sack but thought I'd check in with you first--been a while since I've heard from you. How are things going at your house? Did you get everything completely moved out of your house Becky, and is the deal with the new owners all completed now? [listening for uniqueness]

Also been wondering what kind of advice you got about the drainage around your house to eliminate the basement flooding. I'm worried that that will be a pretty big extensive bit of work [expressing feeling]. Those kind of things make Condo living more attractive don't they...at least that sometimes seems the case here. But then I look at the Lake and the Mountains beyond and wonder how I could put up with the four walls of a Condo ! ! [more feelings]

*I had the helper take all the portable fans down to the base-
ment because I thought the warm weather was over, then
had to go down and get a couple to bring back up here over
the week-end when it got just too warm again. [giving out
reflectiveness].*

*At the next Northwest Watercolor Society meeting an Artist
named John Ebner is going to speak and demonstrate. He's
a favorite Artist of Lynn's so invited her to go as my guest---
Debbie decided she wanted to go too so the girls are coming
here for an early dinner Tues. night and then we'll go on to
the meeting. Lynn has so many things she CAN'T eat so asked
if I would make cabbage rolls so that's one of my projects for
tomorrow [giving out choice]. They aren't hard --just messy to
make and take a lot of time but I will enjoy them too.*

*So much for now---take care and bring me up to date. Hugs,
Aunt Dorothy*

Hi there!

*I was wondering if we were going to hear from you pretty
soon. I agree that it's been awhile [mirroring]. We've been
pretty busy following up on all the moving and the upcoming
work on the house, and Becky's been spending time at her
folks' house to help care for her dad.*

*We did get everything moved out of B's house in time for the
closing. That went fine. The buyers were pleasant and respectful of what they were getting, and both of those helped make
it easier for Becky to leave the house in their hands. But it
still was hard--she spent 25 years there, many of them raising
their only child [feelings]. So you can imagine.*

*One truckload went to storage, one came to our house, and
one went to the Rescue Mission for resale. There were also
quite a few "small" things that went to the church rummage
sale or other spots [choices]. So it was complicated. . . .*

No, we don't have any travel plans in the near future, other than a trip to Chicago to see the grandkids this weekend.

Lincoln sold his car yesterday, which is probably good, because it was beginning to cost a lot of $$. We didn't get out of it nearly what we had into it, but that's often true with cars. [feelings] Now we have to find something to replace it for under $5000. That's going to be interesting [feelings].

When Becky reads your post, she might have even more to say. So we'll be in touch!

Love,
John & Becky

Although I've applied impersonal understanding to analyze parts of this email exchange, at that time, I didn't focus on Aunt Dorothy's specific feelings, choices, or reflections, or on elements of our uniqueness, but just on the pleasure of the contact, the connection. It's good to stay in touch. It's good to know what's happening in her life and share some of mine and Becky's life with someone who loves us. It's good to continue a relationship that's been going on for as long as I can remember. It's good to connect with family. It's all good.

CONCLUSION

On-line communication is so pervasive that, if you want to encourage moments that matter in your life, you have to figure out how to deal with emails, social media, texts, Instagrams, tweets, blogs, games, cell phone conversations, and the other digital options that have surfaced since I wrote these words. The explosive growth of online communication has reduced the frequency of personal contacts both by offering lots of convenient impersonal options and by driving people to limit the depth of contact and to objectify others in an effort to control the barrage and protect their privacy, time, and sanity.

It's also true, though, that some online communication options make personal contact not only possible but very convenient. So you can definitely encourage moments that matter online.

Chapter 4

DATING AND COURTSHIP AGONY
AND ECSTASY

DALE AND SUSAN ARE THIRTY-SOMETHINGS *who have both been divorced for several years, and each is the primary parent for an only child. The two literally bumped into each other in the soccer club parking lot when Dale backed his car into the door of Susan's SUV. Dale readily admitted it was his fault, and their exchange of insurance information was so cordial that they agreed to meet for coffee. One thing led to another and four days after the accident they had sex. Both said they weren't interested in a long-term relationship, and although they slept together twice more, their hook-up relationship was over in a month.*

Susan felt vaguely used, because she suspected that Dale's interest in her was almost completely physical. But she knew enough about hooking up not to be surprised about what happened. Dale had problems convincing himself that, even though he was still alone, he'd had some nice sex with Susan. He was also concerned about how superficial their short relationship had been.

What's Going On?

Until recently, adolescents and twenty-somethings were just about the only people involved in the agony and ecstasy of dating and courtship. But in today's typical life-pattern, long-term relationship development begins with dating in adolescence, moves into serious courtship a few years later, culminates in cohabitation or marriage in 1-3 additional years, disappears from the couple's radar for the months or years that the partnership or marriage lasts, and then, for over half of us, becomes a priority again when the partnership ends or divorce occurs.[53] This means that dating and courtship are primary life concerns for tens of millions of people from puberty through senior citizen status. Junior high students are certainly sexting, but pages of AARP publications also feature dating advice and sex products.

Unfortunately, contemporary culture also generates ever-newer ways to make the process challenging and potentially dangerous. Today, between two thirds and three quarters of college students hook up at some point during their academic careers,[54] where "hooking up" means having casual sexual contact with someone you're not dating, without any expectation of future commitment.[55] The practice is also widespread among thirty-somethings and divorced baby boomers like Dale and Susan.[56] One problem with hook ups is that they are assertively impersonal. Most of the time hook-up partners have been drinking alcohol, and almost half engage in sexual intercourse during the hookup, although participants believe that petting below the waist, oral sex, and intercourse all regularly occur in the process of hooking up. The practice is widespread enough that researchers have identified a "Hook-Up Culture" that is part of North American life.[57] For many people, the practice raises serious moral considerations. But even putting these aside, this culture puts people at risk for all the threats they learned about in junior high health classes, including STDs, HIV, and date rape, not to mention the inevitable psychological and spiritual pains that come from confusing sex and intimacy, distorting what it means to be masculine and feminine, and compromising your own values to meet someone else's expectations.

Pluralistic Ignorance

Hook-Up Culture happens partly because of widespread "pluralistic ignorance," which basically means going along with a mistaken belief in a group consensus. In this case, the mistaken belief is that other people accept questionable practices more than I do, when the fact is, they don't. To put it in researcher-talk, pluralistic ignorance happens when "group members believe that most others in their group, especially those who are popular and opinion leaders, actually endorse the norm [hooking up] and want to behave that way, while they themselves privately feel they are going along with the norm because of a desire to fit in with the group and exemplify the norm."[58] So studies show that many people who are hooking up mistakenly believe that "everybody thinks it's okay," when, if asked individually, most of their friends would say it isn't. In addition, men believe women are more comfortable engaging in these behaviors than in fact they are, and many women mistakenly believe that other women accept hooking up more than they do. This pluralistic ignorance leads some people to experience sexual assault and not to interpret the behavior that way, because they believe that what happened is the kind of thing their peers think is normal.[59]

How do so many otherwise-intelligent people get themselves into the situation of doing potentially dangerous things they don't really want to do just because they think their friends think the activities are okay? The obvious answer is that hooking up is one current way to deal with the sometimes-frightening communication challenge of developing an intimate relationship, selecting a life-partner. Most of us have at least the vague notion that dating and courtship are supposed to lead to a long-term relationship where each person gets to treat someone as uniquely special, admire her beauty and grace, appreciate his competence, enjoy erotic excitement and sexual passion, brag about your partner, get him gifts and plan special times for the two of you, show her off to your friends and family, share secrets, support and be supported, touch. You also get to be the center of another adult's life, to be cared for, honored, valued, affirmed, supported, and unconditionally accepted. What great gifts!

Unfortunately, no parents provide their children with an instruction book that tells them how to keep love in their lives. We naturally want to realize our full human potential in loving relationships, and yet it's scary to put yourself in a position where you can be rejected, especially when divorce statistics say that it's very difficult to successfully maintain a long-term intimate relationship.

So how can we reduce the fear associated with building an intimate relationship so we can handle the process more effectively, humanely, and gracefully? How can we increase the opportunities for moments that matter and make dating and courtship as personal as possible?

DANCING ON THE WIRE

The best way to demystify dating and courtship is to understand how intimate relationships actually work, and the best way to do this is to get a clear picture of the three "both-and" goals that every person in an intimate relationship—knowingly or unknowingly—is working to manage. The three are Expression/Privacy, Integration/Separation, and Stability/Change. Intimate relationships can be understood as ongoing dances that manage these three dialectical tensions.

The term "dialectical tensions"[60] doesn't mean that people are necessarily "tense" about these pairs of goals. They are called "dialectical tensions" because Expression/Privacy, Integration/Separation, and Stability/Change describe the opposing-yet-interrelated objectives or ends we are pursuing as we listen and talk with our partners, make decisions about spending time together and apart, establish online contact patterns, engage in sexual activities, prioritize various independent and joint activities, and do all the other parts of our relational lives.

Once you understand these three, you can confidently handle pick-up lines, plan what to do on a date, test for common interests, identify serious differences, develop sexual compatibility, fit into your partner's family, and manage most of the other challenges of relationship development.

Expression/Privacy

Russell and Angie have been dating for only three weeks. Russell doesn't know that Angie's father and sister both attempted suicide when they couldn't cope with their addictions to alcohol.

Russell:	*Did you hear about Neil getting a DUI?*
Angie:	*Yeah. I wonder if others in his family are also addicted.*
Russell:	*What do you mean?*
Angie:	*Well, alcoholism is a family disease, so I worry about Jean and Pat.*
Russell:	*One DUI doesn't mean he's addicted—or his sister and brother.*
Angie:	*I'm just saying. . . .*
Russell:	*Have you got a lot of history with this kind of thing?*
Angie:	*(Has to decide what to say next.)*

The Expression/Privacy tension reflects our combined desires to express ourselves and to keep some things private. Because Russell and Angie have been dating, Angie gets to deal with this dialectical tension in this conversation. Each of us is naturally inclined to share our thoughts and feelings with the person we want to feel close to, and at the same time each of us feels the need to keep some things to ourselves and to protect ourselves from judgment or criticism. The fact that we feel both ways at the same time is not strange or dysfunctional; it's a common, normal part of human experience. Both sides of these dialectical tensions are often felt at the same time.

Although the Expression/Privacy tension exists throughout the partnership, it is especially obvious in the early stages of relationship development. Between two people, this tension primarily shows itself in the presence and extent of self-disclosure; that is, how much each partner tells the other about his or her past activities, dreams and goals, current struggles, feelings, embarrassing moments, and secrets.

Integration/Separation.

Mishereen and Molly have been together for over a year. They've spent two special fall vacations at the Florida condo that Mish inherited from her dad.

Molly: *I got a text from my sister about the family fishing trip this year.*

Mishereen: *What's that?*

Molly: *I mentioned it last year. Most of my brothers and sisters and their families spend a long weekend in September at a fishing resort in Minnesota. My family's been doing this as long as I can remember.*

Mishereen: *I really like having our own time at the condo, and we can't afford to vacation twice in the same year..*

Molly: *I really like our time there, too. But I miss being a part of this family trip.*

Mishereen: I don't know. I'd feel like an outsider. . . .

The Integration/Separation dialectic acknowledges that people want to feel a part of various social groups and, at the same time, we also want to be self-sufficient. Each of us wants to be close to a relational partner but not too close, or for too much of the time. When a partner asks for space, she's pursuing one pole of this dialectical tension, and when she asks for more attention and affection, she's expressing the other. Again, the fact that she feels both ways at almost the same time is completely normal. As a relationship matures, this tension surfaces each time we connect with our partner's friends or family members. We want to feel accepted by, and be a part of our partner's family, for example, without having to give up ties to our own family or completely changing our traditional ways of being with them. This is what's happening between Misehreen and Molly.

This tension surfaces in the very concrete challenge that every long-term couple has to negotiate, "doing holidays." Will it be Thanksgiving with one partner's family and Hanukkah or Christmas with the other's? Shifts in alternative years? All holidays focused on the partners themselves, with family members on both sides invited to join them? Or does the pattern change each year? These are Integration/Separation questions.

Stability/Change

Brad and Erin have been married for 27 years. They'll become empty-nesters when their youngest moves out next year. For the past several years, Erin's had a fear of flying.

Brad: *You know, we ought to plan a special time for ourselves after Lisa gets married.*

Erin: *What are you thinking about?*

Brad: *Las Vegas is the perfect get-away. It's filled with things to do, and not all that inexpensive, so long as you don't gamble too much. We've never done anything like that.*

Erin: *I know. And I'm not sure I want to now. It's a long way to drive. I think it'd end up being expensive. And I don't feel like a Las Vegas kind of person.*

Brad: *That's part of what'd make it exciting!*

Erin: *If Lisa gets pregnant, I want to be around to help.*

Brad: *Sounds like you're going to keep finding reasons not to do this.*

This third tension combines predictability or security with novelty. Each of us wants both enough stability to meet our security needs and enough change to keep life interesting and exciting. Couples want to know that their partner will be there for them, and they appreciate regular routines, like eating dinner together or calling if they'll be home late. At the same time, boredom is one of the top reasons couples give for breaking up.[61]

Couples manage this dimension of their relationship partly by communicating to outsiders ways in which they are both conventional and unique. In the U.S., for example, many couples still strive for the traditional stability goals of home ownership, children, and a steady job, *and* other couples decide to go against the norm by remaining childless, living on a boat, and moving between jobs every few years.

How To Do Dating and Courtship Well

Chapters 1 and 2 provide a foundation for feeling confident about How to meet Mr. Right, How much to talk about past relationships, How to build trust, When to meet her family, How to talk about sex, When to make the relationship exclusive, Whether to get a dog together, Whether to hire a wedding planner, and the other challenges of dating and courtship. You're well-positioned to respond to each of these when you understand what it takes to move from impersonal toward personal relating—remember giving out and taking in uniqueness, ESP, responses, and mindful reflections.

And there are also specific skills that will guide you smoothly through the dating and courtship process whenever the three tensions show themselves.

Expression/Privacy

As I mentioned, this is the first both-and dynamic that surfaces in every new relationship. The key communication skill is self-disclosure, which means discussing something about yourself that the other person wouldn't know if you didn't tell them. Some disclosure is a prerequisite for any relationship development, and the idea is to contribute and encourage the kinds of disclosure that help achieve yours and your partner's relational goals. "Contribute and encourage" means that it's important to think of self-disclosure as a collaborative activity, not just an expressive one. In other words, it involves both talking and listening. Offer information about yourself and invite your conversation partner to reciprocate. Start slowly. Nobody wants to be the target of a gut dump of inappropriately personal and detailed information that produces a "TMI!" response. Remember, too, that if you stick doggedly to a listening mode, the other person is likely to feel interrogated or psychoanalyzed. Healthy and effective disclosure is reciprocal.

When Becky and I started dating, I first felt like tiptoeing around political issues, because what I then knew about her led me to predict that she'd be much more socially conservative than I am. She opened the door with a brief comment about Planned Parenthood, and we soon discovered commonalities across the board. We continue to have great conversations about local and national issues, candidates, and policies.

Self disclosure is an important part of online relationships, too. In one study, newsgroup participants showed the importance of self-disclosure when they generally agreed with these statements: "I feel I could confide in this person about almost anything" and "I usually tell this person exactly how I feel." They strongly disagreed with the statement, "I would never tell this person anything intimate or personal about myself."[62] When you're online, you have more control over what you disclose, because the other person has so little access to your facial expression, height, weight, age, tone of voice, and all the other nonverbal cues that help define who you are and how honest you're being. Importantly, however, candid and truthful disclosure produces the best results both off- and online. When three researchers studied the success experienced by members of an internet dating service, they found that those who were most satisfied used large amounts of positive self-disclosure along with an openness about their intent. In other words, the best strategy for both partners turned out to emphasize honesty and candor, which unfortunately is the opposite of some people's way of doing online dating.[63]

Mutual disclosure requires engagement and talk time. These are obviously difficult on horizontal media and take special efforts on vertical media. Both parties need to change their daily patterns in order to connect, whether it's face to face or online. If your prospective partner is hard to contact and hesitant to commit time, his or her choices are telling you something, even if it's not what you want to hear. Remember the point that Brian Christian made about the importance of extended talk time. As he put it, *"I tried to make as much engagement happen in those minutes as I physically and mentally could. . . . In other words, I talked a lot. I only stopped typing when to keep going would have seemed blatantly impolite or blatantly suspicious."*[64] Do your full part to contribute to the pool of meaning that's growing between you and your conversation partner.

Here's a summary of some research-based advice about disclosure.[65]

Disclose the kind of information you want others to disclose to you. Disclosure tends to beget disclosure, and relationship develop-ment is enhanced most when disclosure is reciprocal. As a result,

- *Move disclosure to deeper levels gradually. Give the less-intimate experiment time to succeed before you experiment with greater intimacy.*

- *Continue intimate disclosure only if it is reciprocated.*

- *Use I-statements and descriptions of specific feeling--"I feel homesick;" "I'm excited;" "I'm uncomfortable with that" rather than "It's important to stay near home," "That can be exciting," or "Let's change the subject."*

- *Be honest. Work toward unifying your saying, being, and doing. The communication patterns that are established early in the relationship usually persist, in some form, throughout the couple's time together.*

- *Work to have the verbal and nonverbal parts of your disclo-sure match or fit. Remember that when these two parts are incongruent, people believe the nonverbal. Think about what you conclude when someone shouts, "I'm not MAD!"*

- *Disclose relevant content on a relevant topic. Connect the disclosure to the ongoing conversation.*

- *Offer to help the other person*

- *Display cheerfulness and positivity*

- *Display empathy appropriately*

- *Be dependable and sincere*

- *As you work the Expression/Privacy dialectic, realize that you'll be serving two masters: what you're comfortable with*

*and the inevitable changes you'll need to make if you want
to be in a genuine relationship. Ultimately, you can't fit with
someone else without adapting to them, and if the changes
you make violate your own sense of integrity, the relationship
is doomed. Stay aware of this threat so, if it surfaces, you can
talk it through.*

Integration/Separation

Like the other two both-and tensions, this one operates throughout
the relationship, but it gets foregrounded as the couple works out *how*
they want to be together. The integration side of the tension surfaces as
the couple spends enough time focused on each other that they become
fully "out" *together.* Each partner's family and friends learns about the
other partner, and comes to know, for example, that "Aidan doesn't
drink beer with us on Thursdays any more because he's always with
Pat." The couple will also look for ways to display their partnership
by co-hosting parties, co-signing greeting cards, merging Facebook
pages, etc.

Integrating lives takes time. For some, "love at first sight" is a
reality, but most solid human relationships do not progress at electronic speeds. In fact, one of the most widely-cited studies of how
people build relationships identified fifteen primary strategies, many
of which require weeks, months, or more.[66] The three most important ones were increased contact, relationship negotiation, and social
support and assistance. Others included increased rewards, tokens of
affection, personalized communication, verbal and nonverbal expressions of affection, social enmeshment, sexual intimacy, and behavioral
adaptation. Social enmeshment, for example, means getting to know
and spending time with your partner's family and friends, something
that can't be done in a week or even a few months. Sexual activity can
certainly happen rapidly, but genuine sexual intimacy requires enough
time to experience varied levels of arousal, touching, experimentation,

discussion, and adaptation. Social support and assistance involve asking people for help, advice, and comfort, and these requests only make sense as parts of situations that develop over time—a family problem, work challenge, illness, death, etc. The most important strategy is increased contact, which inherently requires time.

As the discussion of uniqueness, ESP, responsiveness, and mindful reflectiveness demonstrates, people are complex. A successful long-term relationship requires that the parties mesh their complexities, and this process can't happen overnight.

One important way to focus on the first pole of the Integration/ Separation dialectic is by integrating your partner's social networks with yours.[67] Networks have always been important, and social media and other internet options make them even more so today. A 2004 study concluded that in the U.S., people have about 23 "core ties" and about 27 other, still significant ties. Most are friends and not kin. They also have another 500 plus ties with friends, acquaintances, and consequential strangers.[68] Networks significantly affect how we cope with health issues, make purchase decisions, deal with bureaucracies, choose music, and even how we manage our weight. This means that spending time with his friends, meeting her family, and participating in group events that are important to him or her are important.

It's also crucial, from time to time, to openly discuss the state of your relationship and the feelings you have for each other. Don't blow "the relationship talk" out of proportion, and do give this topic some talk time. *On the advice of a good friend, Becky and I try to remember on the 1st of every month to take time to ask each other, "How am I doing?" So far, all these conversations have been reassuring, and a few have raised important issues in a positive way. For example, I've learned that it's important to Becky that I pick up after myself in the kitchen, and she's learned that, as she puts it, "I could be less nit-picky" These brief talks have also been opportunities to praise each other.*

One of the fullest developments of the integration pole happens when the couple is defining themselves as together enough that they are willing and able to identify and talk about the personal features of *their relationship*. Friends will learn what each partner identifies as the *unique* parts of the relationship, the benefits or satisfactions that each has never experienced in a relationship before. The couple will find opportunities to share with family and friends important *feelings* they have in common and joint *choices* they've made. They will ask and answer important *questions* together, such as "What will we do if our careers clash?" "How shall we prioritize our political commitments?" "My mom's been sick for a long time. When she dies will both of us take extra time off work?" And they will also share some of the results of this joint reflecting with family and friends.

When the focus is on Integration, the two people move increasingly to the right side of the impersonal----personal scale. Their identities become to some degree enmeshed; each comes to understand him or herself more and more as in-relationship-with the other. In the best circumstances, sexual intimacy is a high point of this experience of connection. Whether embodied in sexuality or not, however, this increasingly intense sense of relatedness is experienced personally rather than impersonally, not necessarily as a mystical union or mythic melding but as a condition that "feels very right," resolves more issues than it raises, offers a sense of being at peace in the relationship. The partners are usually not able to fully explain this experience, to themselves, to each other, or to close family members or friends, and this is further evidence that it involves the personal parts of your brain.

Nonverbal expressions become more important. If either is artistically inclined, he or she may write poetry, paint, sculpt, craft photographs, compose and/or perform music. Part of the real joy of this stage in relationship development is that we get to fully experience some of the personal parts of who we are.

A huge benefit of understanding that this is a dialectic is realizing that these good feelings about Integration will inevitably be accompanied by elements of the other pole of the tension: *If* Integration is happening, *then* Separation isn't far away.

The Separation pole can surface abruptly or subtly. As a partner notices herself getting defined more and more as "part of a couple," she may need to re-assert her individuality—"I want some 'women only' time," or "Let's try a separate vacation for a change." In other cases, one or both of the partners may develop a vague discomfort about losing his or her identity. A partner who knows about the three dialectics won't be threatened when these feelings surface. "Separation" moves should prompt another conversation about the relationship and the couple's expectations, and this conversation can grow out of curiosity rather than fear.

Stability/Change

The both-and desire for predictability and novelty is also present throughout every relationship, and it becomes particularly important when a couple is deciding how long-term they want this relationship to be. When the Integration pole of the second dialectic is dominant, most couples begin thinking and talking about making the relationship stable by exchanging significant tokens—like rings—moving in together, and/or marriage.

On the surface, these moves are all about stability—"'till death do us part." But remember that this is a dialectical tension, which means that all the forces that lead to and publicly proclaim stability will inevitably be accompanied by some forces that manifest change, and it helps for a couple to expect this. One partner's second thoughts, shifting preferences, and commitment fears ought ideally to be accepted as lovingly as possible by the other partner who understands this dialectic.

This dialectical tension also explains how a couple who's been together for many years may get so settled into their routines that their relationship becomes predictable enough to feel stale. *After nearly 20 years of marriage, Pauline and Victor had settled into many patterns, such as making the same seven or eight dishes for almost every dinner, spending every New Year's Eve with Victor's parents, and always giving each other artwork for their anniversary. Although to some extent both enjoyed knowing what to expect from their relationship, they also longed for new experiences. One year, instead of spending their holidays with Victor's family, they decided to volunteer at a homeless shelter and take gifts to elderly patients in local institutions. They found the novelty of doing something different to be a refreshing change to balance the predictability of their lives.*[60]

When issues related to stability and change arise, candid, personal conversation is the only, and happily the most powerful response. Victor and Pauline changed their traditional holiday activities after Pauline expressed her desire to do something that felt more in the spirit of Christmas (giving out ESP), Victor took what she said seriously (listening), and both of them agreed that since it might feel strange (mindful reflectiveness), they'd treat the first year as an experiment. As they participated in the new activities, they shared how they felt (ESP) and how the holiday seemed more about giving to both of them. They decided together to continue the experiment (collaborating).

In the end, as Victor and Pauline's experience demonstrates, a long term relationship can be defined as a mutual commitment to dialogue, a commitment to keep talking, regardless of the initial discomfort some conversations might create.

This commitment is especially important as the couple experiences conflict. It's critical to remember that conflict does not necessarily mean that a partnership is in trouble; in fact, conflict is a natural and normal part of all long-term relationships. As a result, conflict management is one of the most important family communication skills, and I'll talk about it in Chapter 5. As I'll say there, couples who successfully stay together over time are able to do so partly because they've learned to disagree effectively.

There's a great deal of additional research-supported advice about how to work the Stability/Change dialectic. One useful summary comes from the National Communication Association. After interviewing couples married for more than 40 years to find out what made their marriages work, NCA researcher Judy Pearson found that, although each relationship is unique, the following characteristics are crucial:

- *Having realistic expectations about their partners and the relationship. If couples enter into a committed relationship believing that their partner will fulfill their every need, or the relationship will be perfect in every way, their relationship is doomed. The couples Pearson interviewed expected and experienced difficulties that were often prompted by desires for changes, and they supported each other through tough times.*

- *Integrated identity. Many couples stated the need for a shared identity. Frequently, this was accomplished through sharing information with a partner that would not otherwise be available to them. Because compatible couples frequently develop their own special way of communicating with each other, they sometimes do not need to verbally disclose their emotions to each other. Although autonomy was important, it was less so than shared identity.*

- *Continuing intimacy. Many of the couples continued an active sex life. When illness, medication, fatigue, or other factors forced a decrease of sexual activity, they compensated with increases in physical closeness, non-sexual touching, hugging and kissing.*

- *Successful conflict management. For some couples, relational tranquility was so important that conflicts were avoided altogether. For others, vigorous conflict was a common occurrence. Most were between these extremes. The key for these couples was that over time, they had identified which conflict management strategies and tactics worked well for them.*

- *Accepting each other unconditionally. The partners in successful long-term relationships loved, respected, empathized with each other without reservation. They understood and accepted the realities of both stability and change. Although it was expressed in different ways, each couple also frequently communicated their acceptance of each other.*

- *Using positive distortion. All long-term relationships experience conflict, but members of contented couples did not interpret their disagreements and arguments as destructive, but rather, took the inevitable disagreements in stride, and were confident in their ability to resolve them successfully. They did not view change as threatening but as a normal part of their lives together.*

- *Persistence. In their interviews, the couples stated that they were committed to relational success, no matter what. "Many of [the couples] spoke of their absolute determination to stay together, their positive can-do attitude, and their unswerving belief in long-term relational success," says Pearson. Successful couples consistently put the success of their relationship ahead of any other consideration in their lives.*[70]

Couples who stay together successfully understand that relationships take work focused on all three dialectical tensions. As Pearson's research shows, persistent, even dogged commitment is vital. *And* the couple needs to attend daily to the state of the relationship in all the ways she describes.

CONCLUSION

The best way to minimize the agony and maximize the ecstasy of dating and courtship is to de-mystify the process by understanding its three main dialectical tensions, and by applying the understandings and skills outlined in the first two Chapters. Dating and courtship make up just one of the life arenas that you can manage effectively, if you have a clear understanding of communication and if you apply some effective communication skills.

This is true because relationship development and decay are all about communication. Communication enables you to find a dating partner and negotiate time together. Listening, self disclosure, asking questions, empathizing, expressing and exploring beliefs and feelings, identifying what you want and need, supporting, re-negotiating, asking for changes, establishing boundaries, expressing affection, using positive distortion—all these are communication activities that work well when relational partners understand what communication is and when they apply communication skills to promote moments that matter.

In the life arena of dating and courtship, it's important not to get caught up in the pluralistic ignorance-fueled hook-up culture and to use your knowledge of Expression/Privacy, Integration/Separation, and Stability/Change to move gracefully through relationship development. Recognize that just about everybody involved in dating and courtship shares the same hopes and fears, and you have the advantage of understanding that disclosing and maintaining some of your privacy come as a package, just as the other two dialectical tensions do. Don't be surprised or uncomfortable when you experience both-and pulls, and manage the tensions by making your dating and courtship communication as personal as possible.

Chapter 5

FAMILY FRIENDS AND FAMILY ENEMIES

THIS YEAR, AUNT PATTY'S TWO-PAGE, single-spaced holiday letter reports on 114 family members. A brief verbatim excerpt:

> . . .*Mike is still with the State 24 years he works as a Trades Helper and oversees 5 buildings as a lead worker; Kim is still a respiratory therapist working for Mercy Hospital. Mark is at Mercer Color Brenda still at eye clinics Megan 21 is in college in Columbus very active in the music dept. and majoring in History Alex turned 18 a senior in high school and very busy. Matt is still with Commerce Bank Kristin does freelance magazine work from her home office Courtney 13 8th grader Mikaela 11 6th grade they both are in dance and piano and love school.* . .

Aunt Patty offers a mile-wide and inch-deep snapshot of a large, traditional U.S. family.

The holiday letter from Cindy and Sharon also reports on family activities, and in this case the letter is not about blood relatives but members of their "family of choice." This term is used by gay and lesbian couples whose families rejected their sexual orientation, and by others who are estranged because of abusive family dynamics.[71] The term "family" also applies to the approximately 13.7 million single parent households in the United States where almost 22 million children are being raised.[72] And the category is made even more diverse by blended families and interracial unions. In 2013, the Emmy-winning TV sitcom, "Modern Family," featured a nuclear family (mom, dad, three high-maintenance kids), the patriarch with an immigrant trophy wife and her young son, and a gay son partnered with a husband and raising a daughter adopted from Vietnam. This diversity leads one researcher to conclude, "It's reasonable to define family [not by blood relations but] as people who care about one another, organize their lives together, take care of one another, and intend to continue being together and caring for one another."[73]

FAMILIARITY BREEDS EVERYTHING POSSIBLE

Whatever their form, families are the sharpest doubled-edged swords in the cosmos. One edge cuts through painful history, arguments, dysfunction, and fears to embrace members in warmth, support, and unconditional love. The other edge slashes self-esteem, wounds hope, and impales dreams. For example:

Anderson breezes into the room on his way from practice to hanging out with friends. Slow down! His mom shouts. "You're not going anywhere until your room is cleaned!" "Bullshit! Anderson snorts; "I'll be moving out in a month and you can put up with it until then!"

"I can't do this any more," Mark sighs as he meets his life partner Allan for a weekday lunch. "That idiot's scheduled me for the weekend again, and they just announced at the staff meeting that there'll be no

raises." "Crap!" Allan responds, and as he extends his acceptance and support, Mark finds himself tearing up with gratitude. "I really appreciate you being in my life," he says to Allan. "I love you."

Ed is in the kitchen, enthusiastically putting together a recipe that he and his wife agreed was perfect for tonight's potluck. Flour has been mixed with sugar, baking powder, and other dry ingredients; vegetables have been diced; meat has been coked and shredded, and both the stove and the oven are in use. Jenny comes in, glances around, and begins laughing as she grabs the broom. Before she can say, "You just can't cook without making a mess, can you?" he growls, "If you have to ridicule everything I do, get out of here!"

As children, our family constitutes our entire world. Whatever the quality of family life, children accept it as normal. When we grow up, family members retain this larger-than-life aura. We are eager for their approval and overreact to their criticism, because we feel that their judgments are absolute evaluations of our value as human beings. We get defensive because we are afraid that, if someone who knows us as well as they do thinks we're wrong or flawed, they must be right. As Deborah Tannen puts it, "No matter what age we've reached, no matter whether our [family members] are alive or dead, whether we were close to them or not, there are times when theirs are the eyes through which we view ourselves, theirs the standards against which we measure ourselves when we wonder whether we have measured up."[74] And at the same time, we long for and bask in every expression of their love.

This is why families are the sharpest double-edged swords in the cosmos. This is why this chapter is called "Family Friends and Family Enemies." Families are the places where we can feel most secure, most at home, most understood, most appreciated, most loved. And, precisely because family relationships can be so long-term and intimate, family communication can also wound us most hurtfully, even fatally. The happiest and least-stressed family members live with both eyes wide open to all of these possibilities.

WE'RE ALREADY IN THE MIDDLE OF IT

One difficulty in developing this clear perspective is that there's no opportunity even to begin thinking about your family's communicating until you're already conditioned into deep-seated and sometimes toxic habits. Studies of mother-infant interaction show that a variety of patterns are established in the first months of life. One is the happy dynamic where mother is responsive, infant is cooperative, and mother responds positively to the cooperation. Another is where mother is controlling and infant is compliant, and a third where mother tries to control while the infant resists. First patterns like these persist in some form and, as the years pass, families develop predictable ways of, for example, doing tasks together and preferring clear and direct or masked and indirect messages.[75] These patterns differ across families, but in each case, family members view them as normal. By the time we start pre-school, we're experts, but only at how to communicate in our own family, and not until we spend time around other families do we discover that there are different, perhaps better ways. This means that individual improvement in family communication often has to begin with the process of unlearning one or more entrenched patterns.

THE WONDERBAR OF FAMILY COMMUNICATION

Stanley tool company makes a foot-long, flat steel pry bar that is described by its users as a "must-own," "indispensible" "little miracle" tool that is "indestructible," and "never lets me down." One end of the Wonderbar easily pries rusty nails out of concrete floors and the other removes shingles and raises subflooring or decking. When you want to enhance personal contacts in your family, you'll need the communication equivalent of a Wonderbar, a tool to help you pry loose the entrenched patterns that are creating problems, so you can actually experience new possibilities.

The Wonderbar of family communication is a looking and listening lens that empowers you to distinguish between the two parts of meaning in every family communication event: the information part and the identity part. These two parts of meaning make up every communication happening—not just in families. But the two are especially difficult to see, and especially troublesome, in the communication you experience in your family.

Information and Identity

The first step toward improving any uncomfortable or destructive family communication is to pry the entrenched pattern up enough to identify the Information and Identity aspects of what's going on verbally and nonverbally. Julia T. Wood contrasts the two:[76]

INFORMATION PART	IDENTITY PART
"It's raining today."	*I'm here. Do you want to talk? [supporter]*
"I'm starting a new project at work."	*I want you to be aware of what's happening in my career. [partner]*
"I bought some of those berries you love when I went shopping today."	*I care about you. I keep your preferences in mind. [best friend]*
"I heard a funny joke today..."	*Please confirm that I am interesting. Let's enjoy a laugh together. [somewhat needy partner]*
"Could you believe the way Ed and Janet bickered at the party last night?"	*We're not the kind of people who quarrel in public. [proud partner]*

"Do you want to rent a movie this weekend?"	*Let's spend some fun time together [good friend]*
"I'm thinking about cutting my hair."	*Do you think my hair is attractive like it is? Will you be upset if I cut my hair? [wants confirmation]*
"You really should get back to your workouts."	*I care about your health. [supporter] OR I'm worried about your condition.*

The *Information* part is what the label implies—the facts, data, content, substance, decision, or opinion that's being discussed. This is the apparent meaning of the words and sentences spoken, what anyone with a dictionary could figure out. The people in a conversation usually agree on this aspect. The *Identity* part is what's being said about how the communicators define themselves—as superior, inferior, leader, follower, partner, boss, teacher, learner, helper, lover, warden, supporter, etc. We usually glean it not from the words but from the nonverbal parts of the communication—facial expression, tone of voice, posture, etc. Frequently, the people in the conversation do not agree about this aspect.

Another family communication expert calls the Information part "the word meaning" and the Identity part "the heart meaning—the meaning that we react to most strongly, that triggers emotion."[77] In the example of Ed and Jenny in the kitchen, Ed interprets Jenny's laughter as derisive, even scornful. Jenny might have intended just to make light work of her clean up efforts, but he lumps her laugh together with all the other times he believes she's ridiculed him. The information meaning is amusement and the identity meaning is a "You're careless and you make work for me." In order to clarify and improve communication between family members, first distinguish between these two meanings and communicate about both.

"Communicate about both" is the action step. So long as your family communication is going smoothly, just do your part to keep it that way. But whenever you find yourself surprised, threatened, angered, disappointed, or fearful, use the communication Wonderbar to stop yourself and pry apart what you're seeing and hearing. In the silence, sort out the Information parts and the Identity parts. It takes some mindful reflection to identify what the identity messages are. But only when these parts are expressed, can they be addressed. And when they are addressed, your communication will be about "heart meaning," so, if it's done with respect and caring, it's likely to promote a moment that matters.

So Anderson needs to say that he feels pushed out of the home he's grown up in by his mother's constant criticism. This would put the Identity message he's hearing on the table between Anderson and his mom. His mom also needs to say that she wants him to help her be a home-maker by doing his part to keep the apartment clean. Jenny needs to say that she wants to be an equal partner in Ed's cooking, not just the clean up person. Ed needs to say that he wants his efforts in the kitchen to be appreciated.

Conversation about Identity meaning can be challenging, because it's hard not to get defensive. But it can also be very rewarding, especially if you follow these important guidelines.

GUIDELINES FOR EFFECTIVE FAMILY COMMUNICATING

When family communication is on the rocks, it's often because it's moved to the impersonal side of the impersonal---personal scale. The antidote for this is for the people involved to work harder to make it as personal as possible by listening for and expressing uniqueness, ESP, choices, mindfulness, and reflections.

Studies of family communication have identified several research-based insights that illustrate in practical ways how to promote personal contacts in your family.[78] Here are four of the most important:

Maintain Fairness

This principle might seem obvious, but the concept of fairness is so deeply ingrained in Western cultures that effective family communication must include it. U.S. culture especially values the principle of treating people equitably. Although few family members demand moment-to-moment equality, most of us want our family relationships to be equitable over time. Parents want their partners to be as committed as they are and to make the same kind of emotional investments in the family as they do. Brothers and sisters want to be treated fairly. When family members perceive inequity or unfairness, they experience reduced satisfaction and commitment and sometimes engage in activities that threaten the family's survival, such as harsh criticism or infidelity.[79] Both men and women commonly use unfairness as a reason for cheating.

Family members develop perceptions of fairness about financial issues, emotional contributions, material belongings and physical parts of the relationship. Among the most important for adults are housework and child care. These are responsibilities that virtually all couples want to be divided equitably. When they aren't, marital stability suffers.[80] Unfortunately, even in the second decade of the 21st century, there is widespread inequity in many U.S. families about these issues, because studies show that when both partners in heterosexual relationships work outside the home, women still do the majority of child care and homemaking.[81] Although contemporary husbands assume more responsibility than they did 20 or even 10 years ago, they still do less than half the work; in one study the figure was 36%.[82] Couples in same-sex families tend to create more equitable relationships or, at least, to talk about equity more openly than heterosexual couples.[83] All this means that a first place to look for fairness in your family is in the homemaking/ childcare division of labor. If it's unfairly imbalanced, plan a time to talk about it so you can figure out how to change the balance.

The reason that unfairness can hurt so much is that it's ultimately about identity. Most people interpret unfairness as a threat to their definition of themselves as a competent, caring person. Think about your own interpretations. *"People who get taken advantage of must be weaklings" (threatens my identity as strong and competent).* *"When she does so much less than I do, it makes me look stupid to our friends" (threatens my identity as intelligent and effective).* *"The money he makes is great, but it's a lot harder to provide emotional support for the kids, which he almost never does" (threatens my identity as a full partner in the relationship).* This is why you need to attend to fairness in your family and to help create opportunities to talk about fairness issues.

Communicate Confirmation

At the most basic level, confirming messages say, "I recognize your existence as a person." In many Western cultures, this point is made with direct eye contact, comments relevant to the other person's topic, and equitable turn-taking, which means minimal interruptions. The specifics can differ across cultures, though. In some cultures, children confirm an adult's status by keeping their eyes on the floor while the adult is talking. In most Western cultures, if you're online or texting when someone in the room asks you a question, the confirming response is to stop what you're doing, turn away from the screen, establish eye contact, and respond to their question.

Disconfirming messages fundamentally "say" "You're unimportant," and although it's hard to imagine anyone ever using these words, parents, teachers, managers, customers, and service providers disconfirm those around them all the time. It's disconfirming to remain silent when it would be natural to greet a family member, to ignore your sibling's substantive contribution to a conversation, and for parents to talk about a child who's in the room as if she were absent.

In families, confirmation and disconfirmation deal not only with recognition but also with acknowledgement and endorsement.[84] Acknowledgement means that you recognize not only the person's existence but also his feeling, and endorsement happens when you accept another's feelings or thoughts.

Notice the difference between "I'm sorry you feel hurt" and "You'll get over it." The first is a confirming message that acknowledges the person's feeling and "You'll get over it" is almost certain to be interpreted as disconfirming. "You matter to me" is confirming and "I don't care what you do" will probably be interpreted as disconfirming. "Your feeling is understandable" is a confirming message of endorsement and "You shouldn't feel what you do" is disconfirming. When a child says, "Look what I made!" and a parent responds, "I told you to get in here for dinner!" the child virtually always interprets the parent's response as disconfirming.

Like fairness, confirmation and disconfirmation are important because they are such central parts of the identity aspect of communication. Why? Because confirmation communicates respect, and respect is as fundamental a cultural value as fairness. As a young man named Wayne put it,

> *I've gotten a lot of disconfirmation since I came out. When I told my parents I was gay, Mom said, "No, you're not." I told her I was, and she and dad both said I was just confused, but I wasn't gay. They refuse to acknowledge I'm gay, which means they reject who I am. My older brother isn't any better. His view is that I'm sinful and headed for hell. Now, what could be more disconfirming than that?[85]*

Remember that confirmation does not mean agreement, and that even acceptance and endorsement do not mean that you concur with what the person is thinking or feeling. Wayne's parents would not have had to approve of his sexuality in order to confirm Wayne. His mom could have encouraged additional conversation by saying something like, *"Wow! That's a real shock! If you're gay, I'm afraid for you. I'm worried for the pain you'll have to go through. I don't know how I'm going to fully accept it, but I do know that I love you, and I always will."*

Confirmation and disconfirmation matter so much because they too are tied directly to the answer to the Big Question, What does it mean to be human? The first answer to this question is that, "Humans are social animals," which means that humans become who we are in our relationships with others. When we are confirmed, supported, disciplined, comforted, and loved, we develop the identity of a valued human being. Infants and young people who are consistently disconfirmed usually develop low self-esteem and an uncertain sense of self. Each of us has the opportunity and the power to help "believe another person into being."[86] That is, we can help shape who our family members become by the ways we relate with them. Confirming communication has this kind of positive power.

Don't Sweat the Small Stuff

Healthy family communication requires that parents and children, along with grandparents, uncles, aunts, and cousins, are all willing to overlook minor irritations and frustrations that are inevitable when people live together. Each of us has quirks, habits, and mannerisms that can irritate others: leaving dirty dishes in the sink, talking to ourselves while others are around, failing to pick up toenail clippings, forgetting to put out the trash. Effective family communicators develop thick skins about inconsequential irritations and reserve serious talk times for the topics that really matter.

Of course, one person's minor irritation is sometimes another person's major issue. *I leave crumbs around the toaster, and Becky wants them removed so they don't attract insects. For me, it's minor and for her it's major. When I see toast crumbs as simply evidence that the toaster was used, Becky's position will seem like nit-picking. But if I connect toast crumbs to ants, mice, or cockroaches, as she does, then I'm definitely with her: Keep them out of here!* When this kind of disagreement arises, the person believing, "That's major, not minor," needs to explain the connection he or she is making to a serious outcome. Then both can pursue the issue, remembering what's already been said about fairness, respect, confirmation, and making your communication as personal as possible.

Another thing about small stuff is that, occasionally, what looks like a minor quirk can be the tip of a major iceberg. A spouse's continual lateness can be a symptom of adult ADHD. Failure to follow through can be a sign of clinical depression. A son or daughter's lower grades sometimes signal substance abuse. As in many other cases, the key is to get the disturbing behavior on the table between the people involved, and to put it there in ways that encourage conversation rather than defensiveness. Years ago, Jack Gibb described how. He identified five qualities of communication that usually promote defensiveness and five that promote a supportive rather than a defensive communication climate.[87]

The first way to promote a supportive climate is to use *description* rather than *evaluation. Avoid evaluations like "You never pick up after yourself," and try a more descriptive statement like, "When you change clothes after coming home from work, you leave the clothes you take off on the floor."* As a discussion-starter, this is a low-temperature way to encourage a family member to understand how you're responding to their behavior.

Gibb's second suggestion is to substitute *problem orientation* in place of *control*. Rather than flexing your muscles in a win-lose way, get the two of you on the same side vis-à-vis whatever the problem is: *"Our joint checking account has been overdrawn three out of the last four months. What ideas do you have to fix this?"*

The third and fourth ways to reduce defensiveness are to substitute *spontaneity* for *strategy* and *empathy* for *neutrality*. People get defensive when they believe you have something "up your sleeve" (strategy) and you have little appreciation for the impact your criticism has on others (neutrality). So be candid about your perceptions and feelings: *"I know it's hard to say 'No,' (empathy) but I'm worried that Alberto will take advantage of your willingness to give into his complaining about curfew" (spontaneity)*.

The final two ways to reduce defensiveness are to substitute *equality* for *superiority* and *provisionalism* for *certainty*. It's obvious that unequal, one-up messages are likely to promote defensiveness. So are statements like, "That's all there is to it. Period. End of discussion" (certainty). When you have to raise a difficult issue, communicate as an equal and express your convictions with humility and with the realization that things always change.

Small Stuff You *Should* Sweat

Without denying anything that's just been said, it's also important to recognize that several not-obvious, low-key, and everyday elements of family communication definitely deserve the serious attention of anyone who wants to make communication as personal as possible in his or her family. Each family member's small accomplishments or victories, for example, need to be celebrated. *"You made it on time today! Good going!" "You lost almost two pounds last week? Great! I'm proud of you!" "Nice job on the lawn." "You look terrific."*

The small, seemingly-trivial task of simply making time for each other can also speak volumes about caring and support. Dual career parents and young people active in school and sports especially need to build family times into their schedules and routines. Pay attention to how often screens or ring tones interfere with family contact. Explore "screen-free" places or times and engage in activities that put you face-to-face.

Aphorisms like "She talks the talk, but she doesn't walk the walk" and "Little things mean a lot" make sense to us because we share the belief that genuine motives and real beliefs leak out in small and subtle ways. *A guy I knew boasted about his integrity and then took a brownie in the food line and ate it before getting to the cashier, where he only paid for what was left on his tray.*

Finally, consider your habitual, everyday actions—do you smile each time you greet a family member? Remember her special days? Regularly do small acts of kindness? Remember to call? Assume the best rather than the worst? Habitually demonstrate love?

Keep Talking—Forever

Fundamentally, *a relationship is a commitment to conversation,* a pledge to keep talking, regardless of what happens. When a server greets restaurant guests with, "Hi, I'm Josh and I'll be taking care of you tonight," he initiates a low-level, impersonal relationship. If somebody else carries the food to the table and Josh never checks up on how his table is doing, the people there are likely to feel as if he has not held up his end of even this minimal relationship, because he hasn't "kept talking." This is what it means to say that a relationship is a commitment to conversation. And this simple dynamic doesn't change in families; it just gets much more profound.

Of course, less personal and shorter-lived relationships call for lower-level commitment. This means that the last part of this definition varies between a co-worker relationship, a superior-subordinate relationship, a teacher-student relationship, and a relationship between spouses or family members. In your family, the "forever" addition applies.

Parents who have disowned their children, brothers who refuse to talk with their sisters, and aunts who ignore troubled nephews are all violating this family communication guideline. Embarrassing, shameful, and violent family events often do isolate family members from one another. *And* in every case, family members can choose to keep talking. *If Rais Bhuiyan can forgive the white supremacist who shot him in the face and can even visit him in prison, you and I can keep talking with the daughter who's single, pregnant, unemployed, and addicted.* Why would we want to? Because of the moments that are missed when we don't, and the quality of our lives and theirs that are irretrievably lost.

The basic reason to keep talking is that history isn't over yet. None of us knows what will happen next, and it helps to live our family communication lives with this realization clearly in mind. An unexpected death has extinguished many sparks of hope for family healing, leaving family members with heavy burdens of, "If only I had. . . ."

Another reason to keep talking, regardless of what's happened, is that people sometimes change in profound ways. Therapy, treatment programs, and jail time can prompt genuine change, and only if you've kept talking will you share the benefits of this growth. People found guilty are sometimes exonerated, and heart-felt, well-established, value-laden moral convictions can also change. Lifetime Republicans become Democrats, and vice-versa. *A nationally-known, Harvard and Princeton-educated seminary professor I knew, found himself fundamentally changed by his intense and deep study of homosexuality from an anti-LGBT to a welcoming position. This was a huge shift for a professor at a Christian seminary.* Closer to home, when your family members maintain a commitment to keep talking, even the most offended and entrenched may notice changes and be in the position to respond positively to them.

The Keep Talking--Forever guideline needs to be remembered each time we find ourselves stubbornly waiting until a spouse or relative apologizes, refusing to call or write while we lick our wounds, criticizing a family member behind his back, or in some other way withdrawing from family contact. Being in a relationship means communicating. If you really don't want any future contact, then end the relationship. But, also be realistic about what "family" means. In some ways, family relationships can't really be "terminated." They continue, one way or another, even after divorce, estrangement, and disinheritance, just because human communication is thoroughly continuous.

MANAGING FAMILY CONFLICT

"Yeah, but. . ." is a common response to the Keep Talking---Forever guideline. *"Yeah, but what if your spouse refuses to ever talk about anything important?" "Yeah, but what if I can't calm down quickly enough to be respectful and fair?" "Yeah, but my kids are too sensitive to take any feedback?"* These responses and others raise the need for another set of communication skills that enable you to manage the inevitable conflicts that arise in families. Like confirmation and disconfirmation, conflict happens both outside and inside families. Because it's so prevalent in families, though, and because it's so difficult to handle, I want to focus on it here.

As I've said before, conflict is not necessarily a sign that anything's wrong. Whenever people make communication as personal as possible, some of their uniquenesses meet, and when this happens, differences inevitably arise. These differences surface in what people call conflict: *Opposing opinions expressed with strong emotions over high stakes.*[88]

USE CONSTRUCTIVE CONFLICT MANAGEMENT TECHNIQUES

There's a huge difference between *doing* conflict and *managing* it effectively. When you're doing it, you're just in it. You're not being particularly reflective or mindful. You just want to make your point, win the battle, show your superiority, or in the worst cases, hurt the other person like he or she hurt you. When these are your main motives, it can feel almost impossible to be reflective or mindful, and I can guarantee that the conflict won't be productive. It'll hurt the people involved.

There is another way. When you're in a conflict *and* you want to manage the conflict well, you can draw on the findings from extensive, real-world research. The following eight specific suggestions can help make the conflicts you're in as personal as possible.

Listen First

Travis came in because he thought he had an understanding with a colleague we both were working with, and she was refusing to cooperate. "I can't figure out what the hell she's doing!" he said. I asked him, "Do you think she's crazy?" "Obviously not." "Is she determined to hurt you?" "No." "Well, then, your answer is in your complaint. You need to figure out what she's doing. Meet with her and ask her to help you understand where she's coming from."

When you are in the midst of exchanging opposing opinions with strong emotions over high stakes, you actually can remind yourself to start by exploring the *other* person's perspective. You do this by deliberately beginning with some *questions* rather than strong *statements*. This move will enable you to get some perspective and helpful distance on the conflict, and this by itself will greatly improve what happens next.

I've already talked about the benefits of Listening First. Here's why it makes sense in a conflict. When you're in a disagreement, you already know your own opinion and why you hold it. In some cases, you need to be more mindful and reflective about what you really want to have happen. But, because the other person is unique, has ESP, is responsive, and is reflective, you for sure don't fully understand her opinion and why she holds it. Realistically, the conflict won't go anywhere useful until each of you understands the other. So when you want to manage the conflict effectively, start by listening. If necessary, remind yourself that understanding doesn't mean agreement. Then, take a breath or two, ask the other person what they think and feel about the issue, and then apply some effective listening skills.

By skills, I mean that you might encourage the other person to describe a concrete example of what they're concerned about. When their meaning is unclear, ask them to "Say more" or "Keep talking." Repeat some of their key words with a questioning inflection (mirroring) to encourage them to elaborate. Paraphrase both their main point and the emotions that accompany it. *"So you think we've gone to my parents' house on almost all the important holidays and you don't want your mom to keep calling us selfish and unfair, right?"*

Invest some time in this listening effort. It will repay you in at least three ways. First, since this is a conflict with a family member, one of your automatic priorities should be that the relationship be preserved, or even enhanced. Listening first will keep you from immediately attacking, blaming, labeling, criticizing, stereotyping, accusing, and behaving in other ways that are guaranteed to weaken the relationship. Second, listening will increase the other person's respect for you. She'll see that you have enough courage of your convictions and respect for her to allow her to express herself first. Third, careful listening will reduce the frequency of mistaken disagreements and unfair distortions. You'll learn what the other person's position actually is, which will enable you to determine how much and where you agree and disagree.

Make it Safe

Conflicts go sour most often when the participants get defensive and resort to blaming, shouting, accusing, and being overly certain, aggressive, and controlling. Most of these responses grow out of the fear that comes from feeling misunderstood, disrespected, attacked, or ridiculed. When your identity is threatened in these ways, you'll feel some of this fear, and you can be virtually certain that your conflict partner is feeling it, too. If the conflict is to be managed effectively, at least one of the people involved needs to step out of the content of the conversation, help to make it safe for the other person, and then step back in.[89]

A useful book called *Crucial Conversations: Tools for Talking When the Stakes are High* lays out three steps for making it safe: *Apologize, Contrast,* and *Create a Mutual Purpose.*[90] The authors of this book work with a familiar family communication situation—husband wants to make love and wife doesn't. Although she doesn't feel amorous, Yvonne does want the relationship to be better, so she tries raising the issue:

> Yvonne: *CJ, can we talk about what happened last night— you know, when I told you that I was tired?*
>
> CJ: *I don't know if I'm in the mood.*
>
> Yvonne: *What's that supposed to mean?*
>
> CJ: *I'm sick and tired of you deciding when we do what!*
>
> Yvonne: *(walks out).*

When she reflects on what happened in the other room, Yvonne recognizes that they're both making things worse. CJ's response was clearly defensive, but so was her, "What's that supposed to mean?" So she is willing to start her next attempt with an apology. An apology is a statement that sincerely expresses your regret for your role in somebody else's pain or difficulty.[21] It needs to be sincere. Even when you think the other person did worse things than you did, your apology owns your own part in the conflict. You have to give up the goal of saving face, being right, and winning in order to get what you really want which, for Yvonne, is improvement in her relationship with her husband. When it's sincere, an apology goes a long way toward restoring your conflict partner's sense of safety. Yvonne might start her next attempt to talk with CJ with, *"I'm sorry I left the room. That didn't help anything."*

The second step in Making It Safe is to *contrast* what the other person might be, or appears to be thinking with your actual intent. For example, when she raises the issue with CJ again, Yvonne might say,

> *"I don't mean to say that this is your problem. The truth is, I think it's ours. I'm not trying to put the burden on you. I don't even know what the solution is. What I do want is to be able to talk so that we can understand each other better. Maybe that will help me change how I'm responding to you, too"* (p. 86).

When Yvonne contrasts in this way, she addresses CJ's concerns that she doesn't respect him or that she has a malicious purpose and then she confirms her respect and clarifies her actual purpose.

The third step toward Making It Safe is to *Create a Mutual Purpose*. The first part of your mutual purpose is for both of you to keep talking—as in the guideline above. You can help this happen by saying something like, *"It seems like we're both trying to force our views on each other. I commit to staying in this discussion until we have a solution that satisfies both of us."* As with other suggestions, this has to be genuine. When it is, both persons' sense of safety in the situation almost always increases.

The second part of your mutual purpose is a goal or outcome that transcends the one that separates you. Another good conflict management book called *Getting to Yes* calls this your mutual "interests" as contrasted with your conflicting "positions." As these authors put it, "Your position is something you have decided upon. Your interests are what caused you to so decide."[22] A couple might disagree about how to spend holiday time (different positions) and agree that holidays should focus on immediate family members (interests). When conflict parties loosen their grip on their conflicting positions, they can frequently discover shared interests to build on. Sometimes this can help them discover a mutual purpose. In other cases they need to invent one.

Yvonne and CJ may discover that they both want to make love, but each is aroused in very different ways. Or they may discover that their mutual interest is to experience intimacy with each other, and that lovemaking is one, but the not the only way to do this. When the parties discover a mutual interest or purpose, they just need to design common ways to meet this mutual goal.

Often, however, conflict parties need to invent, rather than discover a mutual purpose. The key to doing this is to find an objective that is more general, more rewarding, and more meaningful than the ones that separate them. They begin by summarizing what seem to be the narrower, conflicting purposes, and then outline what it will take to find a compatible goal. For example, to return to our husband-wife conflict, they might work it out this way:

Yvonne: *I don't want anything with you that isn't great for both of us. I just want to find a way to have us both feel close, appreciated, and loved.*

CJ: *That's what I want, too. It just seems like we get those feelings in different ways.*

Yvonne: *Maybe not. What makes you feel loved and appreciated?*

CJ: *Making love with you when you really want to. . . . And you?*

Yvonne: *When you do thoughtful things for me. And, I guess, when you hold me—but not always sexually.*

CJ: *You mean, if we're just cuddling, that makes you feel loved?*

Yvonne: *Yes. And sometimes—I guess when I think you're doing it because you love me—sex does that for me, too.*

CJ: *So we need to find ways to be together that make both of us feel loved and appreciated. Is that what we're looking for here? [Mutual Purpose]*

Yvonne: *Yes. I really want that, too.*

CJ: *Well, what if we. . . . (pp. 95-96).*

The Make It Safe guideline can be applied in almost every serious family conflict. If you begin by Listening First, you'll be well-positioned to understand the other person's goals that are incompatible with yours, and he or she will already feel at least moderately respected. But recognize that your additional efforts to manage the conflict won't go well when the other person is feeling unsafe. So give enough time and effort to this stage to lower the threat-level of the conflict.

Carve the Elephant

Defensiveness often produces global statements—"You always act that way!" "You never listen to me!" "Grow up!" "You sound like your mother!" "How many times have we tried that already? It doesn't work!" When conflicts are left at this global stage, they're almost impossible to manage effectively. You need to divide the elephant into pieces small enough to clean, bandage, scratch, polish, or munch. Carrie and Amy are roommates:

Carrie: *I don't like your attitude. You're always so nega-tive and sarcastic about everything. I'm thinking I should look for another roommate. [Asserts a global problem]*

Amy: *I didn't realize I was getting on your nerves so much. I don't understand what you mean, any-way. What do you mean, "negative"? [Requests something specific.]*

Carrie: *As soon as you walked in the door today, you started complaining about the mess everything was in and how everything is screwed up at work. I'm tired of listening to all that. A simple, "Hi Carrie" would be a whole lot nicer. [A much more manageable request]*

Amy: *I guess I have been pretty short-fused lately. I've been really worried about work and I've started bringing that home.*

Carrie: *Well, you aren't always negative, and I know things have been really rough for you at work. I just get stressed when you unload. . . .*

Even when the overall size of the problem stays large, this move will help you divide it into manageable parts.

Avoid Gunnysacking

This is another way to keep the conflict manageable. A gunnysack is a big burlap bag made to carry potatoes or peanuts. Gunnysacking occurs when a person stores away weeks, months, or even years of resentments and then uses a particular conflict as an opportunity to bring up all the bruises he or she has been nursing and to dump them on the other person, metaphorically emptying the gunnysack over the other person's head.

In the example of Ed and Jenny in the kitchen, it sounds as if Ed might be gunnysacking when he says, *"If you have to ridicule everything I do, get out of here!"* This statement seems to summarize many previous hurts he's experienced when Jenny laughed at the way he hung pictures on the family wall, mowed the lawn, and repaired the loose towel bar in the bathroom. At other times, the gunnysacking can be more explicit: *"Here we go again! Two weeks ago you had to change the reservations I made, yesterday you criticized my cleaning job, and now you're ridiculing the way I cook!"*

The antidote for gunnysacking is to keep current, which means that you do your best to deal with controversial issues as they come up. This can keep a disagreement from becoming the occasion to air every doubt and hurt you've carried for weeks or even years. Try not to let resentments build.

Both Parties Say What They Want to Have Happen

Disagreements can dead-end in such statements as, "Stop being so conservative!" "Be nice to me!" or "Stop wasting so much time!" This kind of order is a dead-end not only because the tone creates defensiveness but also because it's next to impossible to comply. What would count as "being nice"? What activities seem to you like a "waste of time"?

One way to apply this recognition is to ask your conflict partner, "What do you want to have happen?" This is different from asking either, "What are you going to do about this?" or "What do you want me to do?" Each of those questions presumes fault and blame—"Since I/you caused this, I/you can fix it." But every conflict, like the rest of communication, is collaborative; it grows out of the partners' mutual actions. "What do you want to have happen?" focuses on the situation rather than the individuals, on what's already been constructed between them.

You might also respond to this question yourself by suggesting specific alternatives that embody your interests (as contrasted with your position). As you can see, this suggestion is related to the previous two. All three are ways to make the conflict manageable in scope—which obviously makes it much easier to handle effectively. Put this question—"What do you want to have happen?"—and your response to it in your bag of frequently-used conflict management tools.

Relationship Reminders

Relationship reminders are references to the history that's shared by you and your conflict partner. The purpose of these reminders is to keep the disagreement in perspective by explicitly acknowledging the relationship that contextualizes it. *"Let's remember that we're both on the same side here." "Remember, we've got a long history together." "I love you, honey, and I really disagree."*

It's crucially important that relationship reminders be genuine rather than devices or gimmicks. Most people are sensitive to this kind of phoniness, can readily spot it, and get angry when it happens. So don't fake relationship reminders. If you honestly cannot see worth in the other person or value in your relationship, it would probably be best to postpone your conversation until you can.

Defusing

Defusing means pulling the fuse out so the explosive won't go off. You can take steps to defuse yourself, the other person, and the situation.

Defuse yourself by asking yourself these seven questions—or at least as many of them as you can recall when you're in the midst of it:

1. *What are the possible benefits of this conflict?* Conflicts are not all bad. Especially after they're over, conflicts can function to develop confidence in the relationship, get crucial feelings out in the open, nudge or wrench a relationship out

of a rut, and improve the quality of a joint decision. Take 10 seconds to reflect on how this one might be helpful.

2. *Am I remembering that he/she doesn't see this like I do?* From *their* point of view, the other's actions make sense. *They* think and feel that they're being reasonable. Am I remembering this?

3. *Do I understand what they're saying and feeling? Have I actually listened to them?*

4. *What am I doing to intensify or prolong this conflict?* The natural tendency is to blame the other for the all the bad parts of a conflict. But since communication is collaborative, no party is just a spectator or passive recipient. I'm helping build whatever's here—the hurt, the disappointment, the fear, etc. This does not mean that it's all my fault. We're in this *together.* But since my natural inclination is to forget my role, it can help for me to ask myself this question—even out loud.

5. *Am I making myself the target?* Is my locus of control external or internal? Am I taking on personal responsibility for what may be an impersonal, diffuse frustration that they're experiencing? Are they just having a bad day?

6. *Are my goals realistic?* One way to insure failure is to set unreasonable goals. How realistic and reachable are my goals in this conflict?

7. *Am I trying to win this one?* Am I doing all I can to compete, to make the other party lose so I can win? If so, can I ratchet down my intensity?

You can help defuse the other person in three ways: First, continue to listen carefully and thoroughly. Your goal should be to continue to let the other person happen to you while holding your own ground. Try to live fully into this metaphor. Second, explicitly identify where the two of you agree. Disagreement between family members is always nested in larger agreements about priorities, preferences, and practices. Make some of these explicit.

Third, maintain your nonverbal cadence. Other people respond negatively to abrupt or significant changes in the way you are standing, sitting, or gesturing, or to obvious changes in your voice, eye behavior, or facial expression. I'm not saying that you should hide your feelings, but just manage the ways they're expressed. This means that you should keep yourself from wildly rolling your eyes, gasping with incredulity, storming out of the room, making dramatic, "How can you believe that?" movements and gestures, and in other ways expressing off-the-charts self-righteous indignation.

You can help defuse the situation in two ways. One is to move away from anyone who might be seen as an "audience." Praise in public and do conflict in private. The second way to defuse the situation is to deal with as many contextual problems as you can, like noise level or awkward seating. Suggest that both of you sit down. Move to a quieter room. Sit next to rather than across from the other person. Get both of you a cup of tea, coffee, or water. Manage the physical situation to make it as easy as possible to converse productively.

Quiet Time

When nothing else helps enough, call a moratorium on the disagreement and do something else for awhile—an hour, a day, maybe several days. Give everyone involved time to think and feel things trough, to be reflective enough to put the conflict in perspective. Don't wait so long that the issue gets ignored; this can create a festering wound that will get more and more difficult to heal. But when the situation seems to require it, take a quiet time.

CONCLUSION

Happily, most families are populated most of the time by friends rather than enemies. Family relationships often contribute most positively to the quality of our lives. Most of us learn what love is when we are loved by our family. We probably fight with our siblings, sometimes even violently, and we also hear them praise us, defend us, and protect us. We're awe-struck by a family member's generosity. We're humbled by a family member's caring. Most of us model our preferred life-partner on what we've experienced in our family.

Family communication can also hurt, and the potential for pain is every bit as high as the potential for love. This is why it's so important to mobilize our best understanding of communication and our best efforts to make communication with family members as personal as possible.

Depending on how you count them, this chapter contains at least fifteen specific pieces of advice or suggestions. When you're in conflict with a family member--expressing opposing opinions with strong emotions over high stakes—it's hard just to remember any of these, let alone apply them. But I can tell you from years of experience that they can actually help, sometimes profoundly. I've heard accusations and name calling change to productive conversation when one family member really listened to the other. A long-lived and toxic conflict cycle has been broken when the spouses finally responded seriously to the question, "What do you want to have happen?" Hurtful, defensive snarling stopped when a sister apologized, contrasted, and suggested a mutual purpose. The specific suggestions can work.

And, as with all of human life that really matters, effective family communication is ultimately less about any of the fifteen tactics and more about the personally-understood and accomplished outcomes of respect, caring, fairness, confirmation, vulnerability, presentness, candor, humility, and love. In other words, competent, effective family communication is good, and wise family communication is even better.

Wisdom starts with humility, the recognition that you are not the center of the universe, so you'd better figure out where the *other* person is coming from. When humility is expressed as listening, it generates respect and a clear sense that the listener cares. Respect and caring help create an atmosphere of fairness and communicate confirmation.

Wise people are also courageous enough to be present and vulnerable. They let the other person happen to them, because they're confident in their ability to hold their own ground. They open the door to, and at their best, they encourage direct contact, person-to-person meeting. When a wise person learns she's been mistaken, she accepts the learning with grace. Because she is humble and vulnerable, she is willing and able to change positions and opinions.

Hopefully, you've witnessed wisdom happening in at least one or two family communication events involving a parent, grandparent or great-uncle. Wisdom definitely profits from age. But if you're in your teens, your 20's, 30's, or older, you can grow in these directions if you open yourself to connecting with family members in genuine moments that matter.

Chapter 6

ON THE JOB: EVERYBODY'S
LEADERSHIP & LISTENING

W<small>HEN THE VICE-PRESIDENT OF AN ORGANIZATION</small> *I worked for learned that one of his key employees had been downloading child porn on the company network, he was shocked and torn. The employee was a twenty-year veteran and consistently effective mentor. The evidence was incontrovertible.*

When the V.P. met with the President, he learned that a similar problem had occurred a few years earlier in another division of the organization, and it had been handled first with treatment. Only after repeat offenses was that employee terminated. They decided to try treatment first again. With the President's support, the V.P. and the H.R. director scheduled the offending employee for what they expected to be a very uncomfortable meeting.

When confronted, the employee immediately admitted his guilt and acknowledged that he needed help. "Am I going to be fired?" he asked. "I could understand you doing that, but I don't know what my family and I would do." The V.P. explained the alternative that they were considering—involvement of his spouse; compulsory, intense psychotherapy over an extended probationary period; regular progress reports to the H.R. Director; close monitoring of the employee's use of the network; the option of reconsidering termination at any time.

The employee expressed embarrassment, gratitude, and deep remorse. "I've done a terrible thing, and I don't think I'll ever be able to make it right. I know I have a serious problem. I can't tell you how much I appreciate what you're offering me." After a pause, the V.P. replied, "Adam, the truth is, you're worth the risk and the investment. You've given a lot to this place and our people. In most ways, you embody the mission of this place. You're worth it." Then silence and some tears.

Fortunately, this story has a positive ending. With counseling help, Adam and his wife survived this blow to their marriage. Many months of therapy helped Adam re-frame important elements of his life. At a progress report fifteen months after the incident, Adam said that he could still feel in his gut the relief and hope that were there when he heard, "You're worth it."

Moments that matter this intensely are rare on the job, *and* they happen. When they do, they illustrate the power of person-to-person contacts in business settings. And lower-intensity personal contacts can enhance the value-added of staff meetings, performance evaluations, interviews, project meetings, and even sales presentations, whether they're held face-to-face or online.

TODAY'S MANAGEMENT THEORY

This kind of communication is far from the thoughts of most entry-level workers without college degrees. They are typically focused on how to do their job and how to cope with their supervisor. Most new employees with Associate's or Bachelor's degrees, on the other hand, have studied at least a little management theory, and most employees who are promoted to a supervisory position have also learned some management principles. This widespread exposure to management theory means that a high percentage of entry-level, supervisor, and managerial employees have invested at least some effort in studying how to do organizational life effectively.

A multi-billion dollar management theory industry supports their efforts. The ongoing, international struggle to learn how to build motivation and productivity, improve the efficiency and effectiveness of meetings, reduce turnover, and enhance innovation is led by a group of business gurus that includes Peter Drucker, Tom Peters, Ken Blanchard, Jim Collins, Robert Greenleaf, Peter Senge, and especially Steven R. Covey. Interestingly, a great deal of what these theorist-practitioners urge businesspeople to do involves making communication as personal as possible. In other words, one major goal of twenty-first century management theory and practice is to increase the frequency of moments that matter in the informal and formal gatherings that consume over 50% of the on-the-job time of 21st century workers.[93] If one of these gurus were advising the V.P. with the pornography-addicted key employee, they might well urge him to do exactly what he did.

The Most Important Work is Always Done by People

None of these experts believes that if you make communication as personal as possible, you're guaranteed to have organizational efficiency and productivity. Inventory management, global market analysis, supply chain design, innovation, and right-sizing are all required. But notice how consistently the communication advice from leading gurus echoes the suggestions offered in Chapter 2:

- Tom Peters' *In Search of Excellence* reports that the organizations he studied developed open communication systems that *"treated people decently and asked them to shine, rather than treating them as merely factors of production. . . . Fat rule books were being shredded, hierarchies flattened, formalities abandoned."*[94]

- William Isaacs applies findings from ten years of research at MIT to argue that a kind of communication he calls "dialogue" can *"enable people to work together in a highly coordinated and creative fashion, without the need for constant, heavy-handed external controls. . . . Dialogue achieves this by deepening the glue [of shared meaning] that links people together."*[95]

- Isaac's colleague, Peter Senge, extends this commitment to dialogue in *The Fifth Discipline*, and *The Fifth Discipline Fieldbook,* best-sellers that explain how to become "a learning organization." The primary task is to apply ideas from philosopher Martin Buber, psychologist Patrick DeMare, and physicist David Bohm to create an organization characterized by dialogue, defined as *"sustained collective inquiry into everyday experience and what we take for granted." This kind of communication pays close attention to everyday conversation, including "the spaces between the words, not only the words; the timing of action, not only the result; the timbre and tone of a voice, not only what is said. . . . In short, dialogue creates conditions in which people experience the primacy of the whole."*[96]

- Ex-Stanford professor, Jim Collins pinpoints specific features of outstanding companies in another set of bestsellers, *Good to Great, How The Mighty Fall,* and *Great by Choice.* Collins and his coauthors write about companies that significantly out-performed their competition and the market over a 15-year period. The leadership in these companies focuses first on people. As Collins puts it, *"you begin with who rather than what."* Quality of life is also important. *"Members of the good-to-great teams tended to become and remain friends for life. . . . Adherence to the idea of 'first who' might be the closest link between a great company and a great life. For no matter what we achieve, if we don't spend the vast majority of our time with people we love and respect, we cannot possibly have a great life.*[97]

- Ken Blanchard's title is "Chief Spiritual Officer" of the management training and consulting firm that has improved the fortunes of scores of companies, including Applebee's, Burger King, Exxon Mobil, Home Depot, Merck & Co., Staples, and Victoria's Secret. His team emphasizes that high performing organizations demonstrate strength, first, in *"shared information and open communication" and "shared power and high involvement." "Sharing information and facilitating open communication builds trust,"* Blanchard writes. *Empathic listening is crucial, the smallest customer concerns deserve close attention, feelings are an important part of communication, and feedback needs to be continuous and extensive."*[98]

- For many businesspeople, Steven Covey is the king of this hill. Covey's fame began with *The 7 Habits of Highly Effective People*, hailed as the Most Influential Business Book of the Twentieth Century, and it has continued with ten additional best-sellers. Three of the original seven *Habits* encourage moments that matter: *"Think win-win," "Seek first to understand, then to be understood,"* and *"Synergize."* The "8th habit" is *"Find your voice and inspire others to find theirs,"* which highlights your own and others' uniqueness, the importance of feelings, and the centrality of empathic listening.[99] Covey focuses squarely *on "the human side of organizations," especially the danger of "treating people like things," which "insults and alienates them, depersonalizes work, and creates low-trust, unionized, litigious cultures."*[100] Covey's 2011 book argues that, although technology has enabled humans to *overcome "the artificial walls that imprison the human mind. . . , the most challenging walls remain: the walls between people. . .[that] form barriers to trust, communication, and creativity. In today's workplace, we simply can't afford these walls."*[101]

- Robert Greenleaf and his students developed "servant leadership," an approach to organizational management that is praised by many, including Blanchard and Covey. The servant leader, he wrote, is one who wants to serve first, before she wants to lead, especially by enhancing the growth and maturity of her subordinates. *Four of the seven "pillars of servant leadership" identified by executive trainers James W. Sipe and Don M. Frick echo aspects of suggestions in this book: "Put People First," "Skilled Communicator," "Compassionate Collaborator," and "Systems Thinker." Skillful communication, they write, means "listening to understand others and expressing one's thoughts, feelings, and needs with genuineness, respect, and clarity."*[102]

Leadership and Listening

Under headings of "excellence," "greatness," "learning organizations," "high performance," "effectiveness habits," and "servant leadership," these authors discuss almost all the key elements of personal communicating, including uniqueness, everyday conversation, ESP, dialogue, egalitarianism, holism, shared meaning, nonverbal elements of talk, collaboration, empathic listening, and the close connection between quality of communication and quality of life. Two of the main sets of guidelines that mobilize this approach to organizational life focus on leadership and listening. Whatever your role in the organizations you serve, you can enhance your group's effectiveness by using leadership and listening to promote moments that matter.

Person-Centered Leadership

Organizational leadership best practices have been defined by several, long-term research projects that studied leadership in "great" or "high performing" organizations. Companies attain this status by meeting long-term, financial metrics. Jim Collins' original "good to great" companies averaged cumulative stock returns 6.9 times the general market in the fifteen years following their transition point."[103] The "high performing" or "10X" companies his team researched for *Great by Choice* beat their industry index by at least 10 times.[104] "High Performing Organizations" studied by Blanchard's research team were similarly-defined, and a ten-year study of servant-led companies averaged pre-tax portfolio returns of 24.2%, almost 6% more than Collin's original "Great" organizations.[105] These data demonstrate that organizations can use person-centered leadership to encourage moments that matter *and* have high earnings; as Sipe and Frick put it, "servant leadership is great business" (p. 2).

Think Leadership Not Leader

The approach to leadership that these firms take is in some ways counter-cultural. For one thing, successful companies don't focus on "Great Men and Women leaders," but on leader*ship*, which is contributed at every level of the organization. In addition, it's not "command and control" leadership, but the kind that emphasizes collaboration, broad participation, and open communication. *When I talked about this kind of leadership with a group of Ph.D. nuclear engineer-managers who were my clients, many were initially skeptical about what they thought was its "touchy-feely" quality. This group had served in the Navy nuclear submarine corps and thought they could easily apply military rank and discipline to the work of leading civilians. But their CEO was disappointed by the low productivity and high turnover of the teams they led. As he said to me, "I need you to train them to manage human beings."*

All these engineers were highly intelligent, technically competent and dedicated to their work. Unfortunately, they did not have the same level of people skills. Most believed they could best exert influence by giving orders and closely tracking results. After we worked together for some months, most were willing to approach leadership as a collaborative process, but didn't know how to do it.

Ken Blanchard explains the shift that helped these engineers change:

For years we defined leadership as an influence process. We believed that anytime you tried to influence the thoughts and actions of others toward goal accomplishment in either your personal or professional life, you were engaging in leadership. In recent years, we have changed our definition of leadership to <u>the capacity to influence others by unleashing their power and potential to impact the greater good.</u>[106]

This approach makes it clear that leader*ship* is the business of every organizational member. Mailroom, stockroom, loading dock, and secretarial pool employees exert leadership every day. Board members and company officers often get the credit for mission and vision definitions and strategy shifts, but crucial client and customer interactions, high-quality problem-solving, and improved internal processes owe as much to organizationally-local decisions as to global ones.

Apply What Works.

Covey defines leadership as *"communicating* to people their worth and potential so clearly that they come to see it in themselves."[107] Every leadership researcher emphasizes the importance of "skilled communication," "shared information and open communication," "shared power and high involvement," "finding your voice and inspiring others to find theirs," "starting with 'who' questions before 'what' decisions."

Two researchers identified eight common characteristics of "extraordinarily successful" groups, four of which extend personal communication principles and practices: shared leadership, full engagement, embracing differences, and strengthened relationships.[108] These groups were made up of people from 17 to 70 years old, and they focused on topics as diverse as IT, curriculum design, political campaigning, outsourcing, product life cycle management, creating e-government systems, automated medical records, and online health-care support. All the groups had "a compelling purpose," and all produced remarkable tangible and intangible results. Shared leadership was the primary quality that effectively linked purpose and extraordinary results.

As Bellman and Ryan explain,

Watch an extraordinary group in action and you will notice leadership behaviors from across the group. These groups are not top-down or leader-centric. Instead leadership is expressed by many in the group; the lead role shifts with the subject at hand and the expertise required. . . . In these groups, you will see members leading together: Initiating, facilitating, structuring, suggesting, and doing all manner of things to help the group be effective. . . . [Members] typically focus on seeing that the group is being led rather than on being the one constant leader. They turn responsibilities and questions back to the group; they ask others what they would do. They pay attention to group members and try to see that individual needs are addressed (pp. 22-23).

Members are fully engaged in these groups; they do not wait to be asked to contribute. These groups embrace differences by "respect[ing] each other for who they are as human beings," and are willing to "discuss un-discussable issues to get to the bottom of misunderstandings or hurt feelings. They give each other feedback and ask for it in return. They strive for sensitivity but not perfection in their communication because they know others will accept them for who they are." Work in these groups leads to strong relationships; often "the friendships that evolved out of [this] work lasted years beyond people's tenure at the company (pp. 25-29).

You can help lead your group in these directions by making your communication as personal as possible in every meeting.

Lead to Promote Uniqueness —As in all other arenas, giving out and taking in *uniqueness* is potentially the most powerful strategy. Consider how you can enhance your group's communication to get human uniqueness on the table more often. When you consider how you'll share your own uniqueness, recognize that leaders of extraordinary groups model openness to information and ideas along with commitment to the reason that brings the group together. This openness helps get their uniqueness on the table, because, as Bellman and Ryan say, it

> *translates into behaviors such as clarifying your intent and asking others about theirs; expressing what you want and asking others what they want; asking questions and paying attention to the answers; expressing how you feel and asking others how they feel; listening to learn and expecting others to listen too; being willing to change your mind and believing that others will do the same (p. 159).*

When you're responsible for a meeting, look for opportunities to tap into the knowledge, resourcefulness, and creativity of each individual in the group. Include agenda items, record-keeping options, and time preferences of the specific individuals attending the meeting. Be sure each person has opportunities to contribute. Consider beginning or ending a meeting with an opportunity for each person to report on a significant happening in his or her life, one that may or may not be related to the meeting agenda. Search proactively for opportunities to publicize extended accounts of individual contributions inside and outside the organization. Be appropriately open about what's happening in your own life. Evaluate the effectiveness of your day or week, in part, by how successfully you helped put human uniqueness in play in your parts of the organization.

Remember that, ultimately, uniqueness is understood via the personal parts of our brains. It is not so much built out of small parts as grasped as-a-whole, often with the help of nonverbal elements, metaphor, and story. Be sincere about your own motives, so that your "walk" will match your "talk." Look for written, oral, and graphic ways to engage people's personal understanding. Graphically dramatize and tell stories about significant events. Design significant meetings to appeal to all the senses, with room arrangement, lighting, food aromas and tastes, color, and music. Consider linking music and/or images with principles, events, accomplishments, or practices that you want to make memorable. Use your organization's "creative people" (often in marketing, display, visual, or graphics departments) to help you appeal to your colleague's personal understanding in the service of consistently acknowledging uniqueness.

You can develop your own version of the approach taken by the academic leader at an urban university who raised sheep. He's the only associate dean I've ever known with this avocation, and he effectively shared snippets of his rancher life in ways that both made him more approachable and encouraged others to talk about some of their unique interests. Tom was especially adept at telling stories that blended facts about effective animal management with humor, often about his own ineptness. His story-telling helped defuse tension and often suggested apt metaphors. He developed a strong reputation for effective program development, consensus-building, and cost-cutting. Tom succeeded as a leader partly by modeling and encouraging communication that kept uniqueness on the table.

Integrate ESP (emotions-spirit-psyche)—Give out and take in ESP by consistently affirming that the group makes up a *human* system, that humans cannot "be completely objective" and that human systems cannot be effectively treated as complicated machines. These facts have been supported over more than 50 years, not only by research but also by the successes and the failures of scores of individuals and the organizations they have led. It's almost this simple: Companies that proactively acknowledge the importance of the ESP of the humans who make them up succeed, and companies that don't, often fail.

This is why Sipe & Frick's discussion of servant leadership advises people providing leadership at every level to "put people first," in part by "showing care and concern" for who they are as persons. Members of the extraordinary groups studied by Bellman and Ryan reported that they experienced a common set of four feelings in their meetings: energized, connected to the group and the world around them, hopeful, and changed by their group experiences. Their sense of vitality helped make the group's work enjoyable rather than taxing. The feelings of connection led to such comments as, *"We bonded for life" and "When I took this job, I thought I'd only be here for two years. The team and mission have kept me here for seven" (p. 51).*

Your leadership efforts can help your group move in this direction in several ways. Treat your organization's mission and vision statement as an opportunity to have conversations about the human values that the mission and vision assert and the spirit they engender. Look for opportunities to explore group member's passion for your organization's work and their caring for colleagues and their families, mentoring relationships, and long-time customers and clients. Help make emotions part of the organization's responses to consequential events—successful product launches, increases of market share, good press, lost clients, lower stock values, bad press. Effectively expressed emotions from people at every level of the organization help show that the company is not just a machine and its communication climate is human-centric. Include in your own emails, memos, reports, and meeting introductions and conclusions expressions of emotion that are appropriate to the situation.

When you're bringing emotions into the communication mix, it helps to remember three facts about them. One is that emotions are not created by outside forces or caused by others. This is the power of the distinction between external and internal locus of control. Despite what you often hear or say, other's don't "make you mad." Anger emerges in the connection between you and the other person(s) (See the "Between" poem in Chapter 2), and when you forget this fact, the emotions you help bring to the conversation can be toxic rather than helpful.

If others actually controlled your communication, you could never stop in the middle of a heated argument to answer the phone with a reasonably pleasant, "May I help you?" But everybody does this kind of thing. It happens because human choices intervene between stimulus and response. This basic understanding needs to be clear enough to everyone in the conversation that when people communicate about emotions they *own* the feelings in their talk. "She gave a boring presentation" distorts the feeling by making it somebody else's fault. This statement needs to be replaced by something like *"I lost interest in the presentation," or "I couldn't follow her."*

A second crucial fact about emotions is that humans can respond to emotional content in a variety of ways. Choice intervenes here, too. *Eagerness and excitement can be celebrated and shared, and they can also remind those involved to take a second look, so they don't get carried away. Hostility can be met with silence, putting it in perspective --"Let's take a minute to cool off, ok?"— or reframing--"Is there a way to harness all this energy in positive, rather than destructive ways?"* Think of ESP content as an important kind of grist for the conversational mill. Get it on the table, and then use it in productive ways.

The third fact about emotions is that they change. This is obvious, and it's also often forgotten when emotions are getting in the way. The simplest way to use this fact as a leader is to call a quiet time. When that's not possible, find ways to engage the "hot" persons or groups in activities that redirect their energies. If the group's frustrated or exhausted from grappling with an intractable problem, propose an opportunity for fun—a pizza lunch or brief scavenger hunt. If hostility is the problem, suggest a 10 minute moratorium to listen to jazz or offer the group an assignment to text you the most hopeful parts of the struggle they're in. If fatigue is the problem, ask for a volunteer to lead the group in some simple yoga stretches. When emotions are intense, some people won't want to participate in activities designed to help. But the more often your part of the organization approaches destructive emotions this way, the more people will participate. When faced with problematic emotions, the leadership goal of people at every level should be to creatively encourage people to keep talking.

Responses, Mindfulness, and Reflections — Round out your leadership efforts to make the communication as personal as possible by designing ways to give out and take in choices, reflections, and opportunities for mindfulness. As a start, in your own conversations with colleagues, model this skill by communicating *tentatively*. Jack Gibb's study cited in Chapter 5 identified how much tentativeness can reduce defensiveness. The authors of *Crucial Conversations* agree when they advise their readers to talk

> *in a way that expresses appropriate confidence in your conclusions while demonstrating that, if called for, you want your conclusions challenged. To do so, change, "The fact is" to "In my opinion." Swap "Everyone knows that" for "I've talked to three of our suppliers who think that." Soften "It's clear to me" to "I'm beginning to wonder if."*
>
> *Why soften the message? . . .Speaking in absolute and overstated terms does not increase your influence, it decreases it.*[109]

In order to forestall the misinterpretation that they are advising wishy-washy talk, these executive trainers offer "the Goldilocks test" as a way to check your statements for the appropriate level of tentativeness. *"This is probably stupid, but. . ."* is too soft. *"How come you ripped us off?" is too hard. "It's starting to look like you're taking this software home for your own use, is that right?" is just right on the tentative scale (pp.145-146).*

Metacommunicating can also be a skill for giving out and taking in mindfulness. Remember that metacommunication is communication about communication, for example with statements like *"It sounds like we're getting off the topic,"* and *"This was a great meeting!"* Too much of this can drive people nuts, but effective communicators recognize when it's helpful to encourage their conversation partners to talk about their talking. You can help meeting participants make the communication as personal as possible by asking them to describe at the conclusion of a session what they believe were its most and least useful parts. As Chapter 5 explained, you can also practice and model the effectiveness of metacommunication as a conflict management skill by stepping back from a hostile confrontation to identify and express the most important commonalities that connect the combatants (relationship reminders), or by reminding participants (including yourself) of the differences between win/lose and win/win motivations.

A third way to promote responses, mindfulness, and reflections is to affirm the complexity of participants' positions on a given issue, rather than oversimplifying them. Thoughtfully-developed explanations are the goal, not slogans or sound bites. One consultant team helps complexify group members' ideas in part by asking participants to reflect specifically on reservations they have about their core belief about whatever difficult topic that is on the table. Here's how they word this question:

Many people have, within their general approach to the issue, some dilemmas, mixed feelings, uncertainties, or gray areas. Some people find that in their thinking about the issue, an important value related to [the issue] bumps up against another value that they hold dear. Within your thinking about

the issue, are there any dilemmas, value conflicts, or gray
areas that you'd be willing to share?[110]

Consider how you might adapt this script to encourage the same kind of complexifying by participants at your meetings. For example, you could follow-up a strong statement of opinion with something like this: *"That's really clear, and you make a strong case. Is there any place where a value that supports your position bumps up against another important value of yours? When you really think about this issue, do you have any mixed feelings or gray areas?"*

Each of these suggestions for shaping open communication in your organization can be applied by employees at every level. You don't have to be a company officer or even a manager to lead efforts to make the communication as personal as possible. Look for ways to give out and take in uniqueness. Help put ESP on the table, partly by owning and expressing your emotions and encouraging others to do the same. Do the same with mindfulness and reflectiveness by communicating tentatively—not weakly—and affirming complexity in your own positions and those of others.

EFFECTIVE LISTENING

Management gurus also emphasize how important listening is. For some people, this seems as upside-down as the idea of shared leadership. Many believe that improved communication begins when a person learns to *speak* more clearly and persuasively. But the truth is that effective communication begins with effective listening. Why? Because, as I've already said, the basic goal of all communication is the same: to *connect.* It's not primarily to perform, dazzle, or creatively display, but first to *connect* your thinking and the other person's. And since people are inherently unique, you cannot connect effectively until you get out of your own ways of thinking and discover relevant parts of where the other person is coming from. This is why effective communication starts with good listening.

I've already said quite a bit about listening in these pages. Chapter 2 highlights the importance of both "taking in" (listening for) and "giving out" (expressing) features of "the personal." Chapter 3 encourages you to "listen between the lines" of email, texts, and Tweets. It reminds you that listening is 30% talk. Chapter 3 also outlines the "power listening" skills that are summarized by the acronym AMPP—Ask, Mirror, Paraphrase, and Prime. It reminds you to avoid "Why?" questions and pseudoquestions, and introduces Dialogic Listening with the metaphor, "let the other person happen to you while holding your own ground."

Chapter 5 suggests that your family conflict management efforts begin with listening. It mentions again the skills of "Say more" or "Keep talking," mirror responses, and paraphrasing. All these comments reflect how important listening is in every communication arena. In fact,

- *Among the four modes of communication—reading, writing, speaking, and listening—people spend the most time listening—40%-50%.*

- *Although most of us have been taught to read, write, and speak, fewer than 5% have had more than two weeks of formal listening training.*[111]

- *This is why, especially in organizational life, communication effectiveness depends even more on listening than on reading, writing, or speaking.*

The Listening Scale

So here's a way to summarize what's known about listening in a simple model you can use to remind yourself how to listen effectively.[112]

TYPES OF LISTENING				
Listening for entertaininment	Attentive Listening	Critical Listening	Empathic Listening	Dialogic Listening
Inside Your Own Frame of Reference			Inside the Other's Frame of Reference	Co-Laborating

The first three kinds of listening are natural, even habitual for most of us. We listen for entertainment purposes to music, poetry, nature, and sometimes to the hum of a well-tuned machine. We listen attentively when we've got something to gain or lose, as in a required training session or when we're getting treatment instructions from a physician. We listen critically when we want to find weaknesses so we can make a strong counter-argument. A common feature of all three is that our main motive is to stay inside our own frame of reference— stick with the music we like, get prepared for the test, defend our turf, spot comments that we can use for our own purposes. This motive can be helpful and useful, *and* it limits the kind of contact we experience. As one author puts it,

> *When I ask you to listen and you start giving advice, you have not done what I have asked. When I ask you to listen to me and you begin to tell me why I shouldn't feel that way, you are trampling on my feelings. When I ask you to listen and you feel you have to do something to solve my problem, you have failed me, strange as it may seem.*[113]

The most effective listening begins when you get outside your own frame of reference. The model shows that there are two ways to do this, and each has its challenges and payoffs.

Empathic Listening

Steven Covey's research has convinced him of the importance of empathic listening so strongly that, he writes,

> *I've devoted much of my life to teaching [it]. . . . I liken empathic listening to giving people "psychological air." . . . Like the need for air, the greatest psychological need of a human being is to be understood and valued. When you listen with empathy to another person, you give that person psychological air. Once that vital need is met, you can then focus on problem-solving.*[114]

Covey argues that the greatest challenge for the empathic listener is adopting the necessary mind-set. It's the mind-set of the person who, when he hears someone who disagrees with him, walks up to that person and says, *"You see things differently. I need to listen to you."* It's also the mind-set of a line employee who doesn't like a new company policy or is dissatisfied with a performance review and who asks for more information. It's the mind-set of a person with the courage and humility to reach outside his or her own frame of reference.

Importantly, this mind-set cannot successfully be taken on as a manipulative strategy, and genuine empathic listening can't successfully be faked. Why? People generally know when they're being conned, and this kind of insincerity can mark a person permanently. If you honestly don't care about where the other person's coming from, don't pretend that you do. But if you want to connect, maybe even profoundly, practice the genuine form of this kind of listening.

Empathic listening skills are familiar, and I've already mentioned several. Nonverbally, it's important to embody openness by facing the other, keeping your arms and hands open rather than closed, smiling appropriately, looking the person in the eye, sitting or kneeling at their level, and giving them time to speak. The acronym AMPP can remind you of four verbal empathic listening skills already mentioned.

Probes that pull more talk from your conversation partner can also be helpful, such as, "Say more," "For example?" and "Where do you see that happening?"

Talking Stick — Another way to encourage empathic listening is to apply an appropriate version of Talking Stick turn-taking. As Covey explains, some Native Americans have used the Talking Stick for centuries at their council gatherings. As long as the speaker holds the stick, no one may interrupt until the speaker feels heard and understood.

I have used a version of this technique in a circle of over forty engineers, using a wireless microphone as a talking stick. I began with a brief story of the rich history of the Talking Stick and a description of what would be carved into and attached to the microphone, if we were all Native Americans. I intended the story to engage the participants' personal thinking and provide a reflective context for the conversation. I explained that Talking Stick communication is not about winning arguments but about hearing another person's story and understanding his or her heart. The fact that the "stick" gave its holder the sacred power of speech helped make each contribution thoughtful and on point. The reminder not to interrupt helped focus participants on each speaker. The requirement to demonstrate to the speaker's satisfaction that listeners understood him or her encouraged reflection and paraphrasing. The action of passing the talking stick encouraged participants to link what they said with what had been said before. The electronic talking stick clearly helped make the communication personal in this conversation, and a version of this technique can enhance the contact in many meetings.

Paraphrase Before Contributing — Another widely-shared suggestion is to have participants agree to and practice the communication rule that's part of most talking-stick use, that is, before speaking, each contributor to a conversation must paraphrase the prior speaker's ideas and feelings to that speaker's satisfaction. Participants will find that it's fairly easy to restate another person's ideas, but not so easy to get their feelings right. This is what can make the practice powerful. It definitely slows down the conversation, to the point where participants often get frustrated. *And* this practice demonstrates not only that empathic understanding takes effort but also that this kind of listening can identify commonalities among people who thought they disagreed, and it can promote feelings of appreciation and confirmation. It can be deeply gratifying to be listened to empathically.

Dialogic Listening

As the Types of Listening model shows, the other way to get outside your own frame of reference is to shift focus not to "the other person's meanings" but to the meanings that conversation partners are constructing together. Dialogic listening happens when the people involved are willing and able to consciously collaborate, to build meaning together.

Like Empathic Listening, Dialogic Listening requires a specific mind-set, in this case an intentionally collaborative one. You achieve this mindset through your brain's personal understanding. You can guide yourself into this mind-set in two ways. The first is prescriptive, which means that you decide to collaborate because it's "helpful," "useful," "productive," "a good thing to do." For example, you may have thought about the costs and benefits of win/lose, lose/lose, and win/win communicating, and decided that it's better to work toward win/win. Or you might move toward this mind-set by recalling the problem of the two people in the same library reading room, one of whom wants fresh air while the other doesn't want a draft. The librarian opens a window in the adjoining room, and both get what they want. The mind-set reflects your awareness that often the best way to resolve a disagreement is to identify a mutual purpose, so you collaborate toward that end.

On the other hand, you may embrace this mind-set not mainly because it's "a good thing to do" but because it acknowledges what's actually happening. This is the descriptive, rather than prescriptive option. As Chapter 2 clarified, communication is always collaborative, in the sense that people co-labor to produce meanings. We don't make meaning alone. Dialogic listening can begin when you recognize that this is how things are in the human world, so the smart thing to do is to live into this reality.

Making Meaning Together

I've said before that the mind-set that grounds dialogic listening requires letting the other person happen to you while holding your own ground. This metaphor captures two intertwining moves. You open yourself to the other's world of meaning while articulating your own contributions to the conversation. You allow yourself to be vulnerable to the other's rationale, conclusion, and accompanying feelings at the same time as you offer your own rationale, conclusion, and accompanying feelings. You envision yourself seated at a potter's wheel with your conversation partners, and, all at the same time, each pair of hands is working the wet clay. Any of you can ruin what's being turned, *and* it's also possible—and potentially deeply gratifying—for your four, six, or eight hands to shape something none of you could have crafted alone. Allow yourself to live into this image.

Paraphrase Plus — However you arrive at a dialogic mind-set, you can help embody it by practicing several specific listening skills. One is a *paraphrase plus*. I've already said that a paraphrase consists of (1) a restatement of (2) the other's ideas and feelings, (3) in your own words, (4) concluded with an invitation for the other person to verify your understanding. A paraphrase plus includes all of these elements plus the addition of your own response to the question "And. . .?"

The plus part may be an expression of what the other's ideas and feelings elicit in you. It might be an example of the point they made. It might be an added idea that takes their thought in a different direction. The paraphrase plus ends with an invitation to the other to keep the conversational ball in the air. For example:

	Rita:	*We've been meeting for months about this database change. We've heard enough presentations to confuse everybody, and it feels like we're never going to make a decision. I like the fact that we have input, but I wish we'd just pick one so we can get to work learning it!*
(paraphrases)	Muneo:	*So you're saying we should pick one even though there are still questions, because it's impossible to answer everything until we've used the system, right?*
(attacks)	Tim:	*You want to give up our one chance to have some power over IT? That's crazy!*
(paraphrase plus)	Scott:	*It sounds like you appreciate what's happened so far and you're ready to get on with it. I'm tired of the process too, but I'd still like to see all three options in a compare-and-contrast table. What do you think of setting up that comparison and then deciding?*

Another way to think about the paraphrase plus is that you're broadening your goal beyond listening for "fidelity"—being true to what the other person said. If you're paraphrasing for fidelity you're finished with the task as soon as you've successfully reproduced "what she means." A paraphrase plus goes beyond fidelity to what happens next, beyond reproducing their thoughts and feelings to adding your own response so two or more of you can mutually construct meaning between or among yourselves.

Ask for a Paraphrase — Because paraphrasing is potentially so helpful, another dialogic listening skill is to *ask for a paraphrase.* It can be difficult to do this well, because a request for a paraphrase can sound like an accusation: "Okay, why don't you try telling me what I just said?!" This obviously is not going to contribute to the process of sculpting mutual meanings. Instead, try putting it this way: *"Just to make sure we're going in the same direction, could you tell me what you think we've agreed to so far?" Or you might say, "I'm not sure I've been clear—what do you hear me saying?"* After the other person paraphrases you, continue the co-sculpting with an affirmation or a movement further along the thought line. When done in this spirit, a paraphrase plus can help the conversation continue dialogically.

Run with the Metaphor — A third skill you can use in the sculpting process is to *run with the metaphor.* This means that you extend whatever metaphors the other person has used to express his or her ideas and develop your own.

Metaphors are ways of speaking that link two dissimilar objects or ideas in order to make a point. They don't just appear in poetry and other creative writing; we use them all the time. "This place is a zoo," "My vacation was a circus," and "Dialogic listening involves sculpting mutual meanings" all contain metaphors.

The skill consists of listening for both subtle and obvious metaphors and then weaving them into your conversational responses.

When other people hear you take up their metaphors, they commonly feel deeply understood. *In a workshop I was leading, I listened to an engineer describe the part of his job that involved appearing before regulatory boards and municipal committees to answer questions about various construction projects. Part of what Phil said about his job was that it was a "game." I tried to run with his metaphor by asking, "What's the name of the game?" "Winning," Phil replied. That wasn't where I wanted to go, so I tried again. "Okay," I said, "But what kind of game is it—baseball, football, soccer, chess, or what?" "It's football," Phil replied. "What position do you play?" "Fullback." "And who's the offensive line?" "All the people in the office who give me the information I take to the meetings." "Who's the coach?" I asked. "We don't have one. That's the major problem." This was a telling response. In fact, from that point on, the workshop was focused on one of this firm's major management problems.*

Remember that these specific listening skills are like selections on a salad bar (another metaphor!). You don't eat everything, and in different situations you select different dishes. Here's an example of several of these skills being used in a conversation between two employees involved in an intercultural competence training session.

	Sheri:	*That workshop drives me up the wall. I know the stuff's important, but I feel squashed in there.*
(run with the metaphor)	*Julio:*	*"Squashed" as in stepped on, or "squashed" as in there's just too much to do?*
	Sheri:	*"Squashed" as in there is no flexibility. That trainer is so rigid! We can't come in late, there's no time to check texts or email, everybody has to say something every session. I'll bet he wouldn't allow a makeup session if I was in the hospital!*

(ask; say more)	Julio:	*I didn't know he wouldn't allow makeups. Where did you hear that?*
	Sheri:	*Alaysha told me that on Tuesday she tried to arrange to be gone for a client visit and the trainer wouldn't agree to it.*
(paraphrase)	Julio:	*So Alaysha was keeping up with the requirements and he wouldn't let her attend the other group's session?*
	Sheri:	*Well, she'd missed a couple of sessions, but I still think it's pretty unreasonable. I'm going to have to miss two in a row, and I'll bet he unloads on me.*
(paraphrase plus)	Julio:	*I can see why you're worried. If you've got a good reason, though, and can meet when the other group does, I bet he'll agree. I was talking with him about when cultural adjustment has to consider different time assumptions and expectations. That's part of the workshop content. If you talked about it that way, I'll bet he'd respond positively. What do you think?*
(paraphrase)	Sheri:	*So you're saying I can ask for the time and connect it to a point he's made?*
	Julio:	*Yeah.*
	Sheri:	*I hadn't thought about that. Good idea! I appreciate the tip.*

CONCLUSION

There is strong evidence that people in organizations can increase productivity, efficiency, and employee satisfaction and decrease turnover and customer complaints by making their communication as personal as possible. One specific way to do this is with the kind of leadership that management theorists call "who-focused," "high performance," "servant leadership," or "shared leadership." There are opportunities to practice this kind of leadership at every level of the organization. The key is to develop what leadership gurus call "shared information and open communication," "shared power and high involvement," "collaboration," and "dialogue." Do this by searching for opportunities to appropriately get features of the personal on the table in meetings, training sessions, performance evaluations, and informal workplace conversations. Appropriately express your own uniqueness, ESP, choices, and mindful reflections and encourage the people you interact with to follow suit.

Another powerful way to make communication on the job as personal as possible is to model and encourage empathic and dialogic listening. Effective listening is the *sine qua non* of effective communication. When listening is good, communication works; when it's bad, misunderstanding, resentment, disrespect, and needless conflict occur. Develop your ability to adopt both empathic and dialogic mind-sets and to practice the skills that help these kinds of listening happen.

Chapter 7

MOMENTS THAT MATTER IN LEARNING SITUATIONS

I LEARNED ABOUT HARD WORK FROM *watching my dad and how to be organized from my mom. I learned about the importance of family from grandparents on my mother's side, and my dad's folks helped me learn not to complain. I learned that love is the key to good teaching from Walt, my major graduate professor.*

I learned the most about the dangers of cigarette smoking from conversations with Andy, my boss in the Sears tire center, who was teaching me how to mount and balance tires. Almost all I could hear were his wheezing pants and interrupting coughs.

I learned the most about national politics, small colleges, pinochle, and how to tip from Prof Karl, my college mentor. Groups of us spent weekends with Prof traveling to other schools preparing for and debriefing from competition. From these classmates I learned important research skills, how the U.S. Supreme Court interacts with Congress, and that I look geeky in turtlenecks.

169

I learned about feminism from several strong women, and about LGBT culture from Bill, John Paul, and many others. I learned to meld faith and thinking from my housemate John, and the meaning of vocation from Fr. Ralph. I learned a lot about parenting from my daughters, especially when they were teenagers. I learned dozens of important insights about people and families in thirteen years of twelve-step meetings.

Your learning experiences are probably a lot like mine. Classrooms are important for lessons about spelling, math, and geography. Family gatherings, school playgrounds, sports, and clubs are where we learn lessons about respect, discipline, leadership, winning, and losing. Most important learnings happen in moments of personal contact. As Martin Buber put it, "It is not the educational intention but it is the meeting which is educationally fruitful." [115]

LEARNING MEETINGS

Buber's point is that learning is a contact sport. The key connections are person-to-person, as John Dewey noted early in the 20th century. "All education," Dewey wrote, "proceeds by the participation of the individual in the social consciousness."[116]

For generations, teachers, trainers, and professors believed that they could educate best by lecturing, giving assignments, and grading. A revolution began in the last third of the twentieth century when these people finally began to take Dewey seriously, which meant shifting focus from teaching to learning and from educators being the "sage on stage" to being "a guide on the side." One big reason why this revolution was important is that it promoted more moments that matter.

The Experts Agree

In 1916, Dewey told teachers that they have to stop trying to hand ideas to students as if ideas were bricks.[117] Dewey showed that learning

*is not simply motion in one direction, from the curriculum via
the teacher to the student. Rather, learning involves interact-
ing processes, energy moving in a variety of directions: from
student to the curriculum and vice versa, from teacher to
student and vice versa, and from student to student as well.*[118]

For a long time, most teachers continued trying to hand out bricks.
It took decades of efforts by scores of learning theorists, education
researchers, and classroom teachers to shift the focus from teaching to
learning and from the teacher or trainer to teacher-learner partnerships
and communities of learners.

Today, there are still grade and middle school, high school, and
college students, along with business people in required workshops
and seminars, who are suffering under the oppressive weight of teachers and trainers trying to inject knowledge into them by exclusively
lecturing, rewarding rote memorization, and focusing mainly, as one
critic puts it, on "covering the content [rather than] uncovering part of
it."[119] Happily, there are also millions of learners in mentoring relationships, workshops, classes, and seminars that emphasize engagement,
shared power, solving genuine problems, experiential application,
moments that matter. These learners are benefitting, not only from
Dewey's original insights, but from the research, writing, and practice of many contemporary educators who urge teachers, trainers, and
learners to promote personal communication.

For example, in *Discussion as a Way of Teaching,* two award-
winning educators emphasize the importance of conversation. They
highlight nine qualities of what they call democratic discussion, six
of which echo what I've said about encouraging moments that matter.
"Hospitality" is the first, an atmosphere in which uniqueness is valued
and "people feel invited to participate." Equal opportunity to contribute
is a second, and a third is "mindfulness," which "involves being aware
of the whole conversation—of who has spoken and who has not," and

requires careful listening. Humility and mutuality emphasize that learning is "always an uncertain, even uneasy quest," and that participants "care as much about each other's self-development as one's own." Appreciation anchored in respect rounds out the description, along with what Dewey called "hope."[120] Learning situations where this kind of discussion is encouraged promote frequent moments that matter.

The same thing can happen in business organizations. *Herb, a consultant committed to conversational learning, was working with a senior management team at Wright Patterson Air Force Base when the commanding officer (CO) asked for his input during a meeting. The CO had been leading the group through the agenda for several minutes, and Herb responded to his question, "I think we should take a break." The team spontaneously broke into groups of two or three and began talking among themselves. After reconvening and continuing the agenda, the CO again turned to Herb for advice and Herb again suggested a break. When this sequence was repeated for a third time, the CO asked in frustration, "Why do you suggest a break every time I ask what we should do?" Herb replied, "Because that's the only time anything is happening."[121]*

Collaborative, discussion-based, dialogic, engaging, problem-based, learning-focused approaches have been tested in K-12 schools; with math, English, chemistry, communication, sociology, landscape architecture, biology, history, philosophy, psychology, medical, and business students in large and small colleges and universities; and in business organizations in the U.S., Europe, and in several Pacific Rim countries. When learning is tracked in any of these venues, the results are always the same. People learn the most when they are helped to engage in content-focused conversations to co-create moments that matter.

FIVE GUIDELINES FOR DOING LEARNING MEETINGS

You can profit from this knowledge in all of the learning-focused situations you are part of at home, on the job, at school, with friends, in family gatherings, and in the organizations you serve, whether you are operating mainly in the "teacher" role or as a "learner." These guidelines can be useful whenever you and the people you're with are trying to improve your understanding of anything from video game strategies to chemistry formulas, sales techniques, tennis strokes, policy options, or sexual positions. In each of these arenas, more learning will happen when you appropriate a version of five pieces of advice that grow out of the learning theory I've described and the understanding of communication in Chapters 1 and 2:

- *Remember that learning is constructed not received*
- *Be learning-focused*
- *Discover others' genius and share yours*
- *Talk effectively*
- *Get fellow learners to talk*

#1: Learning is Constructed not Received

The mistaken belief that educating means handing students bricks treats a person's mind as a storage bin with empty places waiting to be filled. But research on how people actually learn demonstrates that

- *"new knowledge is acquired by extending and revising prior knowledge,*
- *new ideas acquire meaning when they are presented in a coherent relationship to one another, and*
- *knowledge becomes usable when it is acquired in situations that entail applications to concrete problem solving."*[122]

This is what it means to say that learning is constructed not received.

The first construction move is to link new ideas to prior learning.

The person who knows how to dribble a basketball learns a bounce-pass as a dribble to a teammate, and the beginning sailor who absorbed Bernoulli's principle in physics class sees exactly how to trim a close-hauled jib. They learn when they link the new challenge to some prior learning.

The second construction move is to connect new ideas together into a coherent whole, and the third is to apply them. To put them together,

> *People learn to the degree to which they can actively manipulate facts within some general framework and can relate general ideas to specific events in their experience. We have knowledge, in other words, only as we actively participate in its construction. Students do so by engaging with other students and with the teacher, in a process of inquiry, critical discourse, and problem-solving. The teacher's role is to foster conditions in which students are encouraged to construct knowledge.*[123]

When Ken Bain, Director of the Center for Teaching Excellence at New York University, studied over 60 outstanding educators at two dozen institutions, this was the first "key concept" he found. The best educators don't think of what they're doing as just getting students to "absorb some knowledge." "Because they believe that students must use their existing mental models to interpret what they encounter, they think about what they do as stimulating construction, *not 'transmitting knowledge'.*" [124]

Listen First — When you're a teacher, trainer, or mentor, one of the ways you can apply this principle is by listening first. I've talked about this several times before, and it's especially important in learning situations. Start your interactions with your trainees or students by asking rather than telling, by getting them to describe what they already know about the topic, skill, or operation. Resist the temptation to begin with an overview, a list of the benefits, or a locker room speech. Instead, encourage the learners to talk, and listen carefully to what they say.

You can also help this happen when you're a learner by developing a conversational opening that allows you to help your teacher trainer, or mentor understand some of your prior knowledge that you believe is related to what's being taught, and to confirm whether it is. You can do this with questions, too, and they have the added benefit of reducing the chance that the teacher or trainer will think you're challenging her authority. Try something like, *"Is this operation similar to what I did on the old equipment?" "How does this approach to handling customer complaints connect with what we learned in the orientation program?" or "How's the new database different from the one we've been using?"* Follow up the response you get with additional comments about experiences you have with related content.

As a learner, also look for opportunities to share questions that have arisen as you've applied related concepts or performed related operations. In Chapter 2, this was called giving out reflectiveness, because it helps the other person understand how you've been thinking about or reflecting on the topic. For example, *"I've never understood how the units get assembled for packaging; will we be talking about that?" or "I've always wondered how the basic principles get applied in multicultural situations; will that be part of what we do?"*

This is another place where uniqueness is important. When you're an educator working with multiple learners, your ability to customize your teaching or training is limited. At the same time, the initial efforts you invest in understanding what each learner brings to the table will pay off as you move through the process.

I usually begin my effort to know learners as individuals by extending the traditional "Tell us a little about yourself" activity. Often, I'll spend the entire first session interviewing them, exploring connections between learners and relating my experiences to theirs. One uniqueness-identifying activity is a time-line. Ask learners to draw a horizontal line across a blank sheet and to put their birth date on the left edge, the date of their death on the right end of the line, and today's date where it fits in the middle. Then ask them to identify two "best" and two "worst" events on the left side of today's date (i.e., in their past) and two "bucket list" events on the right. I open the conversation by discussing one or two of my entries. By the end of a 20-minute conversation, the group will know some unique insights about most of the individuals in the room.

When you understand some of the learners' unique strengths and weaknesses, you can use what you learn in several ways, for example by investing extra time with some content, recruiting experienced learners to help you teach concepts or operations that they know well, and providing opportunities for learners to share unique application examples.

Plan Collaboratively — A second way to apply this principle as a teacher or trainer is to postpone completing the organization and schedule of your course, workshop, seminar, or training until after you've met with your students or trainees. Structure is critical, but the organization of the training should reflect both the teacher's prior knowledge and the students'. As a practical matter, it almost always works best to keep plans flexible from beginning to end. The instructor's best ideas about timing and application opportunities can often be improved by input from learners. Stay open to this kind of collaborative development.

Integrate Application — In addition, insert regular opportunities into the workshop or course for learners to demonstrate what they've learned. Avoid the common trap of believing that "They got it" just because you believe you said it so clearly—or even so often. Don't ever limit assessment to only a final exam or concluding skill check.

At various points during the course or training, ask learners to restate principles in their own words, create and effectively handle their own case studies, or perform key operations. This will give you—and others involved—opportunities to respond in kind, from your own perspective, and meet what they say in fruitful interplay. Always remember that they're interpreting everything you say and do through their own lenses, their own prior knowledge.

Use Plus-Delta — Plus-delta is an activity that gives learners the opportunity to let instructors know how things are going. Periodically in the course or workshop, the teacher or trainer asks students to anonymously share two one-or two sentence perceptions: What's going well (the plus) and what might be changed (the delta). Whether you're face-to-face or online, you can arrange to do this electronically. Or you can do it the old-fashioned way on a half sheet of paper. If you are responsible for the training, use time between sessions to reflect on what learners write, and be sure to converse with them about what you've learned the next time you meet. If there is diversity in what people think is going well—"I like the readings." "The readings suck."—share that, along with how you interpret this feedback, and ask students to respond. You may want to explain parts of the class that get negative reviews, and either clarify why you've decided to keep them or how they'll be changed. Two key guidelines are always to show that you're taking the feedback seriously, because it gives you insight into how learners are constructing or interpreting what's going on, and always make the follow-up a conversation.

#2: Be Learning-Focused

Instruction-focused training or teaching mainly considers inputs—the qualifications of the trainer, the number and length of sessions, materials to be read, key assignments and tests. Learning-focused training or teaching concentrates on outcomes—how participants are different when they're finished from the way they were when they started. The best educators think of teaching as *"anything they might do to help and encourage students to learn. Teaching is engaging students, engineering an environment in which they learn."*[125] When you want to move from being instruction-focused to being learning-focused, implement a version of the following five changes.[126]

Change the Balance of Power — The first is to shift the balance of power from teacher-control to as much collaboration as the situation permits. It's naïve to believe that educator and educated ever have completely equal power. All learning events exist in institutional or interpersonal systems that define power relationships. In a business organization, for example, learners are often required to complete training successfully in order to keep their jobs or get promoted. Within the constraints of the situation, though, educators can still adjust power relationships significantly.

When, as suggested above, an instructor begins with questions rather than statements, for example, this simple communication choice can help empower learners, because it gets learner concerns and issues into the talk. The same thing happens when an instructor develops the structure of the course collaboratively. Power relationships can also be shifted in the direction of equality in dozens of other ways. When asked a question he can't answer, the teacher can admit his limitation rather than masking it, and can ask if anyone else can help. Instructors can ask students who have experience related to the content to share what they know.

Empowerment can also happen when learners are told less and encouraged to discover more. This can occur when students are given a scenario or case and asked, perhaps in groups, to find the content in the field that explains, answers, or resolves the problem. As they report what they've found, they have the floor and set the terms of the conversation. As one educator explains, learning *"requires invention and self-organization on the part of the learner. Thus teachers need to allow learners to raise their own questions, generate their own hypotheses and models as possibilities and test them for validity."*[127]

Promote Deep Learning — The function of content also changes when you're learning-focused. Instruction-focused educating often generates surface- rather than deep-learning. This happens when learners participate because they're required to, focus exclusively on hypothetical and contrived problems, and are expected mainly to memorize facts. Deep learning happens when a learner experiences a qualitative change in aspects of his or her ways of seeing, experiencing, understanding, and conceptualizing something in the real world rather than as a quantitative change in the amount of knowledge he or she possesses.[128] Deep- rather than surface-learning should be your primary goal. The most effective workshops and courses leave behind two or three important ideas with broad applications rather than dozens of isolated facts.

Guide on the Side — A third change involves the role of the teacher. Learning-focused instruction acknowledges that the teacher is not the only expert; even beginning students can interact with content by exploring it, relating it to their own experience, and challenging it. Their mindful reflectiveness is as relevant as the instructor's. In addition, outstanding teaching is not determined by how charismatic or even how resourceful the teacher is but by what the students take away from the experience.

The teacher's role shifts, as was mentioned, from "sage on stage" to "guide on the side." Learner-focused teachers talk less; they rarely speak more than 40% of the time. They ask more questions, probe student responses more, and listen empathically and dialogically more often. Physically, they move in the middle of the room and around its sides more than at the front. They practice nonverbal ways of encouraging student talk—nod+silence+smile, "Say more" gestures, quizzical looks. They promote and urge student discovery and celebrate it when it happens with an encouraging smile, a sincere "Thank you" or "Great response!"

Promote Interdependence — A fourth change is in the responsibility for learning. Instruction-based learning encourages students to be dependent on the teacher. In learner-focused situations, students are encouraged to move toward being collaborative and independent learners. The position of independent learning is familiar to every self-taught gardener, trekker, knitter, or boat-builder, and these models can usefully inform learning situations in businesses, classrooms, webinars, and workshops.

Because many learners have been taught by authoritarian teachers and trainers to be dependent, it can take time and effort to develop their autonomy. It can also be challenging to successfully *lead* learners to do more *for themselves.* You need to be willing and able to practice what you preach. *When you ask a question, wait for a response, even if it takes awhile. Sit, at least part of the time, to show that you don't always want to be the focal person. Delegate discussion-leadership to other learners. Consistently demonstrate your commitment to collaboration in every part of the course, workshop, or seminar.*

Evaluate to Enhance Learning — The fifth change focuses on how learning is evaluated. Research shows that assessment directly promotes learning—students remember what they're tested on. But often assessments send the wrong signals. As an instructor, think about what you'd want a learner to say if you ran into her at the mall a year after your mentoring, workshop or course and you asked, "What do you remember?" The assessments you're using—skill checkups, application exercises, projects, papers, tests—should focus there. If they don't, they need to be redesigned.

Make evaluations as authentic as possible. This is easier in a training situation, because you have specific work expectations to meet.

Have all learners demonstrate their competence in the topic of the workshop or training. If it's complex, break it down into parts and set up situations for them to demonstrate skill in each. In a class or course, evaluate responses to genuine rather than hypothetical questions— *"What three steps would our City Manager take if he were applying the model we've discussed?" "What investment strategy follows the highest number of the principles we've covered?" "How would you apply what we've learned to a political campaign? An ad campaign for the local symphony?"*

#3: Discover their Genius and Share Yours

Before the word "genius" came to mean a person with an IQ over 140, it meant the characteristic disposition or distinctiveness of a person—his or her uniqueness. So each of us has our own "genius." The best teaching-learning relationships are those that include uniqueness, where both or all people involved come to know something of each person's individuality.

Walt is a teacher I had whose uniqueness enriched his effectiveness. Before becoming a university professor, he'd been a Marine drill sergeant and combat veteran. Yet he's the educator I mentioned who taught me that love is the key to good teaching. Who would have thought that those qualities went together? Walt wore the same academic outfit just about every day, and he also drove the most flashy Cadillac he could afford. He consistently pushed us in the direction of deep learning, and he loved crossword puzzles. When he was 60, he could easily do 50 push-ups, and he enjoyed cooking spaghetti Bolognese. I learned more working with Walt than I learned working with any other teacher, and it's partly because he was willing to share his iindividuality and encourage me to develop my own.

Making uniqueness a priority means giving it time. Seconds, minutes, and hours are always scarce resources, but you've probably figured out by now that most moments that matter don't happen in two minute exchanges. The pace that we're pushed toward by smartphone ads, multitasking managers, and short-cutting charlatans is techno-logical, not humane. Human contact just about always takes time, and whether you're a teacher or a learner, you'll profit from the minutes you invest in individuality.

One of the greatest practical payoffs of this investment is the abil-ity to keep the conversation going. The time and effort you invest in learning about your student's or your teacher's individuality can help you respond productively to a conversational impasse—a "final word," intractable position, or even a rude insult. It will help you keep the conversation going.

For example, if you know something of the student's genius, you can respond to, *"I give up! I can't answer your question in a way that makes sense to you!"* with something like,

- *"You're ahead of the conversation. Help us catch up!"*

- *"I meant to be probing, not shutting you down. Can you give me another chance?"* or

- *"Great energy! You obviously give a damn about the topic. What's the most frustrating part?"*

Which response you choose depends on what you know about the complaining student. In less intense interactions, individual knowl-edge can empower you to customize questions, adapt assignments, and suggest particularly appropriate applications.

There's an old story that the best school is a log with a master teacher on one end and a student on the other. Large lectures, over-subscribed webinars, MOOCs (massive open online courses), and other numbers-based practices make it challenging to apply this prin-ciple. And yet, every mentoring, training, and teaching situation pro-vides opportunities to discover and share genius or uniqueness, and no single move is more likely to promote moments that matter.

#4: Talk Effectively

The fourth way to promote moments that matter in learning situations is to talk well. As Ken Bain reports from his study of the best college teachers, *"Perhaps the most significant skill the teachers in our study displayed in the classroom, laboratory, studio, or wherever they met with students was the ability to communicate orally in ways that stimulated thought."*[129] The research identified five key skills.

Conversation not Performance — *"More than anything else, the most successful communicators treated anything they said to their students—whether in fifty minute lectures or in two-minute explanations—as a conversation rather than a performance. They interacted with students and encouraged and allowed them to interact with one another and with the material."*[130]

Gary, a professor I knew, practiced this skill over many years in his daily meetings with 225 students. *Gary taught in one of six amphitheater-style lecture halls in a new building equipped with the latest instructional media. He used the projectors and screens to illustrate, highlight ideas, and give assignments, but he spent the bulk of each class in a low-key, well-organized, content-focused conversation with his students. Gary held the small, wireless microphone against his lower lip so he could talk as if he were sitting next to each student in a living room or lounge. When he moved around the room, it was mainly to take the mike to a student who had a question or comment, and he'd stand or kneel next to them and exchange remarks as if they were chatting over coffee or a beer. As he conversed, he'd often ask, "Are you with me?" He watched student's reactions, read their eyes and other body language, and adjusted what he said to the enlightened, confused, bewildered, or even bored looks he saw. He learned students' names and called on them. He quickly became one of the most popular professors on this 35,000 student campus, and after just two years of this kind of teaching, Gary received the university's top teaching award.*

A Sense of the Dramatic — Without moving into performance mode, the best teachers also insert a sense of the dramatic into their talk, partly by using volume and vocal variety to make their talk lively. Like conversation partners on a street corner, they will sometimes whisper, shout, or exaggerate the high/low pitch changes of *"You've got to be kidding!" "Can you imagine what they did next??" or "That's what I'm talkin' about!"*

They also know how to make silence loud. Educators with a flair for the dramatic know when to pause to let a key idea land. They've learned about "wait time," the seconds—or more—that can pass between when a good question is asked and when the first student responds—and they leave that time empty. They know that silence can mean that thinking is happening. Sometimes they emphasize the impact of a pause by holding perfectly still. Sometimes they ask an incisive question and, while students consider it, move to the back of the room, so the student who responds has to swivel in her chair. When they're in an exchange with a student, in a large class or a small one, they often move to a place in the room where the exchange has to pass "through" as many learners as possible, so the one-on-one includes others.

Effective teachers are also good story-tellers. They search for anecdotes that make key points clearly and dramatically. Often, the best story is one that gives its hearers a glimpse behind the curtain of a business or institution. Stories based on "insider knowledge" can also be compelling—an overheard or candid comment from a prominent politician, celebrity, or CEO. The best teachers are also not afraid to tell stories that are outrageous—that feature locally famous people, involve disgusting behavior, or otherwise come close to being offensive. Of course, there are lines that should not be crossed, but most students are tolerant, especially if the story spices up the learning session. *Gary's students consistently remembered his stories about how a particular restaurant chain designed its seating, lighting, colors, birthday celebrations, and sound levels to create enough discomfort that diners would come in, order, eat, and leave rapidly, which enabled the restaurant to turn the tables quickly and increase revenue.*

Changes of Pace — Another insight that the best teachers know is that the attention span of almost all learners is short and getting shorter. At the turn of the 21st century, teaching research recommended changing classroom activities at least every 20 minutes. Media multitasking has reduced that time considerably. According to Bain's research,

> *every ten to twelve minutes, [the best teachers] change the rhythm and content of their delivery, shifting direction or focus, altering activities or subject, punctuating an explanation with stories or questions, ending or beginning an exercise. Some teachers sprinkle in humor; others move from the concrete to the abstract. If they are talking they stop; if they are silent, they say something (p. 120).*

Warm Language — Cool language is detached and impersonal. *"There was this story about this little girl and three bears and how she went to their house when they were gone and tasted and tried everything and then they came home and discovered her."*[131] Accurate enough. Not very interesting.

Warm language demonstrates engagement, involvement, presence. *"Once upon a time there were three bears and a little girl named Goldilocks. Goldilocks got her name from her beautiful blond hair and sparkling smile. After an afternoon's long walk in the forest, she found herself lost, and was getting desperate for cellphone service when she happened upon a neat and tidy little house."*

Cool language works well for previews, summaries, and reminders, and warm language works best to invite, engage, and stimulate.

Good Explanations — When explanations are bad, students feel confused, frustrated, and put off. Good explanations snap lights on in students' heads.

One feature of a good explanation is that it applies the communication principle, *Define before you develop; explain before you amplify.* A clear explanation starts with simple generalizations and then becomes both more complex and more specific. It's also presented in a way that makes it accessible and even welcoming. For example,

> *Locus of control is a psychological term for the way people explain what they do.* (basic definition*) The simple version is that people with an external locus of control point to outside forces as causes for their behavior* (first sub-category defined). *So they'd say, "I had to shout back; she was making me look silly." Or "I'm sorry I'm late. The traffic was terrible."* (simple examples of first sub-category). *Those with an internal locus of control attribute more of what they do to their own choices* (second sub-category defined). *So this person might say, "I'm sorry I'm late. I wasn't able to leave when I'd planned"* (familiar example that contrasts with an earlier one). *Could you give me an example from your own experience of internal and external locus of control* (invites conversation)*?*

Good explanations start with simple ways to help the learner begin to construct an understanding. Often the first pass is not completely accurate or detailed, but it starts the process. Then the instructor uses conversation to add complexity.

#5: Get Learners to Talk

When teaching is performing, the instructor wants learners to be quiet and focused. But when teaching is conversation, the best learning spaces are filled with talk. Of course, talk can be cheap, and the best educators know how to make it valuable by helping it be consequential, informed, topic-focused, and intensely interactive.

The teacher can set the expectation that conversations are consequential by raising genuine, rather than contrived or purely hypothetical questions. *"Why do local politicians work well together even though some are Democrats and some are Republicans?" "How was the Miami Dolphins player abuse scandal similar to the Enron scandal?" "Why are Black students still sitting together in our cafeteria?"* The best teachers don't just ask students to discuss readings, they provoke and guide them into discussing ideas, issues, or problems that an article or chapter can help them approach.

Teachers establish expectations that conversations are well-informed by pressing learners to provide evidence and reasoning to support their claims and rewarding them when they do. Learners who supportively challenge and encourage their classmates in the same ways are also praised. When an enthusiastic learner spins a tale that is obviously memorable but off the point, the effective trainer or teacher will select a sub-point from the story that enables her to help the student get back on the topic, without squelching his energy.

Most teachers committed to conversation choose learning spaces with movable chairs, so learners can quickly scoot into small groups. I've also formed groups in rooms with bolted-down chairs by asking participants to perch on chair backs or move into the open spaces at the front and back of the room. Or you can send them outside or into a common area for a defined time, often with a brief list of discussion prompts.

Think/Pair/Square/Share — Learners used to discussion readily respond to a request to "think/pair/square/share." Individually, students begin by gathering their thoughts about a question or problem (think). Then they discuss their initial ideas with one person sitting nearby (pair). After a few minutes, twos move together into groups of four (square), and the room typically explodes in animated conversation. The instructor circulates to be sure that the talk is on topic and informed. After some minutes, the group comes back together so a spokesperson from each group can share outcomes. This can work in groups of learners as small as 20 and as large as 200, and with topics as diverse as insurance claims, cold calls, production changes, biology, psychology, or government.

Go 'Round & Popcorn — A facilitator can also apply different combinations of "a go-round" and "popcorn." In a go-round, each student has about 30 seconds to a minute to make an initial contribution to the conversation. After everyone has been required and enabled to speak, the popcorn rule applies, which means that contributions can pop up from anywhere. The facilitator applies the same care that makes a space for every learner to speak to the practice of calling on students. The best teachers call on students the way they might do around the dinner table rather than the way they might cross-examine them in a courtroom. In contrast, less effective teachers fall into playing "Guess what's on my mind," a discussion game in which there's only one right answer.

Questioning — "Guess what's on my mind" is also an example of one of the worst possible kind of questions. Equally poor ones are "Are there any questions?" and "Does anybody disagree?" Effective teachers come into the room with a full quiver of good questions, and I talk about this skill in detail in the "facilitation" section of Chapter 8. I don't want to repeat myself here, except to emphasize that some very insightful educators have called the art of questioning "the most important intellectual ability [the hu]man has yet developed."[132]

ANALYTIC OR HOLISTIC? IMPERSONAL OR PERSONAL?

It's impossible to work your way through the lists of 36 specific suggestions without thinking rationally and analytically. So what is the role of personal thinking in learning situations? How does personal understanding help create learning moments that matter?

The answer is that each of the specific techniques in this chapter is a means to a personal end. For example, the whole discussion of genius is about uniqueness—how teacher and learner individuality can help learning happen. The sense that another person is one-of-a-kind can only be grasped holistically and directly, that is, personally. Warm language also promotes contact, the experience of being involved and feeling felt. Think-pair-square-share is the means and dialogue is the end. Almost all of the 36 point toward holistic, immediate understandings; encourage metaphoric, story-based actions; open the door to Aha! moments, and promote personal contact.

And these moments won't happen unless the situation encourages them and the facilitator is willing and able to *connect* with the other learners. The physical space itself needs to be inviting and flexible. Ground rules need to mandate engagement, respect, minimal interruptions, and collaborative thinking. Participants in the workshop, class, or training need to have learned that they're in a safe space where they won't be penalized for not knowing.

In addition, the facilitator needs consistently to model engagement, good listening skills, humility, flexibility, and a concern with genuine issues and problems, not just textbook questions.

CONCLUSION

Each of us can remember being embarrassed or abused in elementary school, put down by an arrogant trainer, misinformed about a critical process, thoroughly confused by an "expert" who couldn't teach, or bored out of our minds by hours of droning lectures. Each of us can also recall exciting Aha! moments when a training activity made clear sense, a master teacher effectively led us through a complicated set of principles, or our participation in a project group helped us learn important new content.

This chapter is meant to show how your learning can be enhanced by applying the same kinds of understandings and skills that earlier chapters have applied to online communicating, families, and your work life. Just like communication itself, learning is a contact sport, whether it happens in a family, on the job, or in a school or classroom. Master teachers know that the best learning happens in moments that matter, between teachers and learners, among learners, and between learners and educational materials—software, videos, case studies, articles, texts, original documents. Effective learners understand that, even though they're often "one-down" in the educational power relationship, they can also help to do learning meetings well.

Whether teacher or learner, when you apply your own version of some of the 36 specific suggestions in this chapter, you'll help to create many more moments that matter.

Chapter 8

PERSONAL POLITICS

MOST OF US THINK OF OUR FAVORITE holidays as times for the family to get together in celebration, love, and harmony. But in many U.S. households, "just beneath the refined veneer of the best dishes and silverware, some politically polarized family members will be sitting at the table, just lying in wait for a perfect moment between the turkey and the pumpkin pie to erupt and begin a political debate." [133] Family political disagreements have become common enough to prompt books like *Red Families v. Blue Families: Legal Polarization and the Creation of Culture*.[134]

This is why many people hope that a chapter called "personal Politics" will help them cope gracefully with Uncle Mike's disgust at a government that "can find money for welfare, but not for Social Security," or cousin Audrey's anger at the mistreatment of Planned Parenthood. And the challenge extends outside families to times with friends and even strangers. A heated political tirade has spoiled many otherwise-pleasant lunches, car rides, or coffee breaks with colleagues or friends. What can a skilled communicator do? Are moments that matter possible in political conversations?

Keeping it Real

The reality is, not very often. Most people with strong political agendas do not want to have a conversation with somebody who has a different view. They prefer to stick with like-minded True Believers. Almost all of Rush Limbaugh's listeners share his views, and the same is true of those who watch Bill Maher. In fact, a recent study shows that this pattern applies to dating and courtship. People place more emphasis on finding a mate who is a kindred spirit on politics, politics and religion, and social activity than they do on finding someone of like physique or personality.[135] This means that the vast majority of conversations between individuals with opposing political views are going to be impersonal, not personal.

And some can be different. But if you know your political views differ significantly from your conversation partner's, and you still want to talk, it will take extra effort to have a productive personal conversation. Everyone involved will need to work on at least three elements:

Metacommunicate

Remember that metacommunication is talk about your talk, and in this case it means, first, finding out whether it makes sense to continue. Ask your conversation partner whether she wants to explore political ideas or mainly to express her political view. Ask out of curiosity, not challenge. You might say something like, *"I'd like to listen to your ideas about _____ and have you listen and respond to mine. I'll bet we can both learn something. And, I know that, at least at the start, we probably disagree. So if we want to avoid just getting in an argument, we'll need to figure out how we want to talk with each other and what we want to get out of this. What would you like to have happen?"*

The other person may well be surprised by your question, and it's possible they'll respond with angry silence. Your question also might prompt a drastic change of topic, or worse. But if you make it clear that you're not interested in being part of a cheering section for ideas that you disagree with, and you *are* genuinely interested in learning from each other, you've given the other person the opportunity to help decide what happens next.

Understanding not Persuasion

The second important step is about expectations. Political advocates who shoot from the lip seem often to expect that their tirade will persuade their conversation partner over to their side. This almost never happens. People's political views are anchored in their experiences and developed over time; they seldom change because of one, two, or even several conversations.

Under somewhat controlled conditions, though, conversations between political opponents can generate enhanced understanding for all participants. Thoughtful study should come before attempts to persuade, *and* it can work the other way around. Opposed expressions of well-considered views can also promote deeper understanding when the advocates are respectful and civil. Whenever you listen carefully to a reflective person you disagree with, it's likely that you'll learn something. So, if both parties are open to this happening, a political conversation can be productive. See if you can agree with each other that you will both work toward understanding not necessarily agreement.

Ground Rules

These steps may be enough to get your conversation going productively. If you want to increase your chances for success even more, though, try spending a little time on ground rules. For example, the leaders of the Pacific Educational Group facilitate what they call "courageous conversations about race." They have worked successfully with school districts all over the U.S. in empowering parents, teachers, students, and administrators to tackle some of the hottest political topics. This group begins by asking participants to commit to four agreements: Stay engaged, Speak your truth, Experience Discomfort, and Expect and accept non-closure.[136]

Stay engaged means committing to remain morally, emotionally, intellectually and socially involved in the dialogue. It means not to let your heart and mind "check out" of the conversation while leaving your body in place. This can be especially difficult in conversations about race, because many White Americans have been conditioned to avoid the topic, while many people of color converse about race every day, but only among themselves. Most people have also been taught that it's not polite to talk about "politics, religion, or sex." So the cultural cards are stacked against you. But if the people in the conversation can commit to staying engaged, they can help make the conversation productive.

Speak your truth means being honest about your thoughts, feelings, and opinions and not just saying what you believe others want to hear. People often don't speak their truth about a political topic because they're afraid of offending, appearing angry, or sounding ignorant. This problem is worsened, because those who identify with the dominant political culture—whether it's Jewish, heterosexual, White, male, youth-oriented, educated, wealthy, or poor—will have a measure of unearned power that supports the opinions they express. This makes it more difficult for those outside this power circle to speak their truth.

For example, in a mainly pro-life group, it can be very difficult for a man who sees both sides of the issue to speak his truth about abortion. Assume that he's had an experience with a sister who became pregnant from a date-rape that was never reported. He recalls vividly how anguished she was about bringing a child into a single-parent world where there was little money and less social support. He also remembers how frightened she was about the uncertainty of adoption and the guilt she'd feel about "giving up" her child. Although he personally dislikes the thought of abortion, he knows that there are valid reasons why it's legal and available. He's not sure he wants to trust others with this personal information, and yet he doesn't want his silence to be taken as agreement. It will take considerable courage to speak even a general version of his truth in this situation.

When participants agree to this ground rule, they are also committing to suffer the pain of hearing some personal truths they would rather not hear. So this is a ground rule about both what you say and how you listen. You may believe that the other person is immoral, overreacting, distorting reality, blaming the victims, or expecting perfection. You may not understand why they can't just cut some slack or have a thicker skin. When hearing another's truth, though, your challenge is to listen for its meaning, not to discount it, no matter how different it is from your experience. And you should be able to expect the same from them as you speak your truth.

Experience discomfort follows naturally. This ground rule acknowledges that, because politics is generally so polarized in our society, serious political conversations necessarily create discomfort for participants. Many people who dislike conflict want to smooth the situation by emphasizing how "people are all alike." But as Chapter 2 clarifies, the first human reality is that each of us is unique, and political commitments are part of what make us that way. The most highly-functioning human groups—families, work teams, committees, friendship circles, clubs, and organizations—affirm their diversity and exploit differences to enrich the group.

When you genuinely don't want to experience this discomfort, don't engage in the political conversation. This is one reason for the metacommunication you start with. Fruitful conversations about real differences can lead to real growth. This won't happen, though, until people feel both courageous enough and safe enough to experience some discomfort.

Expect and accept non-closure means that your goal for the conversation should not be, as I mentioned, to persuade the other person to your belief, or to solve the political problem you're discussing. *The point of the talk is the understanding, acceptance, and respect that, under the best conditions, the talk itself can produce.* In 2001, the *Boston Globe* reported on a 6-year-long dialogue that had been occurring between 3 pro-life and 3 pro-choice leaders. The women began meeting regularly and secretly after a bombing at an abortion clinic. They were guided by a facilitator who helped them follow several ground rules like the ones I just discussed. After over more than 75 months of dialogue, the women wrote, in a consensus article, that none of them had changed her position. And yet, despite their serious discomforts and continued disagreements, they continued to meet

> *because when we face our opponent, we see her dignity and goodness. Embracing this apparent contradiction stretches us spiritually. We've experienced something radical and life-altering that we describe in nonpolitical terms: "the mystery of love," "holy ground," or simply, "mysterious."*
>
> *We continue because we are stretched intellectually, as well. This has been a rare opportunity to engage in sustained, candid conversations about serious moral disagreements. It has made our thinking sharper and our language more precise.*
>
> *We hope, too, that we have become wiser and more effective leaders. We are more knowledgeable about our political opponents. We have learned to avoid being overreactive and*

*disparaging to the other side and to focus instead on affirm-
ing our respective causes.*[137]

This is what mindful and reflective political conversation between opponents can potentially produce. *And* it won't happen without commitment and hard work by everyone involved. It is not easy to make political talk as personal as possible.

Now, let's think together about personal politics in another important way:

THINKING GLOBALLY AND ACTING LOCALLY

Politics weren't the main motivation for the seven LGBT students who traveled together to the 2011 Rainbow Rave Conference and Drag Show at the University of Wisconsin-Platteville. They went mainly for fun, and they weren't disappointed. The workshops were inspiring, the participants were supportive, and the Drag Show was an epic 400-person party with outrageous costumes and great music. On the drive back, their excited conversation focused on the parts of their experience they wanted to bring back to their own city. "Nothing like this has ever happened in Dubuque, and it should." "Would it be allowed?" "If we did something like this, would people come?"

These questions came up mainly because of their town's discrimination history. There had been KKK activity there as recently as 1990. Especially since 2000, Dubuque has become much more cosmopolitan, thanks to enlightened leaders, a strong economy, new public projects, and global employers like McGraw-Hill, IBM and John Deere. But it wasn't yet known as a place friendly to people who are Lesbian-Gay-Bisexual-Transgender (LGBT).

As the foremost political theorist of this generation explained, politics is basically about power, where "A has power over B to the extent that he can get B to do something that B would not otherwise do."[138]

Like most members of marginalized groups, these students wanted more power over how LGBT people were treated in Dubuque, and they didn't want to try to bully anyone. They wanted to offer insights into the LGBT community by creating a safe space for people to share their stories and learn from each other. They were convinced that education could produce more acceptance, and that a conference and celebration like the one in Platteville could help. The first empowering moment happened during the ride home when the students excitedly barraged their adviser, Jess, with their main question: "Could we do this in Dubuque?" "Yes!" she replied. "You have the skills and the passion to pull this off. I'll support you every step of the way."

One year later, the first Better Together Dubuque conference welcomed over 220 to its panels and workshops, and almost 400 attended the late afternoon celebration at the convention center. It was the city's most important anti-discrimination event in 2012, and was widely covered by ABC news, local and regional websites, and print media. Better Together Dubuque was a local and regional political success, with the potential for national impact.

Jess and the students created this political achievement without past experience, money, or established political connections. They'd all been bullied, rejected, and discriminated against because of their sexual orientation, and they'd moved beyond anger to a shared commitment to educate people about positive alternatives by encouraging dialogue. Their main resources were a clear focus, strong commitments, energy, and the willingness and ability to engage people personally by telling their stories and facilitating serious and productive conversations

Individually and together, they reached out, first on their campuses where they found faculty and administrators eager to support them. Off campus, they discovered the local Human Rights Commission, a community group enthusiastic to embrace their Better Together vision. One commission member connected the students to a center that provides sexual assault and domestic violence counseling. The center offered the nonprofit sponsorship that enabled Better Together to apply for and receive grant support. Another commission member linked the students to a large local publisher with a longstanding commitment to diversity. A retired firefighter, a minister, and a part-time law student on the commission became strong allies.

This expanding network of people was fueled by multiple moments that mattered. They energized each other by connecting as persons. They shared stories that revealed deep commonalities—dedication to social justice, determination to grow beyond their serious hurts, passion to act both authentically and respectfully. They facilitated many two-person and small group conversations about LGBT issues in the city and region.

At one of the conference sessions, Jess met an established community member who had helped write Dubuque's original anti-discrimination law, and who was profoundly moved by what was happening. His son and several LGBT friends had been bullied, and at least one had committed suicide. Through tears, this father told Jess about his lonely and hard struggle to promote human rights in an unwelcoming place. "What you've done is huge. This conference has helped change people's lives. It has saved people's lives."

This is the potential payoff of effective political action at the group level. This is what can happen when people think globally and effectively act locally.

Don't Be Stopped By What's Wrong

As I've already noted, political differences now divide people in the U.S. more than race, education level, income, gender and religion.[139] Many argue that the 2012 U.S. Presidential campaign was the most negative in recorded history.[140] National and local legislative bodies are paralyzed by partisan bickering. Huge numbers of citizens join groups to create and praise vicious attacks, complain about the loss of civility, or withdraw from politics entirely. Conservatives and Liberals keep ranting, and their true believers shout for more.

A PARALLEL POLITICAL UNIVERSE

At the same time all this media-fueled political incivility is paralyzing institutions and destroying relationships, thousands of less-prominent members of dozens of organizations are exercising political power in humane, civil, and often very effective ways. Since most media go by the rule, "If it bleeds, it leads," these groups don't get much coverage. But they're out there.

For example, the National Coalition for Dialogue and Deliberation (NCDD) is a network of over 1600 people who bring citizens together across political divides to discuss, decide, and take action together on issues like immigration, abortion, money in politics, and same-sex marriage. In addition to groups on Facebook, LinkedIn, and Twitter, NCDD provides a Resource Guide on Public Engagement, sponsors regional and national conferences, and connects people with blogs and listservs. One NCDD member created LivingRoomConversations. org, to "revitalize the art of conversation among people with diverse views and to remind our fellow Americans of the power and beauty of civil discourse[141]"

A like-minded group in the Boston area staffs the Public Conversations Project (PCP), which affirms

In this world of polarizing conflicts, we have glimpsed a new possibility: a way in which people can disagree frankly and passionately, become clearer in heart and mind about their activism, and, at the same time, contribute to a more civil and compassionate society.[142]

The PCP has lived out this commitment in successful projects with teams of people from the United Nations, city and county governments, religious and legal organizations, universities, and citizens groups in the U.S., England, Mexico, Iceland, Norway, Finland, and New Zealand.

On the opposite side of the U.S., a team of communication professionals in California and Arizona leads the Public Dialogue Consortium (PDC), which enhances the quality of political communication in organizations and communities struggling with these same divisive issues. The PDC uses community meetings, workshops, and trainings to help people practice dialogic communication which, in their words, requires *"remaining in the tension between holding your ground while being profoundly open to the other.*[143]

Sound familiar? These groups and many others are applying versions of the approach to communication that I'm recommending in this book, and they're finding that it works.

In Apple Computer's hometown of Cupertino, California the PDC's dialogue training has significantly reduced conflict and hostility over diversity and immigration issues. Well-developed web resources and sophisticated software streamline citizen contacts with government, and community meetings, block parties, dessert parties, and informal dinners provide openings for the face-to-face interaction that is the foundation of Cupertino's success. Representatives of other small and large cities have come to Cupertino to learn how to replicate what they've done. Now, "When Cupertino citizens do turn to the city government for help, officials find they can be most responsive by combining the advantages of electronic tools with the benefits of person-to-person contact.[144]

The Cupertino experience illustrates again that politics does not have to be warfare, and that personal communication can help accomplish political goals. So whether you are concerned about marijuana legalization, immigration reform, animal rights, health care, energy and the environment, LGBT issues, anti-racism, abortion, police brutality, gun control, or some specifically local issue, you can get involved and make a difference by working to make your political communication as personal as possible.

THE GOAL: BUILDING SOCIAL CAPITAL

The reason this kind of political communication can be effective is that it builds social capital. What's "social capital"? Well, "capital" is a term for the assets or wealth owned by a person or an organization—its property, buildings, or equipment. Human capital is made up of the properties of individuals, and *social capital* refers to connections among people—the trust, supportiveness, reciprocity, collaboration, networks, and sense of togetherness that makes a group strong and effective. This is what Better Together Dubuque built, and it's also what the NCDD, PCP, PDC, and dozens of similar organizations are building.

Organizations, clubs and churches build social capital when members spend relationship-building time together and when they pool resources to solve problems. Cities and counties build social capital when they encourage networks of relationships that enhance mutual recognition and effective partnerships.

Have you heard the expression, "It's not what you know, it's *who* you know?" This statement is about social capital. If you are poor, disabled, belong to an ethnic or religious minority, or are otherwise marginalized, you may suffer in part because you don't have as much social capital as others do. Social capital greases the wheels that allow communities to operate smoothly. The networks that make up social capital are conduits for the flow of helpful information—how to find a job, license a vehicle, find the lowest prices, register to vote, contest a traffic ticket, locate an honest mechanic or babysitter, recycle waste, choose a good internet or cell phone provider.

Social capital matters, because where social capital is high, public spaces are cleaner, people are friendlier, and the streets are safer. Social capital also affects children, because when parents belong to networks of trust, their children have more opportunities, choices, and educational options. Social capital can even increase how much money people have. Where trust and social networks flourish, individuals, firms, neighborhoods, and even nations prosper economically.[145] And there is even a strong relationship between social capital and better health. "As a rough rule. . . , if you belong to no groups but decide to join one, you cut your risk of dying over the next year *in half.* If you smoke and belong to no groups, it's a toss-up statistically whether you should stop smoking or start joining." [146] Social capital is a real asset.

So, how do people build social capital? By making their communication as personal as possible. Social capital is built in families, groups, clubs, and organizations where people gather because of mutual interests, social activities, or economic and political aims— sports teams, child care cooperatives, neighborhood associations, cycle clubs, churches, service clubs, fitness groups, soccer leagues, cooking clubs, PTSAs, sororities and fraternities, retirement groups. These are the places where people pay attention to quality of life issues. Concerned citizens' "interest in dialogue and conversation, and the cultivation of environments in which people can work together, take them to the heart of what is required to strengthen and develop social capital and civic society."[147] This is what Jess and the students did when they created Better Together Dubuque. This is what the PDC has done in Cupertino and what the PDC did in Mexico, Finland, and New Zealand. When your political communication is effective, you build social capital, and this can be tremendously valuable.

BUILD SOCIAL CAPITAL WITH FACILITATION

How do social capital and facilitation fit together? A facilitator is someone who makes it easier for a group to accomplish its goals. PDC members facilitated contacts among all the stakeholders in Cupertino, and Better Together Dubuque facilitated communication among LGBT people, allies, and other Dubuqers.

When a group of people are in a serious conversation, effective facilitation can sound like this:

- *"Let's hear from someone who hasn't spoken for awhile."*

- *"Please share something about your life experience that you think may have shaped your general perspective about [the issue] or your responses to [events at the center of the controversy]."*

- *"Are there other ways of looking at this?"*

- *"I understand you so far. Now tell me a little more."*

- *"It sounds like there are three conversations going on right now. I want to make sure I'm tracking them. It sounds like one is about roles and responsibilities. Another is about finances. And a third is about what you've learned by working with the last person who held this job. Am I getting it right?"*

- *"You look like you might be about to say something. . . ?"*

- *What is the heart of the matter for you?*

- *"Let me summarize what I'm hearing from each of you."*

- *"What have you heard today that has made you think, or has touched you in some way?"*

In these and other ways, facilitation can help get conflicting parties to the table and can help make their contacts productive. Effective facilitation strengthens a group's trust level, their interpersonal networks, and their collaboration skills, the very things that make up social capital. Effective facilitation promotes good conversation, and the most effective facilitation promotes dialogue, as it's been defined here:

THE BEST FACILITATION PROMOTES DIALOGUE

Dialogue Involves:
Letting the other happen to me while holding my own ground. Remaining in the tension between holding your own ground while being profoundly open to the other.

As people move close to the ideal sketched in this box, their communication is well toward the right-hand side of the impersonal-------personal scale described in Chapter 2. They verbally and nonverbally take in and give out important aspects of who they are as persons—their uniqueness, choices, ESP, and reflective mindfulness. In these ways they help make communication as personal as possible and in this way they help create moments that matter.

When a group practices this kind of dialogue, they also embody participative democracy. The big advantage of democracy is that it encourages broad involvement, and research shows that many heads are almost always better than one.[148] Of course, it can be difficult to manage this kind of participation. There are all kinds of ways it can go wrong. But a skilled facilitator can mobilize a group to pursue political goals effectively, whether the goals are related to a traditional political campaign or to the much more prevalent activities of defining an organization's mission and goals, setting a workload policy, talking respectfully about a divisive issue, prioritizing action items, dividing tasks, or solving a collective problem. Good facilitation can empower a group to work these issues with civil, humane, effective, personal communication.

Three Facilitation Skills: Planning, Guiding, and Recording

The rest of this chapter explains how you can apply the approach to communication outlined in Chapters 1 and 2 to political communication situations by using facilitation to promote personal communication and build social capital.

Sometimes facilitators are disinterested third parties who don't have any direct stake in the group's outcomes. At other times, a regular member of the group facilitates its work. Both outsiders and insiders can be effective, so long as the facilitator recognizes the distinction between *content* and *process* and takes primary responsibility for the *processes* the group follows. Basically, content is "what" the group is focused on, and process is "how," which means the ways they communicate.

Planning

Your first task as a facilitator is to understand the group's desired outcome and the background and context of the conversation. This is primarily *content* knowledge.

Process planning is most important. You don't need an elaborate plan for a family talk, but it is important to have even an informal conversation happen at a convenient time and in a place where you won't be interrupted. These are *process* considerations, and when you're facilitating the work of a task force, work group, project team, or political action committee, they become increasingly important.

Some groups also need the kind of conversation ground rules that I talked about earlier. In almost every case, it's helpful to call people's attention to the common-sense guidelines that distinguish good discussion from wasting time, fanning the flames, serial speech-giving, or another of the many ways group conversation can go wrong.

SAMPLE DIALOGUE GROUND RULES

- Everybody gets a fair hearing

- Seek first to understand, then to be understood.

- Especially when disagreeing, paraphrase before asserting your position.

- Share "air time"

- If you are offended or uncomfortable, say so, and say why.

- It's OK to disagree, but not to personalize it; stick to the issue. No name-calling or stereotyping.

- Speak for yourself, not for others.

Another part of planning is to ask group members to help construct an agenda, so you have a roadmap for the conversation (content & process). Get as clear as you can before the meeting about general goals and time expectations. You may even draft a very basic agenda with suggested time frames. But be sure to take the next step. The group will be most willing to follow an agenda that they have helped construct. So ask them, either before or at the start of the meeting, what they want to accomplish, and use what you hear to structure the time. It's usually helpful, unless the agenda is very simple, to post it where it can be seen during the session, and to help members stick to the tasks they've laid out.

When you're facilitating the group's first meeting, you'll also need to plan a way for them to get to know something about each other—an icebreaker (process). Online resources list dozens of them.[149] Sometimes I ask each person to describe two truths and a lie about themselves, and to have the rest of the group determine which is which. A more topic-focused icebreaker asks pairs of participants who don't know each other to spend 3-5 minutes introducing themselves and describing one personal experience they've had with the topic of the meeting. Then ask each to introduce his/her partner to the group, using information from their discussion.

Here's a checklist of other important planning topics:

- *What do participants need to know before the conversation starts? (content)*

- *What room set-up will best encourage participation? (process)*

- *What supplies do you need? Flip charts & pens? Post-it notes? iPads? Refreshments? (process)*

- *In what order should topics be discussed? (process)*

- *If the conversation is to be divided into sessions, how much time should be allocated to each? (process)*

- *Will all participants be in every session, or will you divide the group into breakout sessions? (process)*

- *How will outcomes of one session flow into the next? (process)*

- *How will you achieve closure—summarize and move toward implementation? (process & content)*

Guiding

This is the heart of facilitation. "Guiding" is a term for all the things you do during discussions to help the group's communication work the assigned topic(s) and be as personal as possible. Your three main ways to guide the group's conversation are *questioning*, *listening*, and *responding*.

Questioning — The point of facilitation is to help productive talk happen, and the main way to encourage talk is to ask genuine questions.

The first step toward effective questioning is to distinguish between an answer and a response. An answer finishes the conversation on that topic, while a response moves the thinking along and also encourages or at least enables the conversation to keep going. Effective facilitators are much more interested in responses. Of course, groups do need to get to an ending point or make a decision. But it helps, early on, to encourage people to offer responses to the group, rather than closed-ended answers.

The second step is to remember that there are dozens of kinds of questions, and the conversation will go better when you choose the best ones. The most basic distinction is between "closed" (yes/no, one-word) questions and "open" ones. "Will you take notes for the group?" is a closed question, as is "How many people are we expecting?" Open questions encourage people to talk. For example, "What experiences have you had with city personnel?" or "How did you decide to do that?" Generally, most of your questions should be open ones.

One master teacher at Harvard offers this list of useful questions:[150]

- *Information-seeking questions: "How many people showed up last time?"*

- *Diagnostic questions: "What's your analysis of the problem?*

- *Challenge/testing questions: "What evidence supports your conclusion?"*

- *Prediction questions: "If your conclusions are correct, how might the school board respond?*

- *Hypothetical questions: "What would have happened if we would have gotten the grant?"*

- *Extension question: "What happens when you extend your-reasoning into another budget year?*

- *Priority questions: "Given the limited resources, what's the first step to be taken? The second?*

People who ask questions for a living—counselors, teachers, psychiatrists—are often taught to avoid questions that begin with "Why?" because they tend to promote defensiveness. I mentioned this in an earlier chapter, and I note it again because it's an important guideline for facilitation. People ask "Why" questions because it's important to understand the reasons behind what a person thinks and believes However, you're more likely to learn these reasons when you ask, "How did you decide to do that?" rather than "Why did you do that?" and "Tell us your reasons" rather than "Why do believe that?" "Why" tends to call for a justification, a defense of an opinion. The other formulations just ask for a description of the steps or process that led up to the current view.

Listening — I've emphasized the importance of listing in several other chapters, and I don't want to repeat what I've said. I include listening again in this section to emphasize that two-thirds of the heart of facilitation (questioning, listening) is about taking-in and only one third (responding) about giving-out. So recall or review what's been said in earlier chapters about listening:

LISTENING GUIDELINES

- Listen First
- Listening inside your own frame of reference:
  - For entertainment
  - Attentive
  - Critical
- Listening inside the other's frame of reference
  - Empathic
- Listening to co-sculpt meanings
  - Dialogic

- AMPP—Ask, Mirror, Paraphrase, Prime the pump

- Talking stick

- Paraphrase before contributing

- Paraphrase plus

- Run with the metaphor

- Communicate confirmation

- *Erlebnis* vs. *Erfahrung*: proactive vs. receptive experiencing

Dialogic listening works best to help the group reach a point of closure. Remember that "closure" doesn't necessarily mean that the problem you're discussing is solved. In this case, it means that the group is satisfied with where the conversation has gone and is willing to continue it. Ideally, the group agrees on an outcome that's been tested with the help of the facilitator's best efforts. But the end of this particular conversation may also represent a pause until the group resumes the discussion, an agreement-to-disagree, or quiet time until you take up the task again. All these outcomes can represent success. This is because your goal is to build social capital, and it's produced by conversation, not necessarily consensus.

Nonverbal Parts of Listening. People make quick evaluations of your nonverbal listening cues. They can easily spot the person who's just waiting for her turn to speak and not really taking in what's said. They implicitly understand that insincere questions are accompanied by the wrong kind of eye behavior—too little eye contact or showing visual distraction. When you fill too much talk time, this says you're not really interested in their views, and if you let a group member interrupt others, you'll lose some of the respect that's necessary to good facilitation.

For example, a workshop participant came up to me after a long day of individual and group work to ask about a schedule conflict she had. I stopped what I was doing and turned to listen. I meant to be directly focused on her and to show her I was taking what she said seriously. She only got three or four sentences into her explanation before taking a big step back and shouting at me, "Back Off!!", What I thought were my serious face, steady stare and intense posture all looked to her like aggression.

Remember, if what you say (the words) is contradicted by how you say it (nonverbal cues), people virtually always believe the nonverbal. Strive for congruence among your saying, being, and doing.

Also set up the room to facilitate conversation. Use a variety of a circle or U-shape, not theater-style rows, a long table, or any configuration that puts some people behind others. It's possible to have as many as 60 people in a circle, so long as there's a microphone to pass. If you're working with break-out groups, have them in individual circles and arrange the groups so that when they report, everybody can see and hear everyone else.

Avoid my mistake with the workshop participant by making your head, face, and eyes welcoming and positive. Smile at the beginning of the conversation and as often as you can. Smile when you greet or call on a participant. Smile when you hear something familiar. Smile at the light and humorous moments, to help the group share them. Smile when the group makes progress. Don't look goofy, and do look positive.

Use eye behavior to confirm speakers and help control the conversation. Establish a pattern that a person is encouraged to talk when you're looking directly at him or her. Stick with a person who's making a lengthy contribution, at least up to the point where you think the group needs to move on. Then use eye behavior to shift attention to another participant. Use direct eye contact to communicate respect. Remember that in many cultures "too little eye contact" has universally negative meanings—"He's lying," "She's afraid," etc.

Pay mindful attention to timing, first by managing the starting and stopping times to meet what group members expect. Insert appropriate pauses, give people the time to respond to a question, and distribute time equitably among people with different opinions. Also model what it means to "give a short response," to elaborate a point, and to listen patiently to avoid interrupting.

Be sure that your tone of voice—volume, pitch variation, rate of talking—unfailingly communicate respect for the group's content and its process. Ask questions loudly enough to be heard by all *and* in a conversational tone, to keep the interaction comfortably informal. Paraphrase an inflammatory comment with objectivity, even though you may disagree with it. This will often be enough to encourage the speaker to re-state it in a less inflammatory way.

Responding — The deceptively simple act of responding to a participant's just stated contribution is the third key facilitation skill. You can prepare for responding, but in practice, as one writer puts it, "response is the art of the immediate."[151] This is one facilitation challenge that makes the process exciting. I've found that, while a participant is speaking, I need to be both listening to him or her and paying attention to as much as possible of what's going on. What happened in the last few seconds? How confident does the speaker sound? How did the she conclude what she was saying? How does her contribution link to the one preceding it? Am I convinced that this is a fruitful way for the discussion to be going? Where are we in the agenda? How much time is left? Does this contributor need to be challenged? Encouraged? Should she keep the floor? You have seconds to decide and to formulate a response.

Responses themselves can range among asking a further question, restating one or more of the speaker's points, asking for additional information, evaluating what was said, offering a personal opinion, asking someone else to do any of these, or encouraging a thoughtful pause. It can help to apply a decision tree: As a participant responds to your question, decide whether to (a) continue with another me-her exchange, (b) shift to participant-participant, or (c) pause. Then consider the options (tree branches) of each of these choices. If you take option #1 to continue the exchange with her, you could *support, explore, extend,* or *challenge* what she said (these are the four branches of this decision tree). *Support* could be simple praise—"Good point." Your response might also highlight the value-added of what's said— "Amy's comment gets at the question we had before about timing." Or, it might show the connection or contrast between her comment and something said earlier—"So this idea doesn't overlook the money issue"—or "Amy's comment rounds out the scheduling ideas that Tim and Geena mentioned."

An *exploring* response could clarify assumptions, check on the quality of Amy's analysis, or test the reasonableness of her conclusion. Or you could *extend* the breadth and depth of her comments by asking her to link what she's said with other people's contributions. A *challenge* could cite contrary evidence or ask someone else if they have a rival interpretation.

When you opt for basic choice #2, to shift to participant-partici-pant interaction, sometimes all you have to do is be quiet and let others carry the conversation. Alternatively, you can turn to someone else and re-ask the question you asked Amy, or raise a related question and invite the group to consider it. Or you could provide more structure by asking two other participants to offer their views of the primary issue Amy presented and encourage their continuing conversation. Responses like these facilitate the group's work in two ways: They guide the discussion's direction and they model what some kinds of effective contributions sound like, and how they work.

I was facilitating a conversation among a diverse group of young adults when the issue of white privilege was raised by a Caucasian man named Doug who said that race or ethnicity didn't ever enter his mind—that he was "colorblind." A woman of color named Denise criticized his naiveté, and I responded with an invitation for other group members to share their experiences with this issue. Renaye, another woman of color, echoed Denise's comments, and emphasized that in U.S. culture, whites are the only people who have the luxury of being "colorblind." There are even books and articles written about "colorblind racism[152]" Denise and Renaye began supporting each other's attacks of Doug. When I saw the tears in Doug's eyes, I encouraged Ron to describe what he heard going on among Doug, Denise, and Renaye. Ron's analysis provided enough perspective and time for Doug to compose himself, to the point where I invited his response. His humility and appreciation for the insight sparked a civil and fruitful conversation. At the time, I remember feeling grateful that the response options I chose worked out as well as they did.

Two more response moves round out the basic set of guiding skills: *Reframing* and *Facing Up*. *Reframing* helps group members change the way they're interpreting some events. For example, many group members don't want to give each other negative feedback, because they say they care about members and don't want to hurt them. The facilitator can help them overcome this reluctance by reframing what it means to "care." You can explain that genuine caring is sometimes expressed by effectively giving feedback about possible improvements and withholding this feedback can hurt members by denying them the informed choice to change. Then, ask for responses.

Reframing can also help by downplaying a group's efforts to demonize "the enemy," whether they are "the school board," "the mayor," "mom," or "Wall Street bankers." Politically-intense conversations often grow on—even depend on—stereotyped slurs and negative labels, and these views and labels never produce effective political understanding or action. When it's warranted, the facilitator can usefully reframe the group's beliefs about the "evil people" by putting their motives in context, introducing positive facts about them, or sharing a story of good things they've done.

Facing Up means requiring the group to reflect on something that's happened that the facilitator considers dysfunctional. You might say something like, *"Lynn, a minute ago you said 'I just want to stop the project.' Do you remember that?"* If Lynn remembers, you might continue, *"That particular statement focuses on your position without identifying your interest, which is inconsistent with one of the group's ground rules. What do you think?"* Keep this process from being accusatory by checking your interpretations with the person you're talking with and empowering them to respond.

Facing Up obviously needs to be used sparingly. But group conversations can, as I mentioned above, go off-track in dozens of ways, and one of the facilitator's main jobs is to keep the conversation moving helpfully.

Recording

This task is straightforward. I mention it mainly to remind you that it's part of the facilitator's job. Great things can happen in lively conversations among people who care about an issue, and they can be lost of they aren't recorded. If you ask a participant to take notes, you effectively remove him or her from the conversation *and* you rely on his or her note-taking skills. It's preferable to do the job yourself.

The easiest way is low-tech: Put 1-3 flip charts on easels in front of the room with 2-3 markers at each. Use the pages to write down key points, decisions, and action assignments. Use different colored pens to help organize the notes. Flip chart tablets with adhesive top edges permit you to post filled-out pages around the room. The summary at the end of the conversation is made easy by following the notes you've written. And, equally importantly, group members can *see* the progress and accomplishments they've made, so they're less likely to go away grumbling, "Another wasted meeting."

There are several electronic ways to record group products, including interactive whiteboards, digital tablets, laptops with appropriate software, and even apps for smart phones. These don't usually permit all participants to see what's been recorded, unless each has the right hardware and software in their hands. One advantage of digitally-captured notes, though, is that they can be emailed immediately to every participant. Meeting management software also includes some recording features that can help, if you can use them where and when you're meeting.

CONCLUSION

Personal political communication is difficult. Moments that matter don't occur very often in the political communication that you see and hear the most about. But they can happen between family members and friends who approach their conversations mindfully and reflectively. And they are happening all the time behind the scenes, in political conversations that are not covered on MSNBC, Fox News, or the Huffington Post. Impassioned, civil, humane, and productive conversations occur thanks to hundreds of grass-roots organizations and thousands of service-oriented individuals who are applying common-sense communication rules to public deliberation. Many of these conversations include moments that matter, events of contact where the people involved make their communication as personal as possible. And in the process they build social capital.

The social capital they construct enriches every one of them. It helps grease the wheels that allow communities to operate smoothly. The networks that make up social capital facilitate the sharing of important information, increase friendliness, and even help enhance group health and wealth.

Facilitation is a specific kind of communicating that can build social capital. Three key facilitation skills are planning, guiding, and recording. The specific suggestions for each include:

- **Planning**
  - Understand the background of the discussion and the outcomes the group wants.
  - Choose a suitable time and place
  - Consider proposing ground rules for the conversation
  - Collaborate to produce an effective agenda
  - If it's a first meeting, plan an icebreaker
  - Review details--supplies, timing, room setup, etc.

- **Guiding**
  - Questioning
    a. Focus on responses rather than answers
    b. Ask more open questions than closed ones
    c. Use different question types for different needs
    d. Avoid "Why?" questions
    e. Pay attention to question patterns
  - Listening
    a. Follow advice given in earlier chapters
    b. Encourage empathic and dialogic listening
    c. Pay special attention to nonverbal elements—smiling, tone of voice, avoiding inconsistencies.
  - Responding
    a. Use your responses to participant responses to guide discussion
    b. Use all available options—supporting, exploring,

extending, challenging, etc.

    c. When needed, reframe and help the group face up to dysfunctions

- **Record** key points, decisions, and commitments.
  - Flip charts are still effective
  - Electronic options can also work.

Realistic expectations, mindful and reflective planning, and facilitation can help produce the most healthy and productive political communicating. And, as the stories in this chapter demonstrate, each one of us is empowered to think globally and act locally to help build this social capital in our own communities by applying the approach outlined in Chapters 1 and 2 of this book to the political communicating we experience.

Chapter 9

MULTICULTURAL MOMENTS
THAT MATTER

CONSIDER THE FOLLOWING SNIPPETS from actual conversations:

> *Neighbor:*   *Hey, did you meet that new family down the street?*
>
> *Kelly:*   *[whose family does not attend church] No, I haven't. Did you?*
>
> *Neighbor:*   *Yes, but it was sort of uncomfortable. They're really nice but they're atheist--or I guess not atheist but humanist or Buddhist or something— same thing, though. Anyway, I just feel funny being around people who aren't Christian, you know?*
>
> *Kelly:*   *Umm. . . .I guess so. . .*

Neighbor: [who is female] Hey, how are things going? Are you ready to get started in your new office?

Ann: [whose new job is Director of a City department with 10 employees] Yes, I'm really excited about it!

Neighbor: Well, good luck! Hey, by the way, my friend's wife works over at City Hall. I don't know if you realize it, but the women over there are pretty sharp dressers. Very put together and stylish.

Ann: Uh. . . OK, thanks. I'll keep that in mind.

Client: [Enters Ann's office, with her name and title on the door.] Umm. . . Hi. Is this where I file a harassment complaint?

Ann: Yes, it is. Why don't you have a seat and tell me what happened?

Client: Well, actually, the person who sent me here suggested that I talk to the Director. Is he around?

Ann: I am the Director.

Client: Oh, Ok. I didn't know.

Golfer: [who is White] Hey Al, great article in the paper talking about the NAACP!

Al: [who is Black] Oh, No. . .Sorry, that wasn't me. That was a friend.

Golfer: Yeah. . . . I'm glad you guys were able to save your organization.

Al: Huh . . .yeah. . .thanks.

Golfer: *Yeah. . . the NAACP is an important thing for you guys to have.*

Al: *Uh. . . huh. . . yeah, well, see you later.*

Co-worker: *Hey Al, do you have a minute? I need to ask you a question.*

Al: *Sure. . . . What's up?*

Co-worker: *Well, we're starting a diversity committee and it doesn't have any diversity. So I was wondering if you could join.*

Al: *Well, I'm not sure I'm the best person for the committee. My schedule is really tight.*

Co-worker: *Oh, well, we can schedule the meetings around when you're available. We really need someone who is diverse.*

Al: *Oh . . . Um. . . .*

Monica, a middle-aged, professional African American woman is standing with her husband in the supermarket checkout line. An elderly White woman walks in with a partly-used bag of fruit to return. Without any request or "excuse me," she pushes her cart directly in front of Monica's. When her husband begins to protest, Monica assures him, "She's probably with that man in front of her." They shift to another line. The man in front of her finishes checking out and leaves alone.

Nothing huge is going on here, right? Kelly's neighbor lumps everybody who's not Christian together and expresses discomfort around people who are different from her in this way. Ann's female neighbor assumes that every woman, even if she's a senior professional, is thinking first about style. Ann's client assumes so strongly that the Director must be a man that he misses the title on her office door. The golfer views Al not as an individual but as just one of "you guys in the NAACP," and the co-worker appears to believe that any person who looks "different" can bring the needed "diversity" to his committee—and wants to. The elderly White woman is clearly rude, but is it fair to conclude that the main reason she crowded in front of Monica and her husband was because they were Black? Do you see any blatant discrimination here? Any overt racism? Anything that would violate the law or even make the news?

Only a few decades ago, violent Anti-Semitism, gay-bashing, and the lynching of African Americans often went unnoticed. Today, the Trayvon Martin case and hate crimes like the James Anderson and Marcelo Lucero killings still happen, and, although anti-Semitic incidents are at an all-time low, there were 31 violent assaults against Jewish people in 2013.[153] In addition, almost 60% of LGBT high school students in Iowa report having their property stolen or deliberately damaged at school, and over 33% report physical harassment.[154] Racial and cultural violence is still a serious problem in the U.S.

An equally serious problem is that almost all of those who identify with or appear to be in a cultural minority, whether it's racial, gender, religious, age, disability, or sexual identity, experience microaggressions literally every day. The snippets of conversation capture common, repeated experiences for many of today's cultural minorities, and show that many people who identify with cultural majorities deal with difference very poorly. Online, "The Microaggressions Project" has received more than 15,000 submissions, and in March, 2014, had had 2.5 million page views from 40 countries.[155] In the same month, the *New York Times* quoted a university of Michigan graduate call-ing microaggressions "racism 2.0. . . . You hire the Asian computer programmer because you think he's going to be a good programmer because he's Asian." A Harvard student noted, "It's almost scary the way that this disguised racism can affect you, hindering your success and the very psyche of going to class." [156] "Driving while Black" still gets people of color stopped in many U. S. cities and towns. Women are assumed to be subordinates, and they still earn less than men in similar positions. Loss Prevention Specialists at Wal-Mart and Target commonly follow many more Latinos and Blacks than they do Whites. In the 21st century, microaggressions are one of the biggest challenges to encouraging multicultural moments that matter.

MICROAGGRESIONS AND CULTURAL DIFFERENCES

Microaggressions are communication events that feature brief and commonplace verbal or nonverbal indignities, whether intentional or unintentional, that are readily interpretable as hostile and derogatory toward cultural minorities.[157] Microinsults are subtle snubs that demean a person's cultural heritage or identity, such as when an employee of color is asked, "How did you get your job?" The implication is that the person must have obtained the position through some affirmative action or quota program and not because of ability. "Microinsults can also occur nonverbally, as when a White teacher fails to acknowledge students of color in the classroom. . . ."[158]

Microinvalidations exclude, nullify, or negate the experiences of a minority person. As I noted in Chapter 8, when people of color hear, "I don't notice race at all; I'm color-blind" from a person in the majority culture, the effect is often to negate their experiences as racial/cultural persons. White is definitely a distinct racial color, and, while those of us who are White can go through days or weeks without noticing how our ethnicity affects our experience, most people of other colors in the

U.S. are reminded of their cultural status daily. Virtually no Latinos or Blacks have the privilege of living, parenting, working, loving, and playing in a color-blind world.

Similar invalidations happen when a gay or lesbian person is asked, "Have you ever had normal sex?" when restaurant patrons roll their eyes and slowly shake their heads at the appearance of a racially-mixed couple, and when a well-meaning able-bodied person grabs the handles of an occupied wheelchair without asking, and pushes it up a ramp.

Some individuals with strong cultural identities shrug off micro-aggressions. One reports in *The New York Times*, "I don't get bent out of shape if a white person asks me are you, like, Hindu or something? I just correct them."[159]

At the same time, continuous microaggressions can be difficult to deal with, partly because they often come from well-meaning people who think they are being sensitive and even inclusive. Their *intent* is sometimes good, while the *effects* of what they do are hurtful. For example, when a Latino professional has the occasion to mention her graduate degree, and her White conversation partner replies, "Good for you!" the intent is probably encouragement but the inference can be that most persons of color don't succeed in graduate school. As a White male with a doctorate, I have *never* been told "Good for you!" for earning my degree.

Microaggressions are also difficult to deal with because people inside the majority group can pass off the minority person's inter-pretations as due to "over-sensitivity," or "lack of self-esteem." Unfortunately, these dismissals are often evidence of defensiveness or insensitivity more than they reflect a genuine effort to understand.

Why? Because the charge of "over-sensitivity" ignores the well-documented and crushing cultural histories of racism, sexism, homophobia, religious intolerance, and disrespect of disabled persons that unfortunately frame the lives of many minority individuals in the U.S. These histories provide the context for their negative interpretations. When you and people like you have suffered overt and even violent indignities for decades or centuries, it's understandable that you'd interpret microaggressions negatively. One student of color summarized the experience in a focus group discussion when she noted, "Being Black at this college is like having a second, full-time job."

A third problem with microaggressions is that they can build up over time, to the point where the minority person's explosion is a scary surprise to the well-meaning majority person who does not regularly experience these subtle put-downs. After having her credibility, competence, effectiveness, and suitability for her city job being vaguely questioned over a period of days or weeks, Ann responds to a fairly innocent question, "What's the matter? Because I'm a woman, you don't think I could know anything about the engineering side of this project?! Give me a break, dammit!"

Many historians argue that the defining characteristic of the 21st century is globalization, and this means that each of us needs to deal on a daily basis with people who are different from ourselves. Multicultural competence means consistently dealing effectively with these differences. And this isn't easy. Cultural patterns are even more deeply ingrained than the political convictions I talked about in the previous chapter.

This is why one chapter can't fully cover the topic of multicultural moments that matter. Another limitation is that I'm writing from my own cultural position as an older White U.S. male heterosexual. I've learned from diverse experiences, though, and from my friends who are different from me, that there are at least four steps that will help limit your contributions to microaggressions and strengthen your multicultural competence.

Step #1: Be Aware of Your Own Cultural Identities

Try this before you read further: Jot down your five main cultural identities. I'd list male, White, husband, parent, and writer. These are all central to who I am. They're cultural identities because each comes with historically-based meanings, expectations, and communication patterns that I've learned and that I consciously and unconsciously help pass on to others with similar identities. I'm also a grandfather, Christian, skier, and boater, but, in most current situations, the first five have priority for me.

After you've listed your top five, think about—or explain to someone else—what each means and why these are your main ones. For me, part of what it means to be male is that, when I'm in a conversation with a woman, I try hard not to interrupt, and whenever I've had the chance to appoint a professional co-worker, I've tried to select a female, to balance our leadership. Part of what it means for me to be White is that, where I live (the U.S. Midwest), I have considerable unearned privilege. White people are "the norm" around here. Continue describing each of your five until you can't think of any other meanings.

The reason this exercise is important is that it's impossible to be multiculturally competent until you have a clear picture of where you are standing culturally whenever you interact with others. Your cultural identities emerge from the intersection of your biology, the stories that make up your history, and the cultures that you interact with. Biologically, being tall, short, heavy, thin, attractive, or plain-looking all affect your identity, along with your skin color, eye configuration, hair, and biological sex.

By "stories" I mean what you've been told about "your people" by your elders, and the accounts you give to others about your personal and professional failures and successes; your dietary, grooming, and dress preferences; and the observable indicators of your cultural identity including the ways you get around--bike, car, bus, etc., where you live, and how you spend leisure time. Your identities will also be affected by living in another country or in a large, diverse community vs. growing up in a town of 200 people who are mostly like you.

Five is an arbitrary number, and I ask you to identify five identities to underscore that we are all multicultural beings. This is why the chapter is called "Multicultural Moments that Matter." Each of us could identify ten, twelve, or maybe as many as twenty cultural identities that become relevant in various situations we encounter. But five are enough to make the point.

If this is an unusual or difficult exercise for you, don't skip over it. Instead, take the time to consult some of the many resources that can help you through it, for example:

- the American Field Service at http://www.afs.org/blog/icl/?p=3606;

- the Intercultural Communication Institute at http://www.intercultural.org/documents/competence_handouts.pdf;

- NASFA, the Association of International Educators, at http://www.nafsa.org/_/file/_/theory_connections_intercultural_competence.pdf;

- the National Association of School Psychologists at http://www.nasponline.org/resources/culturalcompetence/defining-cultcomp.aspx

Use these resources to enable yourself to identify and explain your own cultural identities.

Step #2: Learn About Other Cultures

If you've grown up in a small town in central Mississippi, you probably didn't learn much about Japanese or Peruvian culture. If you were raised in a well-defined Jewish neighborhood of New York, you may have limited knowledge of Islamic culture. But even if you have a lot of experience with diversity, it's important for everyone who's going to function well in the 21st century to learn as much as they can about other cultures.

Parents, schools, and other institutions can help. *When my small-town wife and her equally-sheltered husband moved to Chicago with our two pre-school daughters, I wasn't surprised that our daughter Lisa, who was 2, ran to her mommy the first time she encountered a black girl at the bottom of the playground slide. As parents, we took this as a cue to broaden the diversity of our children's experience, and today I'm pleased with my daughters' multicultural competence.*

Institutions can also either ignore or promote multicultural competence. The principal of one of our local high schools recently invited our city's Office of Human Rights to bring his faculty and staff three days of multicultural competence training. I was a member of the diverse team of six facilitators who guided them through exercises about what culture means, cultural identity, microaggressions, and multicultural conflict management. It was clear that, although some of the teachers and counselors knew as much about the topic as we did, many did not. In this case, their institution helped develop their multicultural competence.

You can also build your own knowledge and skill base in a variety of ways. For example, you might review online resources about the distinctions that two Dutch anthropologists made between "individualistic" and "collectivist" cultures.[160] This is a general distinction that has helped many people understand differences between, for example, U.S. and Western European (individualistic) and Northeast Asia (collectivist) cultures. A person identifying with an individualistic culture will prioritize his or her own ambitions over those that might be best for the groups he belongs to. It's logical that such a person would be more likely to get divorced, for example, since he values personal well-being higher than the well-being of the family.

In collectivist cultures, the family, workplace, or even the larger community is prioritized higher than the individual. It's more common for a person who is more collectivistic to sacrifice his or her own ambitions for the sake of the group. So, for example, she might prioritize working over going to school if her family needed the income.

This general distinction can be both oversimplified and overgeneralized into stereotypes. It also offers some useful insights into the behaviors of people who identify strongly with either cultural type.

There are also a multitude of specific cultural differences that it's useful to know about. For example:

- As you've probably learned if you've traveled internationally, cultures differ widely in their treatment of time. Exact time is not reinforced in some cultures, and in others, it is.

- Personal space expectations also vary. In areas of the Middle East and South America, people stand very close when talking.

- Asian female friends often hold hands, but in most Asian cultures, affectionately patting an adult's head is strictly taboo.

- A horizontal shake of the head means "No" in many cultures and "Yes" in Indian culture.

- Enduring silence is considered comfortable in Apache, Japanese, and some Scandinavian cultures and uncomfortable in most parts of the U. S.

- Many of the elderly in the U.S. believe that most people under 25 speak incomprehensibly fast.

- Many North American women are viewed as lacking in professional credibility because they tend to raise their vocal pitch at the end of each sentence—as if everything is a question.

- Men interrupt more than women, and the differences are greatest with intrusive interruptions.[161]

Part of multicultural competence involves being aware of some of these differences. Your culture's way of doing things is not the only way. Which leads to Step #3.

Step #3: Move from an Ethnocentric toward a Cosmopolitan perspective[162]

If you want to enhance your multicultural competence (your ability to deal well with differences), you need to move along the sliding scale from Ethnocentrism toward Cosmopolitanism.

When a person is being ethnocentric, she is "centered" in her own "ethnos" or culture. Ethnocentrism means treating your own culture as "normal" and evaluating values and practices different from yours as "abnormal." *Ethnocentric Whites who are used to serious discussions being carried out in moderated, relatively conversational tones often evaluate African Americans who have loud serious conversations as "rude," and "lower class." Similarly, ethnocentric Asians resist overt expressions of feelings and evaluate enthusiastic Whites as "immature," "overbearing" or "embarrassing."*

A cosmopolitan person sees differences as normal and as sites for exploration. For her, cultural humility is an important part of multicultural competence.[163] She understands that her "normal" way of doing things is not "normal" for everyone. She experiences her own culture in the context of other cultures and evaluates different values and practices within their own cultural context. *For example, if you are White, cosmopolitanism can mean not challenging your Latino conversation partner's macho assertions because you recognize them as part of his culture, or accepting your African American colleague's belief that almost no Whites are really sincere as a legitimate belief, given his experience.* It means responding to obvious cultural differences with humility, empathy and curiosity rather than defensiveness and rejection.

This can be relatively easy for Caucasian males in the U.S. when we're talking about eating with chopsticks or fingers rather than silverware—"Okay; that's just how they do it in that culture." It can be very difficult for the same people when the issue is radical Islam's hatred for the U.S. or the few women CEOs of Fortune 500 companies. A cosmopolitan perspective requires you to grant full humanity and respect to cultural Others you might fundamentally disagree with. You don't have to support or agree with them, *and* it is important to be able to see the world from their point of view.

Multicultural researcher Milton J. Bennett gives the example of a student who confided in him that she was concerned about being ethnocentric in her support of the 2003 U.S. invasion of Iraq. He told her that she might be, and that it would also be possible to make a cosmopolitan judgment about the invasion. *"The test,"* as he put it,

> *was whether she was according full humanity to the Iraqis that she felt should be forcibly dealt with. So I asked, "What is good about Sadam [sic] Hussein from some Iraqi perspectives?" She said, "Nothing is good—he is a monster and all Iraqis think so except some evil people who are profiting from his cruelty." Leaving aside the history of U.S. profits from Iraq, I replied that her concerns were justified—she was being ethnocentric. She was imposing her values on others by making the . . . assumption that her values were the most real. . . . A more [cosmopolitan] approach to the Iraq situation would have been to recognize that Sadam [sic] Hussein is a complex human being whose behavior, while "good" in some Arab contexts because it stands up to the Americans or expresses Arab pride, is nevertheless "bad" in the context of the current world consensus about the use of violence and intimidation in domestic governance. The question then is are you committed to stopping the bad behavior? . . .Are the consequences of interference better than the consequences of not interfering? The answer to all these questions could be "Yes."*[164]

Thankfully, cosmopolitan understanding is usually easier than this. But it does require you to bracket your own values, to treat them as only one legitimate way to understand and evaluate a situation.

I hope you get the sense from what I've said that these first three steps toward multicultural competence require you to become aware of, and comfortable in your own cultural skin. This is vital if you want to make your communication with people who are different from you as personal as possible. It's just a fact that everybody has multiple cultural identities---this is part of the way we're put together as humans. Mine are different from yours. Yours are different from your best friend's, your spouse's, and probably even from your parents' cultural identities.

Not only this, but every person's most important cultural identities vary from situation to situation. *Sometimes an African American male's main cultural identity is that he's Muslim, heterosexual, or disabled. Sometimes a drag queen's main cultural identity is that she's a business owner.* Multiculturally-competent people recognize this about themselves and everybody else, have the resources to respond with humility, empathy, and curiosity, and are ready to celebrate the diversity that these facts generate.

Step #4: How to Invite Multicultural Moments that Matter

I use the word, "invite" as a reminder that, since communication is always collaborative, you can't completely control the quality of contact that you have with someone who is different from you, *and* you *can* increase the probability of person-to-person contact. *When your conversation partner has a strong cultural identity, for example, as a Native American, and is in a group of like-minded and culturally-similar allies, it's less likely that he will be responsive to your best efforts to bridge whatever gaps may exist. It's more important for him to maintain the respect of his friends. When a young White male has repeatedly experienced skepticism about his understanding from mid-dle-aged African American males like you, it's likely that he will also reject your best efforts to connect. All you can do is all you can do.*

Because communication is also continuous, though, don't give up after only the first few tries. Especially if the topic and the relationship are important, keep doing as much as you can do. Your basic goal, as with every other situation, needs to be to take in and give out relevant aspects of what make you and the other *persons*—uniqueness, choices, ESP, and mindful reflectiveness. This ought to be your general guide. Remember, too, that what's at stake is the quality of your life and the other person's. Here are some specific suggestions:

Expect Different Interpretations — Whenever you notice that the cultural differences between you and your conversation partner are significant, expect that she's not interpreting what's happening the way you are. This is part of the common sense that I talked about in the Preface. In most of the U.S., gay men know that straight men don't interpret eye contact, dress, grooming, touch, or gestures the same way most gay men do. Virtually every differently-abled person knows that most people without disabilities have no clue how important things like curb cuts, door widths, and bright lighting can be. If you can enter into obviously multicultural situations expecting different interpretations, you're much less likely, when they surface, to respond defensively or impatiently. When you interpret the situation as "normal," you can have your best efforts ready to deal with whatever arises.

Think in Advance About How You Might Be Interpreted — *If you're a female manager talking with a group of mostly males about the importance of emotional intelligence, you can predict the kind of resistance you're likely to meet. If you're a high school teacher talking with a culturally-diverse group of students about the school's dress code, you can do the same.* Often, the problem is the difference between *intent* and *effect* or culturally-based misinterpretations of the intent. You can counter this by clarifying, in inclusive terms, the intent of the opinion you're expressing or the policy you're describing.

In the first case, you might cite some of the research evidence of the importance of emotional intelligence to customer relations and sales success to emphasize that it's much more than "touchy-feely psychobabble." In the second case, you might remind the students of the gang activity that led to the dress code or the ways extreme dress has disrupted school activities in the past. The point is to do your communication homework in advance.

Validate, Appreciate, and Be Curious About Other Interpretations — *"That's bullshit! This is just another way management's pushing us out of our comfort zone!" "Why are the rules at this school always so White?"* When, despite your best efforts, a cultural misinterpretation arises, your goal should be to demonstrate the values I noted earlier: humility about your own cultural commitments, empathy for others, and curiosity about the differences. In fact, if you take away only one idea from this chapter, I hope it will be the importance of these three attitudes.

The best way to demonstrate humility is by listening. Rather than defending your view, encourage the person who disagrees to say more about his concerns. Pay attention to his reasons, and, if you're talking with more than one person, before you respond, ask if there are others who share his views or have different concerns. The point is to get the resistance on the table, where something can be done about it. This kind of listening also demonstrates your mindful reflectiveness, and by example, it encourages the others to do the same. Hopefully, you were also mindful and reflective before you opened your mouth.

Humility also means recognizing that you, or the policy you're describing, could be mistaken. Remember that, whether you're at work, in a family situation, or among friends, one of your goals should not be just "to win," but to keep the relationship working and, where possible, enhance it. If this is not part of your goal, reconsider saying anything in the first place

When it is part of your goal, you'll need to work with the other interpretations to determine how much agreement or consensus you can reach. This is when you apply empathy and curiosity. Use the specific suggestions about conflict management offered in Chapter 6. Especially remember Relationship Reminders and the question, "What do you want to have happen?" Also consider the dialogue commitments in Chapter 8, Stay Engaged, Speak Your Truth, Experience Discomfort, and Expect and Accept Non-Closure. Do all you can to figure out where the other person is coming from, rather than defending your own position. And express genuine curiosity about the differences.

Assume Positive Intent — Indra Nooyi, Chairman and CEO of Pepsico, comments,

> *In business, sometimes in the heat of the moment, people say things. You can either. . .assume they are trying to put you down, or you can say, "Wait a minute. Let me really get behind what they are saying to understand whether they're reacting because they're hurt, upset, confused, or they don't understand what it is I've asked them to do." If you react from a negative perspective—because you didn't like they way they reacted—then it just becomes two negatives fighting each other. But when you assume positive intent, I think often what happens is the other person says, "Hey, wait a minute, maybe I'm wrong in reacting the way I do because this person is really making an effort."*[165]

Assuming positive intent can be very difficult. Despite the facts that Indra Nooyi is female and a person of color, she has considerable power, and this makes it easier for her to assume positive intent. She can shrug off microaggressions or just "take the hit" and move on.

The principle is too effective, though, to limit its use only to powerful people. Whenever you recognize that you're clearly in a multicultural situation, one where differences make a real difference, the other person—or people—involved probably realize this, too. Sometimes their goal is to defend, distort, or destroy and not to move toward understanding. But much of the time, the other people are doing their best, just as you are, even if they're doing it in what seem to you to be strange or hurtful ways.[166] It can genuinely help if you are able to assume that their intent is positive.

This means that when a Black male hears a younger White woman expressing some version of the "Black men are scary and dangerous" theme, both can profit from assuming the other person's intent is positive. Because the U.S. has a history of so many Black men being lynched because of white women's fears, it is important for both parties not to sweep this discomfort under the rug. He might gently open the door by asking her what she's afraid of. If she didn't intend to express fear, she should respond to his question with as little defensiveness as possible and clarify what led to her comment. The man might also enlighten her by offering a candid expression of how he feels when he hears this theme. For example, *"I hear you. And as a Black man, when I hear this kind of fear from a white woman, I'm hurt and afraid. I don't want to die because of white violence. And I don't want to be silenced. Can we talk more about what you just said?"* The point of this response is to address the cultural issue in a way that's authentic and that keeps the conversation going. The Black man may discover that her intent is not positive. And her willingness to reflect on and reconsider what she said combined with his statements that display candor (*"I'm hurt and afraid."*) along with empathy and curiosity (*"Can we talk more?"*) may help both parties grow.

Assuming positive intent also means that, when a woman hears a man patronizing her, she needs to try to assume that he's doing his best. And, when a straight woman who considers herself an LGBT ally is told by a lesbian friend that she "couldn't possibly understand this situation," she needs to try to assume that she's hearing pain and fear that might be diminished if the conversation continues.

Every time you try to assume positive intent, you may feel naïve, foolish, or at risk of being bulldozed. Remember the importance of humility, empathy, and curiosity, and do it anyway. You'll be surprised at how often it helps.[167]

Apply the Platinum Rule — The Golden Rule—"Do unto others as you would have them do unto you"—is a valued ethical standard in many cultures. It's good in that it helps you think seriously about the impact of your choices on others. And it's limited, because when taken literally, it promotes ethnocentrism.

If I do unto you strictly what I would want you to do unto me, my thinking and behaving remain within my own cultural framework. *I know what "respect" means to me, for example, and part of it is direct eye contact—looking me in the eyes. But in your culture, direct eye contact may be a sign of challenge or hostility. If I treat you the way I want to be treated, in this case it's likely to make things worse.*

So effective multicultural communicating requires you to "Do unto others as *they* would have you do unto them." This is the Platinum Rule. It's an even higher ethical standard than the Golden Rule. In order the practice the Platinum Rule, you need to be sensitive to, learn about, or ask about what's appropriate in the *other* person's culture, and then follow their lead.

If you carefully followed Step #2 in this chapter, you might be thorough—or lucky—enough to know what you need to know. But it's more likely that you'll need to ask the other person. *"We're talking about a sensitive topic here, one that you and I understand differently. How can we discuss it in ways that don't step on each other's cultural toes?"* In almost every case, the caring that you communicate by asking will go a long way toward bridging the differences between you.

It's Never a Sure Thing — You might manage to be humble, empathic, and curious, and you might apply all five of these suggestions, and the outcome of this conversation may still disappoint some people. You might be disappointed the most! Or, if you are in a position of power in the system, you may still have to enforce the problematic policy or carry out the culturally offensive practices. In other words' what's here will not fix every problem. Multicultural moments that matter are sometimes very difficult to develop. If you've made your part of the communication as personal as possible, though, the people involved should not feel as disrespected or depersonalized as they would if you didn't.

When This Chapter Isn't Enough — If you recognize the challenge and are concerned enough to pursue this topic beyond what's here, Good going!

As you investigate other resources, be aware of the differences among those who have dedicated their lives to improving multicultural communication. You'll find differing opinions about the best ways to learn more and do better.

For example, Glenn E. Singleton and his colleagues at the Pacific Educational Group (PEG) believe that multicultural relationships in the U.S. generally, and specifically the educational achievement gap that disadvantages students of color will not be improved unless and until people have what they call "courageous conversations about race."[168]*Although they acknowledge that other kinds of discrimination are damaging, this group insists that focusing on race, and especially on institutional racism, will not only improve the U.S. culture's most pressing problem but also reduce the negative impact of other "isms." Importantly, the PEG can document successes they've had with school systems across the country.*

Milton Bennett and Michael Hammer take a significantly different approach. Bennett designed and tested the "Developmental Model of

Intercultural Sensitivity" (DMIS) to explain the movement from ethnocentrism to what I called cosmopolitanism (he calls it "ethnorelativism"). Hammer produced and validated the Intercultural Development Inventory (IDI), a psychological test that identifies where people are on the DMIS scale and offers graduated educational programming to help them move along the continuum. The approach taken by these researchers and their colleagues emphasizes incremental group learning rather than direct "conversations about race" and deemphasizes the effects of non-inclusive institutional culture. Bennett and Hammer also have research data to demonstrate that their approach works.

A third approach is urged by those I quoted at the beginning of this chapter who focus on microaggressions, and still another set of options is forcefully expressed by those who criticize microaggression research and teaching.

In other words, dedicated, well-informed, and research-based people have widely divergent opinions about how to best build multicultural competence. If you are serious about achieving more self-development than this chapter provides, it's important to know that there are many different ways to work these problems. You can do your own research in order to decide which approach works best for you.

CONCLUSION

In the 21st century U.S., not all minority groups or individuals experience discrimination in the same way. For example, mixed race individuals can often choose which of their cultural identities to foreground. Neighborhoods of some large cities are very LGBT-friendly, while others are overtly hostile to Whites or Latinos. But generally, discrimination of any kind has become unpopular enough, illegal enough, and shameful enough to push many of its primary manifestations into the category of microaggressions. Racism, sexism, homophobia, ageism, and other forms of discrimination have not gone away, and many of them have gone under the table. The primary difficulties that many persons in a cultural minority have to confront today are continuous thoughtless stereotypes, subtle put-downs, and nonverbal insults or invalidations.

On the one hand, microaggressions can be easier to reduce, because they're smaller. On the other hand, they're also often unconscious and well-intentioned, and this makes them much more difficult to eliminate. I hope your first goal is to become aware of them and to search your heart and mind about whether they are part of your communication life.

Four additional steps can help you invite multicultural moments that matter.

- **#1 Be aware of your own cultural identities**. Each of us has multiple cultural identities, and different ones become important in different situations. Reflect on yours, and understand what each means to you.

- **#2 Learn about other cultures**. When you become aware of specific cultural practices that are different from yours, you also learn, by contrast, more about your own culture. You learn that there's not just one "right" way to do things, and that even "strange" practices can make perfect sense to people in other cultures.

- **#3 Move from an ethnocentric toward a cosmopolitan perspective**. Learn to evaluate cultural practices in their own context, not just from the perspective of your own culture. The key is to treat cultural differences with humility, empathy, and curiosity. Humility means acknowledging that other cultures can be as "right," "good," and even as "appropriate" as your own. Empathy means understanding another's cultural world from their point of view, not just your own. Curiosity means responding to difference with questions rather than criticism. When you notice something different that makes a difference, learn more about it before you put it aside.

- **#4 Invite multicultural moments that matter**. Specifically,
- Expect different interpretations.
- Think in advance about *how* you might be interpreted.
- Validate, appreciate, and be curious, about other interpretations.
- Assume positive intent.
- Apply the Platinum Rule.

One of my main reasons for revising *U&ME* was to add this chapter. I didn't include multicultural situations as one of the life arenas in the original edition partly because I don't want to write or talk as if I truly understand the lives of people who routinely experience discrimination.

My fear was overcome by my realization that this is too important a topic to ignore or omit. So I gathered together what I've learned over the years in personal and professional friendships with scores of marginalized people who've taught me a great deal. I've also asked several people who belong to marginalized groups to review and edit what I've written. Their input has been crucially important, and I still take full responsibility for what's here. I hope that these ideas and suggestions can help you, at least in some small ways, make your multicultural contacts as personal as possible.

Chapter 10

SPIRITUAL/RELIGIOUS MEETINGS AND MIS-MEETINGS

ON THE THIRD SUNDAY IN MARCH, Liz, a twenty-something Episcopal Service Corps intern from Knoxville preached for her host congregation in Chicago. In her sermon, Liz reported that, when she began the internship, she expected that its most important part would be gaining job skills and having real-life work experience. "But the most important aspect that I will walk away with," she said, "will be the amazing communities that I've experienced." She elaborated,

> *My community at home with my 4 housemates, is a haven, and a place of renewal for me. We work to be fully present with each other and support one another day in and day out. . . . Monday through Friday, we gather to eat, we discuss our days, talk about our lives, we tell jokes, we laugh, and we pray together. . . . . there are some days, when knowing I'll be able to complain at dinner, has gotten me through the day.*

Liz told the story of three months of making more and more commitments, getting further and further behind, feeling more and more stressed, and then being asked by her supervisor, Bonnie, to run through this sermon.

I stood at this lectern and tried to gather my thoughts and begin, I couldn't. I fumbled and I mumbled and I blushed and I knew that what I was saying didn't make any sense. So Bonnie had me sit down and was encouraging and firm in that way that only Bonnie can be and I was faced with the craziness that has been my life for the past three months, and it was a moment when grace pierced through my life.

So we talked and I cried, and then I called my mom and I cried, and then my mentor in Knoxville and I cried, and Lora, my program director and I didn't cry this time, and then I went home and talked to my housemates, where I almost cried when I told them what had happened and they physically held me and they emotionally supported me. . . .

And later that night, as I read through all of my materials again and processed what I was feeling, I began to hear what God was trying to say to me, what God is trying to say to us. I can't do all of this on my own—we can't do all of this on our own; we need community. . . .

I encourage you, whether you feel like you're running and running and running or if you feel calm and collected—to connect with your family, to connect with your community. Give yourself permission, give yourself time to take a break from all of the running and running in your life. . . . I am extending a special invitation to all of you to come and be a part of our Tuesday Night Community. . . . I'll be at the double glass doors, by Bonnie and Andrew's office, behind the green card table, with Katy and baby Beth, waiting to welcome you when you come.[169]

The central event of Liz' story is "a moment when grace pierced through" her life, a moment that mattered between Liz and Bonnie. As I heard her talk, I experienced some similar moments with her. Liz made available to me in her talk some of her uniqueness, emotions, spirit, choices, and reflections, and I met her with my own reflections and emotions about moments of grace in my life. I felt invited by Liz into her community and specifically welcomed to the green card table by the double glass doors on Tuesday night.

Millions have had similar experiences of contact in a variety of spiritual and religious gatherings. Many of these are not part of any organized religion. To cite just one example, the web contains scores of testimonials from women and men who have attended Law of Attraction meetups in the U.S., Europe, Australia, and South America. These workshops and support sessions are organized around the spiritual belief that by focusing on positive or negative thinking, one can bring about positive or negative results. Participants listen to inspirational speakers and engage in two-person and small group activities designed to use affirmations and other skills to translate positive thinking into better relationships, more professional success, and increased happiness. Many say that these meetups significantly enhance their lives. As two participants put it,

> *Only last week someone told me how she wished she had my confidence- and how I must have been 'the confident one' at school. It was very funny to hear but also very validating about what I have learnt from you. . . .*

> *Since coming to my first workshop a year ago and then attending weekly groups, my whole way of living and thinking has changed. . . . I feel appreciative, powerful and loved- like anything is possible.*[170]

MEETING AND MIS-MEETING

Examples like these demonstrate why many spiritual and religious gatherings can be ideal settings for moments that matter. In many ways, everything lines up. People show up to such gatherings hoping for something special. Whether the event is New Age, Muslim, Jewish, Baha'i, Christian, Buddhist, Unitarian Universalist, twelve-step, or spiritually-oriented in other ways, people attend in order to enter a space that's different from the rest of their lives. Some come with specific hopes and needs, most want to be around fellow-believers, and for many, a highlight of such gatherings is direct, immediate, personal connection—with speakers, others present, and often with the Divine. Liz's sermon describes one young Christian person's experiences with this kind of contact.

Each week, millions of people have similar experiences at Jewish and Muslim prayer services, LOA meetups, drum circles, scripture studies, twelve-step meetings, religious social action activities, Native American spirituality groups, and other spiritual or religious events.

And there are volumes of reasons why people reject organized religion. Many disagree with the social and political positions that are taken by specific institutions. *In 2012, the Vatican ordered the Roman Catholic Leadership Conference on Women Religious (LCWR), which represents 80% of the nuns and sisters in the U.S., to do more to promote Church views on abortion and birth control. One nun and 20-year LCWR member commented to a friend of mine that she sees this review as further evidence that the church and its sacraments are "dominated by a hierarchy of old men." This sister finds it more "life giving" to walk along a scenic creek than to attend Catholic Mass.*[171]

Other people complain about the hypocrisy of "holy" people, the anti-science orientation of some churches, rejection of questioners or doubters, and too many requests for money. For 42% in one survey, services are just "too boring or unfulfilling."[172]

Recent polls say that 80% of the people reading these words believe in some higher power, and almost 25% of the U.S. population reports that belief in God is the most important certainty in their lives. Yet, only about 40% attend religious services regularly, and this number hovers around 20% in Europe.[173] Another 40% of North Americans belong to a "spiritual but not religious" group[174] Most of us are believers, yet, for a variety of reasons, we stay away in droves from many organized spiritual and religious events.

One author observes that many of those who are alienated from organized religion turn to spiritual practices because, if they don't experience contact with the Divine, "they yearn for it."[175] This yearning suggests that humans may well have a deep-seated need for this contact. Many un-churched and disconnected people bump up against this need when they personally encounter a terminal illness, death of a loved one, or other traumatic event. As the saying goes, there are few atheists in foxholes.

So, the potential for spiritual and religious meeting is great, and the practical reality is that these gatherings are filled with mis-meetings. Clearly, the challenge of more completely realizing the potential of spiritual and religious connection is beyond what any single chapter can accomplish. Yet, the approach to communication that's developed here can enrich what happens in spiritual and religious gatherings enough to at least improve the experiences of some of those who don't find these gatherings compelling or fulfilling. There are several ways to enhance moments that matter in spiritual and religious events.

SPIRITUAL AND RELIGIOUS *TALK*

One way is to pay more attention to everything that is spoken and heard in a spiritual/religious gathering, including chanting, singing, reading, praying, and speaking in order to help more contact happen in these events. For convenience, let's call this spiritual and religious *talk*. In most traditions, spoken and heard elements are intimately entwined with space, design, color, symbols, apparel, rhythm, and melody. Individual and group silence is also important, but Jewish and Muslim prayer services, Roman Catholic and Protestant church services, twelve-step meetings, New Age meetups, Baha'i services, and even Quaker meetings include both spoken language and sung lyrics. In their talk, participants and their leaders re-affirm beliefs, witness to gifts or insights, build community, offer praise, share sacred texts, pray together, interpret readings, develop moral admonitions, and participate in sacraments.

Rabbi Jonathan Sacks explains why Judaism, Christianity, and Islam all give great importance to live speaking and listening.

> *What made the three Abrahamic monotheisms different is not that they believed that God reveals himself but rather that he does so in words. They believe that language is holy. . . . Language is the unique possession of [hu]mankind. What makes Judaism, Christianity, and Islam different from other faiths is that they conceive of God as personal, and the mark of the personal is that God speaks. Language. . .redeems our solitude, affirming that in the vast echoing universe we are not alone.*[176]

A Muslim scholar agrees about the importance of what is uttered and heard when she notes, *"The Koran has long had an oral as well as written dimension, its acoustic substance existent in people's sonic memories as much as, perhaps more than, in visual text."*[177]

This point that the God of Islam, Judaism, and Christianity uniquely *speaks* and *listens* explains why chanting, reading aloud, preaching, and singing are so important in these forms of worship. This emphasis on speaking-and-hearing is reflected in such traditions as the importance of reading scripture aloud and singing together, and the Old Testament rule that you don't speak God's name. The Bible and Qur'an describe the earliest meetings between God and humans as speaking-and-hearing events—God spoke to Noah in Genesis (Genesis 7) and Allah spoke to Moses with direct speech (Surat An-Nisa 4:164). This emphasis on speaking and hearing continues in the New Testament, for example, when Mary goes to Jesus' tomb to mourn and doesn't know the man she meets there until He *speaks her name* and she replies, "*Rabboni (teacher)*" (John 20:16). The stories that are so central to the scriptures of these faiths were originally spoken and heard, and many parts of worship preserve this tradition.

Spoken and heard words can take on special power when combined with rhythm and melody. Some of the simplest combinations are the chants that are part of Hindu, Islamic, Jewish, Byzantine, and some Western Christian traditions. Rhythmic chanting calls people to prayer, encourages a meditative state, focuses attention on an icon or symbol, or opens contact with the Divine. As one writer explains, "*Chanting of mantras is not merely a continuous process of repeating words, it is an effective tool to awaken our senses and connect with celestial powers.*"[178]

MINIMIZING MIS-MEETINGS

Mis-meetings happen when this kind of power is un-realized, when people could have met personally and didn't, when an opportunity for contact is missed, despite the fact that the situation encourages people to make their communication as personal as possible. You can help minimize mis-meetings in spiritual and religious gatherings by paying attention to reading, singing, praying, and preaching,

Reading Sacred Texts

Every religion is anchored in sacred texts, which record various forms of Divine speaking and comments about it. Scripture reading is the part of the gathering where this speaking can be re-created so that a version of the original speaking-hearing event might be re-experienced. As one researcher explains, the serious reader of a sacred text

> *considers him or herself as the audience of the Holy Word,*
> *and what was rationally a book written centuries before*
> *now becomes a personalized letter. . . What is praised as the*
> *Eternal Book has a transcendent Being as its author. That*
> *book is read as if it were written at that very instant. . . .*
> *Everything is pertinent, every word and comma (even a pause*
> *of silence) has a meaning. . . .*[179]

Mis-meetings sometimes happen because of the ways sacred texts are shared. Many contemporary places of worship are proud to have technology that permits worshippers to read the text on a large screen. Those that don't, provide a written copy for each individual. This practice has obvious advantages and, as I mentioned in Chapter 1, it also dilutes the spoken-and-heard elements of sharing sacred texts. Reading from a printed page or screen is an individual event, while listening to a reader can be a communal experience. Reading print is a visual experience, while listening, when reading is done well, can draw you into the text in personal and even intimate ways. When texts are read poorly, this can't happen.

Many challenges affect what's experienced. Some Jewish readers struggle with Hebrew. Some Christian readers are bamboozled by an unfamiliar translation. When readers in any faith tradition race, mumble, or drone their way through a text, the potential for spoken-and-heard contact is almost completely lost, and mis-meeting happens.

One way to enhance the frequency of moments that matter in the spiritual or religious gatherings you attend is to give more care to the reading of sacred texts. Oral reading creates a new opportunity for speaker and listeners to co-create again the profound meaning of the text. The meaning helps define a part of the common culture that the worshipping group shares, which is a big reason why reading is important and the role of reader is significant.

The reader needs to remember that he or she has an important identity in the service. The sacred text could have been read silently, but the liturgy or order of worship requires that it be *spoken*. The difference can be important. When someone reads a sacred text aloud, he or she takes on the role of one who re-tells an ancient story, proclaims a truth, serves as an intermediary of holy words. In order to live into this identity, the reader should always pre-read the text, not only to work out difficult pronunciations and sentence structures, but also to grasp its overall meaning. The goal of the reading should be figuratively to guide your listeners to experience what's said with you, to understand it fully, and to respond appropriately.

Readers should also attend to their choices—where to pause, where to speak more slowly and more rapidly, where to add vocal intonation and emphasis. The point is not to impersonate the prophet, psalmist, or Divine but to bring the text alive for your listeners in order to make this communication as personal as possible.

Sacred text reading should also never be rushed. The point is not to be oratorical or pompous, but it is almost impossible to read a sacred text aloud too slowly. One easy way to slow yourself down is to imagine yourself in the centuries-old line of people who've read these words aloud before you. It's just about impossible to hold this image of yourself and rush through what you're reading.

It's easy to tell when someone is reading the verses or lines rather than reading he text's meaning. A person reading lines will often drop their voice's volume and pitch at the end of every line, verse, or sentence, which creates a sing-song pattern, rather than changing volume and pitch to reinforce central ideas. Over-formal pronunciation of minor words like "the" and "a" can distance listeners. The contact-potential of the reading is also diminished when a reader pauses only at the end of lines or verses, and makes all pauses equal, or when she vocally emphasizes words that are not central to the meaning of the reading, for example, "Do *unto* others as you would have them *do* unto you." These sound patterns force the listeners' attention on the fact that lines or verses are being read, rather than inviting them to join the event of speaking and hearing important ideas. On the other hand, when a reading transparently channels the text's meaning, with pauses at important thought-junctures, pitch changes that emphasize important ideas, and a conversational tone, listeners can connect much more closely with what's being read.

Moments that matter can also be encouraged by readings in spiritually-focused gatherings outside church. For example, the prescribed opening and closing that are read at each twelve-step meeting function in some ways like the sacred texts of a religious liturgy. Participants hear principles repeated every meeting, which, like a familiar call to prayer or creed, provide both direction and reassuring familiarity in the community. At the start of every Al-Anon meeting, for example, the family member struggling with alcoholism hears

> *The family situation is bound to improve as we apply the Al-Anon ideas. Without such spiritual help, living with an alcoholic is too much for most of us. Our thinking becomes distorted by trying to force solutions and we become irritable and unreasonable without knowing it.*

And at the end, each hears

> *We aren't perfect. The welcome we give you may not show the warmth we have in our hearts for you. . . . Talk to each other, reason things out with someone else, but let there be no gossip or criticism of one another. Instead, let the understanding, love, and peace of the program grow in you one day at a time.*[180]

Heard often enough, these reassurances begin to take hold. Participants connect in both their struggling and their hope.

Sacred text reading-and-listening obviously cannot create the same meeting-potential as an intimate conversation. And it definitely *can* promote richer contact than what frequently occurs. The mythic status of sacred texts, frequent inclusion of metaphors and stories, and nonverbal elements of the reading event (the reader stands, often walks solemnly to a special reading location, sometimes ceremonially opens and closes a book or unrolls a scroll, etc.) all appeal to personal understanding. In these ways, the reading event opens the door for worshippers to connect with others present and with the Divine. This is the potential for meeting that can be realized when reading is done well.

Singing

Individual soloists or members of a choir often experience their involvement as a ministry, a way of sharing their faith with others. Choirs can also function as prayer and meditation groups, as members collaborate creatively to engage listeners with contemporary praise melodies, majestic hymnody, throbbing gospel rhythms, or a cappella harmonies.

The people who hear well-performed songs can also be uplifted, edified, and even transformed by effective performances. Some worshippers close their eyes, move to the rhythms, and raise their hands in praise as they are lifted up by well-sung music.

Group singing can be unusually powerful. The most direct contribution to moments that matter can happen when those who make up the gathering join in song. *Researchers found that when people engage in synchronous activity, they create a bond that facilitates cooperation, and when group singing was compared with marching and dancing, the singers had the strongest communal experience.*

They reported that they felt as if they had more in common with the
others, and they trusted them more.[181]

The impact of group singing comes from both the verbal parts
(lyrics) and the nonverbal ones (melody & rhythm). For example,
Zemiros are Jewish hymns, usually sung in Hebrew or Aramaic, and
sometimes in Yiddish or Ladino. The community often experiences a
powerful connection by singing together in one of their faith's original
languages or the language of their forebears. Zemiros are also sung
around the family table during Shabbos and Jewish holidays, and here
the connection comes as much from synchronized vocalizing with
loved ones as it does from the language of the lyrics. Pizmonim are
another set of traditional Jewish songs for praise or teaching that help
create community at bar mitzvahs, weddings, and other ceremonies.
Sung music carries important parts of Jewish culture.

One Muslim use of song that strongly moves many of its adher-
ents—and those of other faiths—is the call to prayer. *The Azan is the*
first call to prayer, and consists of repeated, hauntingly melodic utter-
ances that translate, "Allah is most great" (chanted four times), "I
bear witness that there is none worthy of being worshipped except
Allah" (twice), "I bear witness that Muhammad is the Apostle of
Allah" (twice), "Come to prayer" (twice) "Come to success" (twice),
and so on. The Azan is sung in a sweet, melodious voice with plain-
tively elongated vowels, elaborated moves up and down the scale,
and passionate conviction. Those inside and outside the faith call it
"so beautiful" and "so moving." One comments on the personal-
understanding experience of hearing it well-sung: "It brings a sense
of peace, just like a Buddhist chant or a Christian choir would."[182]

Lyrics also bring poetry to worship. The verses of many sacred
songs are moving poems of praise, celebration, reassurance, encouragement, or challenge. Consider, for example, the simple contemporary Christian praise hymn,

By His grace I have been touched
By His word I have been healed
By His hand I've been delivered
By His spirit I've been sealed

Or the reassuringly familiar,

Through many dangers, toils, and snares, I have already come
'Tis grace that brought me safe thus far, and grace will lead
me home.

When the melodies of these hymns are familiar enough to keep powerful lyrics running through the worshipper's head, the communal effects of the service can be felt well after it's over.

In most spiritual and religious gatherings, the point of singing together is connection, and the contact experience happens via tone and rhythm, which is why it's difficult to describe or explain in words. Because group singing can create this kind of connection, even those who believe they "can't carry a tune in a bucket" can be encouraged to join in. Most people at these gatherings understand that some worshippers can sing better than others, and the potential benefits of participation in unison singing far outweigh the risks or costs. Those who opt out of the group singing at a spiritual or religious gathering are limiting what they get out of the experience.

Praying

Group or unison prayer is another common element of most spiritual and religious gatherings. Some prayers are sung, of course, and some song lyrics are prayers, so praying and singing overlap. But, for example, one of the powerful parts of a twelve-step meeting happens when the group says out loud together, *"God, grant me the serenity to accept the things I cannot change, the courage to change the things I can, and the wisdom to know the difference."*

"You are not alone" is one of the main messages of twelve-step programs and as the whole room speaks these words together, strong support resonates through almost every person.

This kind of personal connection can happen whenever a group performs a liturgy or ritual together. One downside risk of liturgy is that standardized actions and utterances can be repeated so mindlessly that they lose their meaning. Most of us have witnessed a part of a liturgy that was said so fast and in such a sing-song or monotone that it's empty of impact.

The upside potential of unison praying in a liturgy is that those reciting the words can experience a connection with both everybody else saying the same things and with the rich history of their tradition. So if a unison prayer is new to you, be patient. It takes time to settle into a liturgical practice to the point where you get everything it has to give. But if you want to experience the connection and community that a spiritual or religious gathering offers you, it can help to join the prayers.

If the unison prayer is familiar to you, you can keep it from becoming a flat recitation by being intentionally mindful. Every liturgical prayer will richly repay close attention, so try engaging with the prayer's meaning rather than just parroting the familiar words.

For example, millions can rattle off the words of Christianity's Lord's Prayer with little thought, but if you consider that, according to the tradition, this is the perfectly whole prayer, all you ever really have to pray, it can be impressive and reassuring. So you can enrich your experience of it by reflecting on the details of what it says.

- *The first word, "Our" underscores the communal elements of the faith. It isn't, "My Father," it's "Our Father," which makes the point that everybody saying it is in this together.*

- *The fact that it says "Our Father" rather than "Our Mother" or "Our God" raises the gender issue. When I asked a theology professor about this issue, he said the primary point for him was that "Jesus called Him father," and that was authoritative. I'm not sure this settles the issue for me, but it is persuasive. At this point in my learning, I want to honor the concerns of those who raise gender issues and the traditional "Our Father" works for me. At the same time, I agree that it's still an open question.*

- *"Hallowed be Thy name" is rich with meaning, if you want to pursue it. This phrase recalls the ancient mystical belief that saying a name meant that the namer had captured and controlled the named. It's obviously not proper to treat God that way, so the rule was established that you treat God's name with special care, i.e., that you "hallow" it. In the Old Testament, God's name, "Yahweh," appears to have been derived from the older, Semitic root hawah, which means "to be or to become."[183] So you end up with a pretty unusual situation. The Bible reports that when Moses asked God to reveal His name, God replied, "I will be what I will be," which is often translated, "I am that I am" or just "I am." This is pretty intriguing if you think about it. Imagine the conversation:*

Moses: *"What's your name, God?"*

God: *"I am that I am."*

Moses: *"Yes, I've got that. But what's your name?"*

God: *"I am."*

Moses: *"No, no; that's not what I mean. Like, I'm 'Moses.' And you are. . . ?"*

God: *"I am."*

Moses doesn't have to be a rocket scientist to figure out that he's talking with Someone pretty special, Someone directly engaged with Being itself. And all this can emerge when you reflect on just the second line of this one traditional prayer.

All the other prayers that are important parts of established liturgies will similarly reward mindful reflection. And when you get a clear sense of what you're saying when you're praying them, you can experience two levels of profound meaning, one about the messages in the words and the other about the community you're part of. Unison prayer is another part of spiritual and religious gatherings that can produce moments that matter.

Preaching

In varied forms, sermons are also part of the religious practices of the three Abrahamic faiths, and similarly of Buddhism, Hinduism, Baha'i, and most other religious traditions. Unfortunately, people have suffered so much from poor preaching that one of the three dictionary definitions of "sermon" is "a long, tedious speech delivered with passion to uninterested people."[184]

Clerics with political agendas also exploit the power of the pulpit to advocate, not only for theologically-related causes—e.g., pro-life and pro-choice—but also for explicitly political ones. Black preacher Jeremiah Wright was widely condemned and praised for his sermons accusing the U.S. government of being partly responsible for 9/11.[185] In 2011, Muslim preachers were credited with effectively promoting the Arab Spring in Egypt. And the pulpits of small and large congregations regularly host sermons that both attract true believers and repulse worshippers with conflicting political agendas.

Without denying that preaching regularly generates frustration, anguish, and even rage, I want to emphasize the possibilities that it offers for promoting moments that matter. Most preaching is not a political diatribe. Most is done by devoted women and men who want to serve their listeners spiritually. And many understand that one of the best ways to serve is to help create opportunities for listeners to connect in community. The example of preaching that begins this chapter shows that Liz is one of these.

One meaning of the Latin word for "sermon" is "conversation," a point emphasized by a growing number of preachers. One of these wrote a book called *Preaching with a Cupped Ear*, in which he describes a kind of preaching that embodies "on-going and open conversation within the community of faith rather than an argument directed at" them.[186] The idea is that a preacher can fruitfully think of the sermon as starting in the conversations that make up the spiritual/religious community. This is why he or she has to start by listening with a cupped ear. When the preacher's first move is to listen, "to be subject *to* the events that make up the life of the congregation, their preaching can . . . be a communica*ting*. . . an ongoing interaction . . ." (p. 104).

I'd call this a dialogic approach to preaching, because it starts when the preacher lets the congregation happen to him or her and culminates when he or she holds her own ground while in the pulpit. This quality can surface in different ways. A question asked in a Tuesday afternoon counseling session or Thursday evening study of the Qur'an can be addressed during the next service. A community concern—empty shelves at the food bank, lack of volunteer workers, schedule conflicts with weekend school activities—can be connected with related scripture.

A more literal version of conversational preaching happens with the call and response that accompany the preacher's talk in many African American churches. A black preacher's analysis of this phenomenon emphasizes that this pattern of speaking is based more in music than in language. Traditional approaches to preaching emphasize how to build a sermon on scripture, research it thoroughly, and organize it into "three points and a poem." Rev. Evans Crawford shifts focus from what goes *into* the sermon to how it is *heard. He explains that, when he wants to help young pastors learn to preach in ways that encourage authentic responses from listeners, they focus together on timing, pause, inflection, pace, and other musical qualities of speech.*

This is a personal approach to sermon preparation and delivery.
When it is done well, the melody and rhythm of the preacher's voice
signal when a response is appropriate and the talk provides a pause so
listeners can respond out loud. Crawford determines the success of a
sermon mainly by evaluating how effectively it encourages responses
that begin with something like "Help 'em, Lord!" and build through
"Well?" ""That's all right!" "Amen!" to the point where listeners
authentically respond "Glory Hallelujah!"[187]

At twelve-step speaker's meetings, one or two members share their stories in some detail, and these talks have some of the flavor of preaching. The speaker recounts in his or her own words what it was like, what happened, and what it's like now. Often these talks are deeply intimate, offering contact that is rich with uniqueness, Emotions-Spirit-Psyche, responses, and reflections. Frequently, what's said resonates in profound ways with the listener's life experiences. Participants are often deeply comforted to learn that they are not alone. They hear stories that parallel theirs, excuses they've heard before, and suggestions they've not yet thought of. They come to realize that, with the protection of anonymity, fellow-sufferers are willing, even eager to support them.

CONCLUSION

Spiritual and religious gatherings offer many possibilities for moments that matter. Too often, this potential is unrealized, and as a result, people drift away from their family's tradition, try to practice their faith in isolation, only drop by their place of worship occasionally, or treat holy-days as only times for secular recreation and entertainment. The lost opportunities, combined with the evidence that humans might be hard-wired for spiritual/religious activity can motivate efforts to make things better.

Spiritual and religious gatherings can promote more personal communication when careful and humane attention is paid to reading, singing, praying, and preaching. Each of these activities can powerfully connect people, with each other and with the Holy One they worship.

Chapter 11

AS PERSONAL AS POSSIBLE

THIS BOOK IS ABOUT IMPROVING the quality of your life, which means your health, happiness, success, self-esteem, longevity, connections with others, gratitude, serenity, and peace in the sense of *shalom*. Nothing is more critical to your quality of life than your relationships, and nothing is more critical to your relationships than how you communicate.

Remember Brian from Chapter 2? He discovered that, if he wanted to establish the kind of *personal* connection that's impossible for a chatbot, he needed to talk and listen in ways that demonstrate uniqueness. Remember Samantha and Ryan from Chapter 3? After learning some scary lessons on Facebook, they now prefer face-to-face exchanges and do most of their online communicating with email. Remember Jess from Chapter 8? She'd been bullied and marginalized most of her life, and then, after she and her friends invested a year of effort in the Better Together Dubuque conference, a powerful community leader told her, "What you've done is huge. This conference has helped change people's lives. It has saved people's lives." Remember Liz from Chapter 10? She cried out of frustration, guilt, and lack of confidence, and then, in the close company of her housemates, she realized, "I can't do all of this on my own. We can't do all of this on our own; we need community."

Each of these people enriched the quality of their life and the lives of people around them. Each did it by enhancing their relationships, and each did that by making their communication as personal as possible.

Most of the time, they weren't aware of it while it was happening, but they helped move their contacts with others toward the right-hand side of the impersonal---------personal scale. They did this by paying attention to what Chapter 2 calls their communication partner's uniqueness, ESP, choices, and mindful reflectiveness at the same time as they gave out appropriate aspects of their own uniqueness, ESP, choices, and mindful reflectiveness. This is what you can also do to enhance the quality of your communication, the quality of your relationships, and ultimately the quality of *your* life.

THREE STEPS TOWARD AN IMPROVED QUALITY OF LIFE

Communication improvement is not rocket science, *and* as you'd expect when the potential payoff is this great, advancement requires some thinking, some courage, creative adaptation to changing circumstances, extensive practice, and the permanent willingness to try again. Remember that your goal is progress, not perfection, and go at it with the help of these three steps:

Step 1: Always remember that human communication is continuous and collaborative.

Continuous

The fact that it's continuous means two things. First, just as each of our lives is a link in a chain that reaches into the past and, especially if you have children, into the future, each time we communicate, we take part in a chain of events that began before us and will continue after we finish talking or texting. This isn't just an abstract meditation. Concretely, it means that you didn't "start" the communication event you're in, and neither did the other person(s). Past experience, expectations, and familiar patterns all shape what's going on.

So What #1? When something confusing or upsetting happens, try looking at the communication around it as a *response* rather than a first-strike. Every time you broaden your perspective this way, what's going on gets easier to understand. For example, I've just been copied into an email that says a friend of mine has been fired. A few days ago, I heard her talk about what was happening, and if the result is now that she's gone, I'm upset and confused. But I know more went on before I talked with her, and after. Her separation from this job is also a *response,* part of a chain of events that I know I need to learn more about before I complain about the process, condemn the person who was responsible, or react in any other way.

So What #2 about communication being continuous is that, so long as anyone can perceive you, you cannot *not* communicate. People can—and do—just about always interpret (make meaning) from what you say or don't say, do or don't do, and how. This means that a lot of communicating is unintentional and nonverbal. You can use this insight to avoid being surprised when people misinterpret you and to try to get more explicit about your intent, and the other person's. You can also use it to understand, when you're interviewing for a new job or meeting a new person, that the other person starts forming her first impression well before you say, "Hi!" The online implications of "You cannot *not* communicate" are also obvious and important.

Collaborative

Some people don't believe that communication is really collaborative. They think that when a grouchy male authority figure shouts, SHUT UP! the meaning is simple, clear, and coming from only one person. But the only thing that's individual about this event is the *psychology*—what's in his head when he shouts those words. And the psychology could include lots of feelings, including anger, fear, frustration, instinctive reaction to noise when he wants quiet, and so on.

The *communication* is different from the psychology. As Chapter 2 explains, the *communication* is what emerges *between* the shouter and the people he's shouting at. The whole group may immediately go silent, and then what's between the shouter and the people—at least on the surface—is command-and-obedience. Or some may get quiet and one or two might shout, "SHUT UP YOURSELF!" Or his daughter, who happens to be one of the group, may cringe with embarrassment. Or his spouse or superior may start striding toward him to calm him down. Or everybody in earshot may just keep doing what they're doing. Each option describes a different *communication* outcome.

This is also not just an abstract meditation. It means that no single person determines what happens when people communicate, because it's always a joint product. "It's all her fault" is always an oversimplification. It can sometimes be helpful to understand what came before a communication outcome—who said what, who didn't reply, who used what racist labels, who put the message on Facebook, who talked to the boss, or whatever. *And* none of these efforts will do much about the outcome itself—the anger, frustration, resentment, relief, appreciation, or happiness. If you want to something about what happened in the past, you need to focus on what you say and do *next*. Why? Because communication is continuous. It's both collaborative and continuous.

Step #2: Make your communication as personal as possible by giving out and taking in aspects of your own and the other person's uniqueness, ESP (emotions-spirit-psyche), responsiveness, and mindful reflectiveness.

Impersonal communication is sometimes best—in the checkout line, at the cafeteria, driver's license office, subway station, bank. But humans are hard-wired to understand things and people impersonally *and* personally, analytically *and* holistically, at-a-distance *and* up-close-and-personal. This is what it means to be a human being: To possess two very different ways of understanding. Most modern culture pushes us in impersonal directions, which means that our lives are unbalanced toward what philosophers and psychologists call "rational" understanding and brain scientists call "impersonal" understanding.

One important way to improve the quality of your life is to restore some balance by helping to make more of your communication as personal as possible. This is the key to exerting some direct influence over your quality of life.

You can do this by paying attention to what you "take in" when you communicate and what you "give out" As much as you can, to the degree that the situation permits, take in (expect, notice, listen for, probe) the distinctively human qualities of the other person(s), and at the same time give out (express, say, share) relevant aspects of your own human qualities.

What are these human qualities?

Uniqueness — You will notice the other's uniqueness the minute you make it a priority. Your uniqueness shapes everything you say and do, so why not own up to this truth? The other person's uniqueness also shapes everything he says and does, so why not listen for and ask about that?

Emotions-Spirit-Psyche (ESP) — These are the unmeasurable parts of yourself and the other person. Emotions are the most obvious unmeasurable parts, but it's also important to tune into the other person's special energy, distinctive enthusiasm or negativity, always-present worry or confident smile. Sometimes ESP is obvious, like when she's seriously angry or he can do nothing but weep. But most of the time you have to pay attention to what's beneath the surface, what's less-than-obvious.

Responsiveness — Humans can both react and respond. Reactions are primitive, knee jerk, habitual, while responses show something of who you are as a person, because when you're responding, your choices intervene between what happens and what you say and do about it. When you cough up something (It just happens), do you spit on the floor? When your job's really hard, do you just quit? Most of these times you *choose* otherwise. Help get choices into your listening and talking.

Mindful Reflectiveness — We can all proceed mindlessly on automatic pilot and take life unreflectively as it comes. Or we can pay mindful attention to what's happening here-and-now, and be reflective about what we're thinking, feeling, and doing. Most of the time, we do some of each. When you want to make your communicating as personal as possible, it's important to be both as mindful and as reflective as you can, and to encourage your conversation partners to do the same.

Step #3: Keep at it. Expect your efforts not to succeed every time. Try another way. Be dedicated and patient.

Remember that every time human uniquenesses meet, there will be differences. Often, people agree because they're only responding in their role of "cab driver," "clerk," "secretary," "student," or "boss," rather than personally, as a unique cab driver, a clerk with feelings, a secretary with strong values, a mindful and reflective student. This is why whenever you make your communication as personal as possible, you'll discover that the other person has different expectations, priorities, beliefs, some that are trivial, and some that aren't. Acknowledge the differences. As much as you can, embrace them because they add richness to the mix. Exploit the differences for what you can learn from them.

Whenever differences surface, you can choose to dig in your heels and stick to your guns, which will make contact difficult (and is what Chapter 9 called ethnocentrism). Or, you can adapt by doing something different. Choose the second option as often as you can. Display humility, empathy, and curiosity. Listen more than you'd planned. Accept that the other person notices things you missed. Add her insights to your analysis of the situation. Give importance to things you first thought were trivial. Expand your definition of what's at stake. Think about effects on people that you were ignoring. Re-evaluate your belief that you've thought about all possible options. Acknowledge that you're going to have to put it another way, strengthen your argument, make room for another value, find an example or metaphor that better clarifies what you mean.

Adaptation and flexibility are not about being wishy-washy. They are about promoting, encouraging, and enhancing personal contact, moments that matter.

Remember that these moments can be positive or negative. They're not all warm and fuzzy. Feelings that are on the table between two people can be intense. Letting the other person happen to you can be uncomfortable. Don't allow yourself to be verbally abused, and do acknowledge and accept genuine expressions of negative feelings. Stay civil. If it gets out of hand, call a quiet time. *And* take your turn to hold your own ground, to express your opinion clearly, explain your

position fully, define your boundaries plainly. The point is to be assertive, not aggressive and also not passive. Recall how I learned about
"dignity" (Chapter 1): Uncomfortable and even painful moments that
matter can be helpful.

Be patient with humanness. People are complicated and they can
be puzzling, messy, frustrating, and even incomprehensible. Hang in
there. Remember that the definition of a "normal person" is "somebody you don't know very well." Your efforts to make the communication as personal as possible will often fail the first, second, and third
time. Have faith that the fourth, fifth, or sixth effort will succeed. Why
not give up? Because what's at stake is the quality of your life.

CONCLUSION

Sometimes your efforts to make your communicating as personal
as possible won't work because the toxic patterns are so entrenched.
Sometimes they won't work because your efforts are incomplete or
awkward. Sometimes they won't work because you chose a bad time
or place. Sometimes the other person(s) is/are too frightened, or too
committed culturally to being closed or distant.

But the potential exists in every situation for you to connect personally. Why? Because humans are all the same in two critical ways:
We're all social animals, so we want this kind of contact, and we
all can grasp the world both impersonally and personally, so we're
capable of achieving it.

This is true not just of old people, Caucasians, women, or social
service providers, but *all* humans. *How* we connect personally varies widely among Israelis, Japanese, and Southern Californians, but
five similarities ground all the differences: Each human throughout
the world is unique, unmeasurable, responsive, and mindfully reflective, and each becomes who he or she is in relationships with others,
relationships built in our everyday listening and talking.

Every morning you and I are given another day of possibilities. We can count on part of our day being spent in impersonal contacts— with advertisers, bus drivers, clerks, cashiers, some people we work with, and sadly, some friends and family members. When we let everyday pressures control our lives, they usually get more and more filled with these various kinds of mis-meetings. And the quality of our lives suffers.

And we can also choose another option: To take advantage of the day's possibilities by making more of our communicating as personal as possible. To balance all the impersonal contacts with more personal ones. And in this way to improve the quality of our lives.

We can do this with confidence because we know that down deep, everybody wants human connection, just as we do. This is why our efforts to make our communicating as personal as possible will often be returned in kind. Not always, but often. It works when you do.

ENDNOTES

CHAPTER 1: MOMENTS THAT MATTER

1 D. J. Siegel, *The Mindful Brain: Reflection and Attunement in the Cultivation of Well-Being.* New York: W. W. Norton, 2007, pp. 76, 123, 129, 167, 287, 288.

2 D. Rock, *Your Brain at Work.* New York: Harper/Collins, 2009, p. 163.

3 A. Steptoe, A.Shankar, P. Demakakos, & J. Wardle, "Social Isolation, Loneliness, and All-Cause Mortality in Older Men and Women," *Proceedings of the National Academy of Sciences, 110,* 2013, 201-219. doi:19.1073/pnas.1219686110.

4 Ken Cissna and Rob Anderson highlighted the conceptual importance of thinking in terms of "moments" in "Theorizing about Dialogic Moments: The Buber-Rogers Position and Postmodern Themes," *Communication Theory, 8* (1998), 63-104. doi: 10.1111/j.1468-2885.1998.tb00211.x.

5 L. Baxter & C. Bullis, "Turning Points in Developing Romantic Relationships," *Human Communication Research, 12,* 1986, 469-493.

6 M. Irvine, "Is Texting Ruining the Art of Conversation?" http://www.bigstory.ap.org/article/texting-ruining-art-conversation.

7 T. Hsu, "Restaurant Pays Patrons to Put Away their Phones," *Dubuque Telegraph Herald,* August 19, 2012, p. 4B.

8 N. Carr, *The Shallows: What the Internet is Doing to Our Brains.* New York: W.W. Norton, 2011.

9 S. Turkle, *Alone Together: Why We Expect More from Technology and Less from Each Other.* New York: Basic Books, 2011.

10 M. Buber, *Meetings,* Ed. M. Friedman. LaSalle, IL: Open Court Press, 1973, p. 18.

11 M. Buber, *I and Thou,* Trans. W. Kaufmann. New York: Charles Scribner's Sons, 1970.

12 J. Stewart, K. E. Zediker, & S. Witteborn, *Together: Communicating Interpersonally, 6th ed.* New York: Oxford, 2005; J. Stewart, *Bridges Not Walls: A Book About Interpersonal Communication 11th ed.* New York: McGraw-Hill, 2012.

13 H. Prather, *Notes to Myself.* Los Angeles: Real People Press, 1970, n.p.

CHAPTER 2: MAKING YOUR COMMUNICATION AS PERSONAL AS POSSIBLE

14 B. Christian, *The Most Human Human: A Defence of Humanity in the Age of the Computer.* London: Viking, p.4.

15 D. Price-Williams, "In Search of Mythopoetic Thought," *Ethos, 27,* 1999, 25-32; E. Cassirer,, *The Philosophy of Symbolic Forms: Vol. 2., Mythical Thought.* New Haven: Yale University Press, 1975; M. Foucault, *The Order of Things: An Archeology of the Human Sciences.* New York: Vantage, 1973.

16 J. B. Taylor, *My Stroke of Insight: A Brain Scientist's Personal Journey.* New York: Viking Penguin, p. 30.

17 Taylor, p. 30.

18 I. McGilchrist, *The Master and His Emissary: The Divided Brain and the Making of the Western World.* New Haven: Yale University Press, 2009, p. 28.

19 C. Keysers & V. Gazzola, "Towards a Unifying Neural Theory of Social Cognition," *Progress in Brain Research, 156* (2006), 382.

20 McGilchrist, p. 55. On mirror neurons, see V. S. Ramachandran, *The Tell-Tale Brain: A Neuroscientist's Quest for What makes*

Us Human. New York: Norton, 2011; & Ben Thomas, "What's So Special About Mirror Neurons," *Scientific American Blog*, http://blogs.scientificamerican.com/guest-blog/2012/11/06/whats-so-special-about-mirror-neurons/

21 R. J. Winter & E. Greene, "Juror Decision-Making," in F. Durso, Ed., *Handbook of Applied Cognition, 2nd ed.* (pp. 739-761). New York: John Wiley, 2007.

22 McGilchrist, Part I.

23 P. Watzlawick, J. H Beavin, & D D. Jackson, *Preagmatics of Human Communication.* New York: W. W. Norton, 1969. See also K. J. Gergen, S. M. Schrader, & M. Gergen, *Constructing Worlds Together: Interpersonal Communication as Relational Process.* Boston: Pearson, 2009.

24 You may wonder whether I am developing an analytic, *impersonal* response to a *personal* challenge. I've said that interpersonal contact is holistic, metaphoric, immediate in quality, and yet I'm breaking into some parts (analyzing) the central feature of "personness" in order to help you promote this quality. If you're wondering about this, I would say two things at this point in the development of these ideas. First, nonfiction books—and many fictional ones—inescapably appeal in part to impersonal understanding. Books like this one are divided into chapters, organized by headings and subheadings, and their claims are supported by empirical evidence and expert opinion. I don't think I could reach most readers if I wrote only poetry. Second, the first and dominant quality of "the personal" in this model is "uniqueness," which can be grasped only holistically (personally). So the impersonal features of my discussion of personal communicating are meant to work in the service of developing personal understanding.

25 Christian, p. 94.

26 Some national cultures downplay this feature. They make up what two influential anthropologists call "collectivist" cultures. (I mention these in Chapter 9.) In these societies group membership is privileged over uniqueness, and young people

learn early on who is included in their "we" and who makes up the significant "they" groups. Members of collectivist cultures tend to downplay the use of the word "I," score as more introvert on personality tests, discourage showing emotions, and get most of their information from their acquaintances. Example collectivist national cultures include Guatemala, Indonesia, Taiwan, South Korea, and Brazil.

On the other hand, "individualist" cultures value uniqueness. In these cultures, the use of the word "I" is encouraged, selves are seen as independent, people score more extrovert on personality tests, showing happiness is encouraged and sadness discouraged, and media are the primary source of information. Example individualist national cultures include the United States, Australia, Great Britain, Canada, Hungary, Italy, France, Norway, and South Africa. Buber was writing from the perspective of a moderately individualist culture, but people from cultures around the world have embraced the potential for meetings-between-unique-others that he encouraged. See. G. Hofstede, & G. J. Hofstede, *Cultures and Organizations: Software of the Mind.* New York: McGraw-Hill, 2005.

27 McGilchrist, p. 52.

28 R. Bhuiyan, http://www.worldwithouthate.org

29 Siegel, *The Mindful Brain*; E. J. Langer, *Mindfulness.* Cambridge, MA: Da Capo Press, 1989; E. J. Langer, *The Power of Mindful Learning.* Cambridge, MA: Da Capo Press, 1997.

30 T. N. Hanh, *You Are Here: Discovering the Magic of the Present Moment,* Trans. S. C. Kohn, Ed. M. McLeod. Boston: Shambhala, 2010, p. 2.

31 Siegel, pp. 15-23.

32—J. Mandelbaum, "Interpersonal Activities in Conversational Storytelling," *Western Journal of Communication, 53,* 1989, 120.

33 F. Goodrich & A. Hackett, *Anne Frank: Diary of a Young Girl.* New York: Dramatists Play Service, 1958, pp. 79-80.

CHAPTER 3: MEETING AND MIS-MEETING ONLINE

34 T. Bolton, http://www.registerguard.com/web/opinion/27924203-47/eugene-faculty-peak-union-letters.html.csp

35 http://www.digitalbuzzblog.com/infographic-social-media-statistics-2013; http://www.pewinternet.org/2013/12/20/social-media-update-2013; http://www.businessinsider.com/social-media-engagement-statistics=2013-12

36 Skype statistics, 2013. http://aaytch.com/pages/borderless

37 M. Brownlow, http://www.email-marketing-reports.com/wireless-mobile-smartphone-statistics.htm

38 J. Hanas, "The Race for the Second Screen: Five Apps that are Shaping Social TV." http://www.fascocreate.com/1679561/the-race-for-the-second-screen-5-apps-that-are-shaping-social-tv

39 L. Weeks, http://www.world.secondlife.com/group/fabdd1d-5047-3d26-9e8f-f633051b5dad

40 A. Duggan & J. Brenner, "The Demographics of Social Media Users—2012," http://www.pewinternet.org/Reports/2013/Social-media-users.aspx

41 E. Chow, K. Glueck, I. K. Lerner, R. Levin, C.Rosales, & S. Tang, "Senior Watch," *Northwestern,* Summer 2011, 16-28.

42 M. Laitman, "Generation Net: The Youngsters Prefer their Virtual Lives to the Real World," http://www.laitman.com/2012/03/generation-net-the-youngsters-prefer-their-vitual-ives-real.html.

43 Turkle p. 87.

44 H-G Gadamer, *Truth and Method, 2nd rev. ed.* Trans. J. Weinsheimer & D. G. Marshall. New York: Crossroad, 1989, pp. 60-70, 346-362.

45 C. Wallis, "The Impacts of Media Multitasking on Children's Learning and Development: Report from a Research Seminar." New York: The Joan Ganz Cooney Center at Sesame Workshop, 2010.

46 D. Rock, *Your Brain at Work: Strategies for Overcoming Distraction, Regaining Focus, and Working Smarter All Day Long.* New York: Harper-Collins, 2009, p. 36.

47 P. Paul, "From Students Less Kindness for Strangers?" http://www.nytimes.com/2010/06/27/fashion/27studiedEmpathy.html?_r=0

48 Samantha Baraglia, personal communication, 2.17.12

49 A. Sinno, R. Sinno, & J. Stewart, "Social Media: Where Interpersonal Communication Meets Mass Communication," in J. Stewart, Ed., *Bridges Not Walls: A Book About Interpersonal Communication, 11th ed.* (pp. 61-71). New York: McGraw-Hill, 2012.

50 K. Patterson, J. Grenny, R. McMillan, & A. Switzler, *Crucial Converesations: Tools for Talking When the Stakes Are High, 2nd ed.* New york: McGraw-Hill, pp. 162-167.

51 T. Watkins, "Going Beyond 'Why'." http://thecoachingsource.com/2011/08/16/going-beyond%E2%80%9Cwhy%E2%80%9D/

52 J. Stewart, K. E. Zediker, & S. Witteborn, "Empathic and Dialogic Listening," in J. Stewart, Ed., *Bridges Not Walls: A Book About Interpersonal Communication, 11th ed.* (pp. 485-494). New York: McGraw-Hill, 2012.

CHAPTER 4: DATING AND COURTSHIP
AGONY AND ECSTASY

53 M. Friedman, "Men in Marriage," http://www.meninmarriage.com/article05.htm 2011.

54 C. Heidman & L. Wade, "Hook-up Culture: Setting a New Research Agenda," *Sexual Research & Social Policy, 10,* 2010. Doi: 10.1007/s13178-010-00242.

55 E. A. Armstrong, P. England, & A. C. K. Fogarty, "Orgasm in College Hook Ups and Relationships," in B. Risman (Ed.), *Families as They Really Are.* New York: Norton, 2009.

56 Heidman & Wade, 2010.

57 Heidman & Wade, 2010.

58 T. A. Lambert, A. S. Kahn, & K. J. Apple, "Pluralistic Ignorance and Hooking Up," *Journal of Sex Research, 40,* 2003, 129-133.

59 Lambert, Kahn, & Apple, 2003.

60 L. A. Baxter & B. Montgomery, *Relating: Dialogue and Dialectics.* New York: Guilford, 1996; L. A. Baxter, "Dialectical Contradictions in Relationship Development," *Journal of Social and Personal Relationships 7,* 1990, 68-88; L A. Baxter & E. P. Simon, "Relationship Maintenance Strategies and Dialectical Contradictions in Personal Relationships,' *Journal of Social and Personal Relationships, 10,* 1993, 225-242.

61 C. T. Hill, Z. Rubin, & L. A. Peplau, "Breakups Before Marriage: The End of 103 Affairs," *Journal of Social Issues, 32,* 147-168.

62 M. R. Parks & K. Floyd, "Making Friends in Cyberspace," *Journal of Computer Mediated Communication, 4,* 1996, 80-97.

63 J. Gibbs, N. Ellison, & R. Heino, "Self-presentation in Online Personals: The Role of Anticipated Future Interaction, Self-disclosure, and Perceived Success in Internet Dating," *Communication Research, 3,* 2006, 150-159.

64 B. Christian, *The Most Human Human: A Defence of Humanity in the Age of the Computer.* London: Viking, 2011, p. 191.

65 M. Rabby & J. B. Walther, "Computer Mediated Communication Effects in Relationship Formation and Maintenance," in D. J. Canary & M. Dainton (Eds.), *Maintaining Relationships Through Communication* (pp. 141-162). Mahwah, N. J.: Erlbaum, 2003; S. Petronio, *Bounaries Of Privacy: Dialectics of Disclosure.* Albany: SUNY Press, 2002; V. J. Derlega, S. Metts, S. Petronio, & S. T. Margulis, *Self-Disclosure.* Newbury Park, CA: Sage, 1993; R. A. Bell & J. A. Daly, "The Affinity-seeking Function of Communication," *Communication Monographs, 51,* 1984, 91-115.

66 J. H. Toulhuizen, "Communication Strategies for Intensifying Dating Relationships: Identification, Use, and Structure," *Journal of Social and Personal Relationships, 6* 1989, 413-434.

67 Social networks are very important to long term relationships. The probability of divorce can be predicted with some accuracy by examining how poorly or how well the couple's personal networks are blended. M. R. Parks, *Personal Relationships & Personal Networks.* Mahwah, N.J.: Lawrence Erlbaum, 2007, pp. 198-205.

68 L. Rainie & B. Wellman, *Networked: The New Social Operating System.* Cambridge, MA: MIT Press, 2012, p. 135.

69 K. Floyd, *Interpersonal Communication: The Whole Story.* Boston: McGraw-Hill, 2009, p. 337.

70 J. Pearson, "How to Create Lasting Love," *Communication Currents, 6,* 2011. http://www.natcom.org/CommCurrentsArticle. aspx?id=747

CHAPTER 5: FAMILY FRIENDS AND FAMILY ENEMIES

71 K. Weston, Families We Choose. New York: Columbia University press, 1997.

72 American Academy of Child & Adolescent Psychiatry (aacap), "Facts for Families & Children with Lesbian Gay Bisexual, and Transgender Parents." http://www.aacap.org/cs/root/facts_for_families/children_with_lesbian_gay_bixexual_and_transgender_parents doi: 10.1080/01926187

73 J. T. Wood, "What's a Family, Anyway?" in *But I Thought You Meant. . . Misunderstandings in Human Communication.* New York: Mayfield, 1998, p. 96.

74 D. Tannen, *I Only Say This Because I Love You.* New York: Random House, 2001, p. 246.

75 M. Forcada-Gues, B. Pierrehumbert, A. Borghini, A. Moessinger, & C. Muller-Nix, "Early Dyadic Patterns of Mother-Infant Interactions and Outcomes of Prematurity at 18 Months," *Pediatrics, 118*, 2006, 107-114.

76 J. T. Wood, *Relational Communication: Continuity and Change in Personal Relationships, 2nd ed.* Belmont, CA: Wadsworth, 2000, p. 193.

77 Tannen, 2001, p. 247.

78 S. A. Anderson 7 R. M. Sabetelli, *Family Interation: A Multigenerational Developmental Perspective, 4th ed.* Boston: Allyn & Bacon, 2007; A. Aron, C. C. Norman, E. N. Aron, C. McKenna, & R. E Heyman, "Couples' Shared Participation in Novel and Arousing Activities and Experienced Relationship Quality," *Journal of Personality and Social Psychology, 78,* 2000, 273-284; J. Gottman, "Why Marriages Fail," in K. M. Galvin & P. J. Cooper, Eds., *Making Connections: Readings in Relational Communication* (pp. 258-266). Los Angeles: Roxbury, 2003; A. Y. Napier & C. A. Whitaker, *The Family Crucible: The Intense Experience of Family Therapy.* New York: Harper Trade, 1989.

79 S. Sprecher, "A Comparison of Emotional Consequences of and Changes in Equity Over Time Using Global and Domain-Specific Measures of Equity," *Journal of Social and Personal Relationships, 18,* 2001, 477-501; P. Anderson & L. Guerrero, Eds. *Handbook of Communication and Emotion.* San Diego: Academic Press 1998.

80 B. J. Fowers, "His and Her Marriage: A Multivariate Study of Gender and Martial Satisfaction," *Sex Roles, 24,* 1991, 209-221.

81 M. Perry-Jenkins, C. P. Pierce, & A. E. Goldberg, "Discourses on Diapers and Dirty Laundry: Family Communication About Childcare and Housework," in A.Vangelisti, Ed., *Handbook of Family Communication* (pp. 541-561). Mahwah, NJ: Erlbaum, 2004.

82 Y. Kamo & E. Cohen, "Division of Household Work Between Partners: A Comparison of Black and White Couples," *Journal of Comparative Family Studies, 29,* 1998, 117-132.

83 M. Huston & P. Schwartz, "Relationships of Lesbians and Gay Men," in J. T. Wood & S. W. Duck, Eds., *Understanding Relationship Processes: 6. Off the Beaten Track: Understudied Relationships* (pp. 89-121). Thousand Oaks: Sage, 1995.

84 K. N. L. Cissna & E. Sieburg, "Patterns of Interactional Confirmation and Disconfirmation," in J. Stewart, Ed., *Bridges Not Walls: A Book About Interpersonal Communication, 4th ed.* (pp. 230-239). New York: Random House, 1986.

85 J. T. Wood, *Interpersonal Communication: Everyday Encounters, 5th ed.* Belmont, CA: Wadsworth, 2007, p. 224.

86 R. May, *Love and Will.* New York: W. W. Norton, 1969.

87 J. Gibb, "Defensive Communication," in J. Stewart, Ed., *Bridges Not Walls: A Book About Interpersonal Communication, 11th ed.* (pp. 352-358). New York: McGraw-Hill, 2012.

88 K. Patterson J. Grenny, R. McMillan, & A. Switzler, *Crucial Conversations: Tools for Talking When Stakes are High, 2nd ed.* New York: McGraw-Hill, 2012.

89 Patterson et al., 2012.

90 Patterson et al., 2012, pp. 82-96.

91 Remember that no person "causes" another to respond a certain way, so an apology should not be, "I'm sorry I made you feel bad." One person's behavior can obviously affect the other person, though, so you might well regret what happened: "I'm sorry that happened." or "I'm sorry we're in such a bad place over this." The point of an apology is to own your part in the painful or difficult situation.

92 R. Fisher & W. Ury, *Getting to Yes: Negotiating Agreement Without Giving In.* Boston: Houghton Mifflin, 1981.

CHAPTER 6: ON THE JOB: EVERYBODY'S LEADERSHIP & LISTENING

93 S. F. Lee, 2012, http://www.shirleyfinelee.com/MgmtStats

94 T. J. Peters & R. H. Waterman, *In Search of Excellence: Lessons from America's Best-Run Companies.* New York: Harper/Collins, 1982, p. xxii.

95 W. Isaacs, *Dialogue and the Art of Thinking Together.* New York: Currency, 1999, p.10.

96 P. M. Senge, A.Kleiner, C. Roberts, R. B. Ross, & B. J. Smith, *The Fifth Discipline Fieldbook: Strategies and Tools for Building a Learning Organization.* New York: Doubleday, 1994, p. 353.

97 J. Collins, *Good to Great.* New York: Harper/Collins, 2001, p. 62.

98 K. Blanchard, *Leading At a Higher Level.* Upper Saddle River, NJ: Prentice-Hall, 2007, pp. 10, 13, 44, 139, 154.

99 S. R. Covey, *The 8th Habit: From Effectiveness to Greatness.* New York: Free Press, 2004, pp. 5, 192.

100 Covey, 2004, p. 16.

101 S. R. Covey, *The 3rd Alternative: Solving Life's Most Difficult Problems.* New York: Free Press, 2011, p. 91.

102 J. W. Sipe & D. M. Frick, *Seven Pillars of Servant Leadership.* New York: Free Press, 2009, pp. 5, 48.

103 Collins, 2001, p.3.

104 J. Collins & M. Hansen, *Great By Choice.* New York: Harper/Collins, 2011, p. 3.

105 Sipe & Frick, 2009, p. 2.

106 Blanchard, 2007, p. xix.

107 Covey, 2004, p. 98.

108 G. Bellman & K. Ryan, *Extraordinary Groups: How Ordinary Teams Achieve Amazing Results.* San Francisco: Jossey-Bass, 2009.

109 Patterson, et al., 2012, p. 14.

110 M. Herzig & L. Chasin, *Fostering Dialogue Across Divides: A Nuts and Bolts Guide from the Public Conversations Project.* Watertown, MA: Public Conversations Project, 2006, p. 124.

111 Covey, 2004, p. 191.

112 Extending Covey, 2004, p. 192.

113 Covey, 2004, p. 193, quoting Ralph Roughton, M.D.

114 Covey, 2011, p. 48.

CHAPTER 7: MOMENTS THAT MATTER IN LEARNING SITUATIONS

115 M. Buber, "Education of Character," in *Between Man and Man,* Ed. M. Friedman Trans. R. G. Smith. New York: Macmillan, 1965, p. 107.

116 J. Dewey, "My Pedagogic creed," *The School Journal, 54,* 1916, 77.

117 Dewey, 1916, 4.

118 S. M. Fishman & L. McCarthy, *John Dewey and the Challenge of Classroom Practice.* New York: Continuum, 1998, p. 20.

119 M. Weimer, *Learning-Centered Teaching.* San Francisco: Jossey-Bass, 2002, p. 46.

120 S. D. Brookfield & S. Preskill, *Discussion as a Way of Teaching, 2nd ed.* San Francisco: Jossey-Bass, 2005.

121 A. C. Baker, P. J. Jensen, & D. A. Kolb, *Conversational Learning: An Experiential Approach to Knowledge Creation.* Westport, CT: Quorum Books, 2002, p. 6.

122 C. R. Christensen, D. A. Garvin, & A. Sweet, Eds., *Education for Judgment: The Artistry of Discussion Leadership.* Cambridge, MA: Harvard Business School Press, 1991, p. xiv.

123 Christensen, Garvin, & Sweet, Eds., 1991, p. xii.

124 K. Bain, *What the Best College Teachers Do.* Cambridge, MA: Harvard University Press, 2004, pp. 26-27.

125 Bain, 2004, p. 49.

126 Weimer, 2002.

127 C. T. Fosnot, Ed., *Constructivism: Theory, Perspectives, and Practice.* New York: College Teachers Press, 1996, p. 29.

128 Weimer 2002, p. 11.

129 Bain, 2004, p. 117.

130 Bain, 2004, p. 118.

131 Bain, 2004, p. 122.

132 N. Postman & C. Weingartner, *Teaching As a Subversive Activity.* New York: Doubleday, 1969, p. 23.

CHAPTER 8: PERSONAL POLITICS

133 http://www.beliefnet.com/Love-Family/2004/11/Surviving-A-Red-Blue-Holiday Bash.aspx#A7dAhoJmev5WWcwd.99

134 N. Cahn & J. Carbone, *Red Families v. Blue Families: Legal Polarization and the Creation of Culture..* New York: Oxford, 2010.

135 http://psychcentral.com/news/2011/05/11/political-views-influence-relationship-partner-choice/26073.html

136 G. E. Singleton & C. Linton, *Courageous Conversations about Race.* Thousand Oaks, CA: Corwin Press, 2006, pp.58-65.

137 http://pubpages.unh.edu/~jds/BostonGlobe.htm

138 http://www.nytimes.com/2014/02/08/us/politics/robert-a-dahl-dies-at-98-defined-politics-and-power.html?_r=0

139 K. Liptak, "Study: Polarization Highest Level in 25 Years," http://www.politicalticker.blogs.cnn.com/2012/06/05/study-polarization-at-highest-level-in-25-years/

140 D. Slack, "RIP Positive Ads in 2012," http://www.politico.com/news/stories/1112/83262.html

141 http://www.livingroomconversations.org

142 M. Herzig & L. Chasin, *Fostering Dialogue Across Divides: A Nuts and Bolts Guide from the Public Conversations Project.* Watertown, MA: Public Conversations Project, 2006, p. iii.

143 K. Pearce, *Public Engagement and Civic Maturity: A Public Dialogue Consortium Perspective.* Raleigh, NC: Lulu, 2012, p. 28.

144 A. Phelan, *Access Cupertino: Citizen Engagement for the 21st Century.* Washington, DC: International City/County Management Association, 2010, p. 3.

145 M. K. Smith, "'Social Capital,' The Encyclopedia of Informal Education, 2005-2009." http://www.infed.org/biblio/social_capital.htm

146 A. Rothstein, *Social Traps and the Problem of Trust.* Cambridge: Cambridge University Press, 2005, p. 206

147 Smith, 2005-2009, p. 205-209.

148 A. Banerjee, "11 Important Advantages of Group Decision-Making." http://www.preservearticles.com/201205182375/11-important-advantages-of-group-decision-making.html

149 See, e.g., http://www.icebreakers.us

150 C. R. Christensen, "The Discussion Teacher in Action: Questioning, Listening, and Response," in C. R. Christensen, D. A. Garvin, & A. Sweet, Eds., *Education for Judgment* (pp. 153-172). Boston: Harvard Business School Press, 1991.

151 Christensen, 1991, p. 166.

152 E. Bonilla-Silva, *Racism Without Racists: Color-blind Racism and the Persistence of Racial Inequality in Contemporary America, 3rd ed.* Lanham, MD: Rowman & Littlefield, 2010.

CHAPTER 9: MULTICULTURAL MOMENTS THAT MATTER

153 http://www.cnn.com/2014/04/14/us/
kansas-shooting-suspect-profile/

154 http://www.iowapridenetwork.org/climatestudy.html

155 http://www.microaggressions.com/

156 See, for example, "Power, Privilege, and Everyday Life" at
microaggressions.tumblr.com/, and http://nyti.ms/1r2vWBr

157 D.W. Sue, C.M. Capodilupo, G. C.Torino, J. M Bucceri,
A. M B. Holder, K. L. Nadal, & M. Esquilin, "Racial
Microaggressions in Everyday Life," *American Psychologist,
62* (2007), 271-286; J.F. Dovidio & S. L. Gaertner, "Aversive
Racism and Selective Decisions: 1989-1999," *Psychological
Science, 11* (2000), 51-75; D. W. Sue, "Racism and the
Conspiracy of Silence," *Counseling Psychologist, 33* (2005),
100-114; D. W. Sue, *Microaggressions in Everyday Life: Race,
Gener, & Sexual Orientation.* Hoboken, N.J.: John Wiley, 2010.

158 Sue, et al., (2007), p. 274.

159 An unidentified Harvard student quoted in http://nyti.
ms/1r2vWBr

When you're comfortable with your own intercultural
competence, there's also the opportunity to engage the person
in a conversation about what happened—how the person's
comment might be interpreted, whether that's what he or she
intended, and what alternatives there might be.

160 G.Hofstede and G. J. Hofstede, *Cultures and Organizations:
Software of the Mind.* New York: McGraw-Hill, 2005.

161 K. J. Anderson & C. Leaper, "Meta-Analyses of Gender Effects
on Conversational Interruption: Who, What, When, Where, &
How, *Sex Roles, 39* (1998), 225-252. And in some families,
interruption demonstrates engagement in the conversation.

162 These are terms used by W. B. Pearce in *Making Social Worlds: A Communication Perspective.* London: Blackwell, 2007. Also see "Cosmopolitanism" at http://centerforinterculturaldialogue.org

163 J. Oetzel, "Defining and Communicating What 'Intercultural' and 'Intercultural Communication' Means to Us," *Journal of International and Intercultural Communication, 7* (2014), 15.

164 M. J. Bennett, "Becoming Interculturally Competent." In J. S. Wurzel (Ed.) *Toward Multiculturalism: A Reader in Multicultural Education.* Newton, MA: Intercultural Resource Corporation, 2004.

165 I. Nooyi, "The Best Advice I Ever Got," http://money.cnn.com/galleries/2008/fortune/0804/gallery.bestadvice.fortune/7.html

166 One of my African American friends reminds me that sometimes he just can't assume positive intent. For various reasons, some people are clearly racist, sexist, or strongly biased in other ways. In the U.S., African Americans, LGBT persons, Native Americans, and Latinos are most frequently targeted. As I noted, lynchings are less common, but violence still happens. It's important to protect yourself *and* to remember that the cycle won't be broken until individuals take the risk of doing things differently. And often improvement can begin when you assume positive intent.

167 Often, multiculturally competent minority persons work to avoid the risk of being misinterpreted. For example, a Black man notices that the elevator is empty except for a single white woman, and he waits for another elevator. An able-bodied host moves to greet a disabled guest rather than waiting for him to approach her. A male manager in charge of planning a meeting assigns a female manager the first opportunity to talk.

168 Singleton & Linton, *Courageous Conversations About Race.* Thousand Oaks, CA: Corwin Press, 2006; G. E. Singleton, *More Courageous Conversations About Race.* Thousand Oaks, CA: Corwin Press, 2013.

CHAPTER 10: SPIRITUAL/RELIGIOUS MEETINGS & MIS-MEETINGS

169 L. Embler, "Christian Community." Sermon preached at All Saints Episcopal Church, Chicago, IL, March 25, 2012. Used with permission.

170 Law of Attraction Centre. http://www.lawofattractioncentre.com/testimonials/

171 B. Sisco, personal communication, April 11, 2012.

172 J. Bellamy, A. Black, K. Castle, P. Hughes, & P. Kaldor, *Why People Don't Go To Church.* Adelaide: Outlook, 2002, p. 13.

173 D. Barna, "New Statistics on Church Attendance and Avoidance." http://www.barna.org/barna-update/article/18-congregations/45-new-statistics-on-church-attendance-and-avoidance?=church+attendance

174 L. D. Vander Broek, *Breaking Barriers: 1 Corinthians and Christian Community.* Eugene, OR: Wipf & Stock, 2002, pp. 15-16.

175 R. C. Fuller, *Spiritual But Not Religious: Understanding Unchurched America.* New York: Oxford, 2001, p. 19.

176 J. Sacks, "Turning Enemies Into Friends," *After Terror: Promoting Dialogue Among Civilizations.* New York: Polity Press 2005, pp. 113-114.

177 S. R. Finnegan, "Response from an Africanist Scholar, *Oral Tradition, 25,* 2010, 9.

178 N.Namazi, "Understanding Islamic Chants," http://completewellbeing.com/article/understanding-islamic-chants/

179 V. Evola, "Cognitive Semiotics and On-Line Reading of Sacred Texts: A Hermeneutic Model of Sacred Literature and Everyday Revelation, *Consciousness, Literature, and the Arts, 6,* 2005, 4.

180 *Al-Anon Family Groups.* New York: Al-Anon Family Group Headquarters, Inc., 1984, pp.149-150.

181 S. S. Wiltermuth & C. Heath, "Synchrony and Cooperation," *Psychological Science, 20,* 2009, 1-5.

182 O. Suleiman, "Most Beautiful Azan Ever Heard." http://www.youtube.com/watch?v=mUHDYlJHaOQ

183 M. Campbell, "Behind the Name: The Etymology and History of First Names," http://www.behindthename.com/name/yahweh

184 *Random House College Dictionary, rev ed.* New York: Random House, 1984, p. 1202.

185 "President Obama's Former Minister Headlines Local Series," http://pittsburgh.cbslocal.com/2013/04/26/exclusive-president-obamas-former-minister-headlines-local-series/

186 J. F. Bullock, *Preaching with a Cupped Ear: Hans-Georg Gadamer's Philosophical Hermeneutics as Postmodern Wor[l] d.* New York: Peter Lang, 1999.

187 E. Crawford, *The Hum: Call and Response in African American Preaching.* Nashville: Abdington Press, 1995.

CPSIA information can be obtained
at www.ICGtesting.com
Printed in the USA
LVHW011755230120
644586LV00014B/937